Finding the Woman Who Didn't Exist

Finding the Woman Who Didn't Exist

The Curious Life of GISÈLE D'ESTOC

Melanie C. Hawthorne

UNIVERSITY OF NEBRASKA PRESS · LINCOLN AND LONDON

Library of Congress Cataloging-in-Publication Data
Hawthorne, Melanie.
Finding the woman who didn't exist : the curious life of Gisèle d'Estoc / Melanie C. Hawthorne.
p. cm.
Includes bibliographical references.
ISBN 978-0-8032-4034-6 (cloth : alk. paper) 1. Estoc, Gisèle d', 1863–ca. 1906.
2. Women authors, French—19th century—Biography. 3. Women sculptors—France—19th century—Biography. 4. Bisexual women—France—Biography.
5. Male impersonators—Biography. 6. Women anarchists—France—19th century—Biography. I. Title. II. Title: Curious life of Gisèle d'Estoc.
PQ2240.E76Z65 2013

843'.8—dc23   2012032678

Set in Monotype Fournier Pro by Laura Wellington. Designed by A. Shahan.

To Eunice Mahoney, *who has been such an inspiration*

Contents

Illustrations

Acknowledgments

This book was a long time in the making, and along the way I have accumulated many debts. There are many people to thank, and some are acknowledged in notes to the text, but special mention must be made of Christian Laucou, who was one of the first people to set me thinking about the enigma that was Gisèle d'Estoc. I also had help along the way from Philippe Oriol, Gilles Picq, and Richard Shryock. Eleanor Albert helped out with some photos, Cheryl Morgan put me up (and put up with me), and Lynn Higgins introduced me to my dedicatee. Several units at Texas A&M University supported the research that made this book possible, including the Department of European and Classical Languages and Cultures, the Office of the Dean of Liberal Arts, and the Glasscock Center for Humanities Research. Parts of the book were presented as work in progress at scholarly conferences such as the Nineteenth-Century French Studies Colloquium and the Workshop on Cultural Production in Nineteenth-Century France at the University of Florida Paris Research Center, and I am grateful to those communities of scholars in general for their support and interest. Many librarians and archivists smoothed the way for me, including J. Fernando Peña, curator of collections at the Grolier Club in New York. As always, I owe a huge debt to the members of my writing group: I hope this will be an addition to the collective cv that you will be proud to share credit for. And I owe a special thank you to Mathilde Huet, someone I am now pleased to call a friend, who shared so generously her own research. As for the title? Thanks, Patty!

Finding the Woman Who Didn't Exist

Introduction

This is a book about Gisèle d'Estoc. If you have never heard of her, you are not alone, and you may be wondering (to paraphrase the Victorian "nonsense" poet Edward Lear) who, or why, or which, or what is Gisèle d'Estoc?[1] This book offers some answers to these questions. The short version is this. First of all, the answer to the question "*What* is Gisèle d'Estoc?" is that it is a pseudonym, but resolving this question only gives rise to another one: "Then *who* is she?" That is the question some people have been asking for over a century, as they tried to identify the person behind the mask once and for all. You will find out in the course of this book why people cared about finding her, and you will discover that we now know that she was really Marie Paule Alice Courbe (1845–94), who rubbed shoulders with the famous and not so famous of fin-de-siècle France, and who tried her hand at creative endeavors of her own (mainly as an artist and writer). But I am getting ahead of myself by telling you the answer to the riddle of her identity. In fact, we haven't always been sure who she was; that is, we didn't always know that she was Marie Paule Alice Courbe. As this book makes clear, for a long time the person known as Gisèle d'Estoc was confused with another person, so that there were several theories, not always compatible, about her true identity for quite a while. So the deceptively simple question of who is Gisèle d'Estoc in fact resolved itself into the more complex question: "*Which* (one) was Gisèle d'Estoc?" I hope that by the time you finish reading this book, you will agree that the correct answer is that she was indeed Marie Paule Alice Courbe, and you will understand why other identifications have been rejected even though they seemed compelling at the time they were articulated. Finally, then, there is the question, "*Why* Gisèle d'Estoc?" Why bother searching for someone who seems to have disappeared from history without being missed? Why write the biography of a nobody?

The enterprise of writing the lives of others, or biography, has been around for centuries, but who merits such attention is a concept that has changed over time, reflecting broader cultural assumptions.[2] Those at the helm of society—monarchs, emperors, great statesmen (and they were nearly always men), military leaders—have always been obvious candidates for study because of the impact of their actions on everyone's life. The educated (and sometimes not-so-educated) public was interested in the accomplishments of such people and the forces that shaped them and that they in turn helped shape. Similarly, religious figures such as saints were commemorated in hagiography because their virtuous lives served as an example (or exemplum) to others. One of the earliest texts in the language we now call French was written to praise a good girl called Eulalia who became a saint ("bona puella fuit Eulalia . . ."). But these historical and religious people were exceptional, inspirational. While we might aspire to be like them, we knew we were unlikely to match their attainments, and what was interesting about them was their being such exceptions. Although the subject of modern biography has expanded to include artists and writers as well as popular musicians and film stars (the saints of contemporary society, perhaps), we still essentially think of these people as somehow different from the rest of us (no matter how much we might want to imitate them), and their interest lies in this difference.

In the last century or so, the democratic impulse to assert that everyone is equal has legitimized a widening of scope in the biographical enterprise. The belief that leaders were set apart from commoners by different blood or divine choice has ceded to the notion that we are all made of the same stuff, more or less, and that each has a part to play.[3] The exceptional and celebrated will always have their place, but we are increasingly interested in others like us. What was it like to be an ordinary, unexceptional person at different times and in different places? What was it like to be the kind of person we are more likely to identify with or to have among our ancestors? Now, we are interested in the life of the typical as well as that of the unique. The life of a nobody no longer seems so devoid of interest, but there remains a need to articulate why *this* nobody as opposed to *that* one should command our attention. Some recent biographies of what we might call unexceptional people illustrate the genre and its raisons d'être. The life of Elizabeth Marsh (1735–85) was not particularly remarkable in and of itself. True, she was captured by pirates and confined in a harem, and she lived to tell the tale and even publish a narrative of her experience, but in most respects one can say that she lived and died without leaving much of a mark on the world. Yet in the hands of a skilled historian and storyteller such as Linda Colley, the story of Elizabeth Marsh becomes a paradigm for demonstrating that globalization—which we think of as a recent phenomenon—was already well under way in the eighteenth century. Colley's book *The Ordeal of Elizabeth Marsh: A Woman in World History* has also been credited with establishing a new genre of biography, the economic biography, in which the life story of a person shows the way international trade and finance evolved around the globe.[4]

Then there is the case of the social outcast who occupies a marginal place in society, the kind of homeless panhandler who is a common sight on urban streets. Most of us would like to think that we need not identify with such a person, but a fear lingers that he is more like us than we might care to acknowledge, that but for the grace of God (or some other set of circumstances that, precisely, we hope to learn more about from the biographical enterprise) we might in fact have a great deal in common with such a person, even as we hope to be spared his fate. Alexander Masters shows us one such person in *Stuart: A Life Backwards*, turning the abject loser into a subject who wins us over by making us care about how a fellow human being (and therefore implicitly any one of us) could be brought so low. To do so, Masters tells the life in reverse, beginning with Stuart's present (adult) condition and working backward to show how it came about. The early life of an unremarkable person thereby takes on a new interest when we see it as the explanation of how later events that we are already familiar with came about. This is true in the celebrity biography, too, of course. We care about the early years because we already know how Marilyn Monroe turned out later. But in the case of an otherwise unknown person, we need to know early on what is at stake when we invest in the narrative. What is the payoff for caring?

French historians and biographers such as Alain Corbin and Gillian Tindall have pursued accounts of a specifically French Everyman (though again, these are ordinary *men*, not women), particularly those from the nineteenth century, a time far enough removed to be forgotten but not so far that all records have been lost. Corbin plucks someone—Louis-François Pinagot (1798–1876)—virtually at random from the archives purely as an exercise in seeing just how much can be discovered from such records and other sources about a person who did not distinguish himself in any public way. Pinagot is, as Corbin puts it, "un pauvre sabotier qui a vécu, toute sa vie, dans la région la plus misérable d'un des départements les plus déshérités de France" (a poor clog maker who lived his whole life in the most wretched region of one of the most deprived *départements* of France) (225).[5] In addition to basic information culled from censuses and the *état civil*, from court papers and army conscriptions, Corbin extrapolates from information about how different kinds of clogs were made, and from what we know about the wages and conditions of spinners and glove makers in general in order to build up a picture of Pinagot's life. The re-creation asks us, among other things, to imagine what it must have been like to be a single parent fined the equivalent of two weeks' pay (5.70 francs) for the crime of having stolen some wood to keep warm, or to lose what might be an entire week's income (2.20 francs) for stealing branches from a tree felled by snow (142).[6] As I write this, it is 46 degrees Fahrenheit outside, and I shiver at the thought of what it would mean to rely on wood that I must find and collect myself every day to stay warm, especially if I could harvest only what grew on land that belonged to me. There is no evidence to suggest that anyone in Pinagot's world thought such a fine (half a month's income) excessive or unusual, no mention of collective protest or social movement of discontent—and more chilling than the reminder of what it means to be without central heating is the realization that, had I been part of this "lost world" (Corbin's term), I, too, would probably have found such justice meet. In some ways, I rejoice that such a cold world is now lost, even as I suspect that it is not remote enough, but I need the biography of Pinagot to be reminded of the comforts I take for granted.

Becoming nothing but a name in the archive like Louis-François Pinagot is a fate we all might share eventually, but Corbin reassures that no matter how ephemeral our own particular life might be, no matter how quickly the tide of time comes in and washes the sight of our footprints from the sandy shores of memory, we are not entirely lost to future history (so long as historical records survive). Gillian Tindall explores a case of one whose footprints we no longer see, though reassuringly he proves far from lost to us. Her subject, Martin Nadaud (1815–98), was a mason from the Limousin who became the first working-class member of the French parliament. Not quite a nobody, then, but at the same time not enough of a somebody to be widely and easily recalled. Tindall is so perturbed by the fact that no one seems to remember Nadaud that "once or twice in the night" she wonders if he really existed or if she "had somehow invented him" (16). But she knows better, and the cold light of day provides plenty of evidence of his existence and impact. With the help of public records that offer documentation about the public person, Tindall also re-creates the private person, the ordinary man who started out as a typical humble mason from the provinces who took part in the annual migration to Paris in search of work in the building trade.

Biography has also been inspired by the feminist movements of the twentieth century to pay closer attention to the experiences of women and to the role of gender in shaping lives. In part this corrective came about because the assumption that "women are just like men only different" has been challenged by discoveries in many domains that suggest that the paradigm in fact looks quite different. This is no less true of biography than of other fields. Accounts of women's lives have raised important questions about the enterprise of biography itself: about what "belongs" in the story of a life; about the distinction between public and private; about how to evaluate nontraditional sources of information such as hearsay and gossip, which are sometimes the only places information remains about what happened to those were overlooked in their own lifetime; and about the many ethical issues raised when a person starts telling stories about someone else's life. A pioneer in the field of women's biography, Carolyn Heilbrun, famously described in *Writing a Woman's Life* how the trajectory of life stages can look different in the lives of men and women; for the latter, aging can bring increased rather than diminished power, as younger women are used to having to watch what they say when dependent on others. In her biography of Eleanor Roosevelt, Blanche Wiesen Cook had to decide whether omitting what she discovered about her subject's affective and sexual preferences was a form of discretion or of distortion (she chose the latter and broke a long-standing tradition of silence about Roosevelt's private life). Ethical issues can take many forms, especially as biography itself can be seen as a dubious undertaking, characterized (humorously) by Mina Curtiss as stemming from a somewhat unhealthy desire to read other people's letters.[7] Diane Middlebrook's groundbreaking biography of the poet Anne Sexton benefited from Middlebrook's access to records kept by her subject's therapist, but her decision to use that normally confidential material was not without controversy. In pursuing information about the lives of women writers who had not been thought to merit much attention during their own lifetime, Emily Toth has confronted the tricky issue of how much weight to give to gossip and rumor in her biographies of Kate Chopin and Grace Metalious (quite a lot, she suggests). Other biographers have had to consider the ethical implications of having intimate relations (or not) with sources whose information might be compromised or withheld as a result of the choice.[8] Nor are these kinds of issues confined to the sometimes "puritan" Anglo-Saxon world. In France, recent biographies of well-known and much-loved authors that delve into previously untold stories have shaken up the way popular authors such as Colette and Simone de Beauvoir are seen.[9]

Being a little too interested in "other people's letters" is only the beginning of the exploration of what motivates biographers, and here, too, women have been at the forefront of a movement to understand the personal, sometimes hidden, often underestimated or overlooked stakes that drive the author. One of the most outstanding examples in this subfield of the genre is surely Eunice Lipton's *Alias Olympia*, in which her search for impressionist Edouard Manet's model Victorine Meurent is intertwined with autobiographical reflection and analysis. Opinion about this approach is divided, with some praising and others deploring this foregrounding of the author's persona, but whatever the verdict, Lipton is to be credited with drawing attention to the fiction of authorial objectivity in biography. Her creative approach has been much emulated, not always as successfully, it must be said, but often with interesting results. Recent examples in this genre include Ann Wroe's *Being Shelley* and Maria diBattista's *Imagining Virginia Woolf*. Some of these contributions have been in the field of French studies, with efforts that range from Michele Zackheim's novel *Violette's Embrace*, in which the narrator describes her discovery of the writer Violette Leduc, to the more scholarly example of Janet Beizer's recent analysis of how the biographer may want so badly to discover the words of her subject that she (sometimes inadvertently) supplies them herself, filling silences with her own ventriloquized voice rather than allowing the silences to remain. Such different approaches have fostered what might be called a "nonlinear" approach to biography—that is to say, ways of recounting a life that don't follow strict chronological order. It is an approach I explore in this book, too. Here, the story of Gisèle d'Estoc's life begins long after her death, with a rumor that she was only a hoax, that she had never really existed. From this starting point, I trace the attempts to prove her existence and to establish her true identity, with the story of her birth—normally the starting point of a life—coming only at the end of the narrative. Along the way, I hope to show why this life, despite the difficulty of apprehending it, is so compelling as to make literary historians keep worrying at the knots it offers.

For the proliferation of biographies of women has also resulted from the fact that so many fascinating lives have been overlooked. How could the story of a woman who cross-dressed and lived as a man in order to pursue a career in the male-dominated field of jazz music fail to be interesting? In the hands of a superb biographer such as Diane Middlebrook, the subject is not merely interesting, it is absolutely compelling, and *Suits Me*, her life of Billy Tipton, is an example of the heights that good biography can attain. Thanks to the injection of gender as a factor in biography—both the coming-of-age of a generation of talented women biographers and the creation of a reading public interested in women's lives—the last part of the twentieth century was marked by an explosion of outstanding biographies of women, including works by Deirdre Bair (Simone de Beauvoir), Victoria Glendinning (Vita Sackville-West), Lyndall Gordon (Charlotte Brontë, Emily Dickinson, Mary Wollstonecraft, Virginia Woolf), Kathryn Hughes (George Eliot and Mrs. Beeton of cookbook fame), Hermione Lee (Edith Wharton, Virginia Woolf, Willa Cather), Brenda Maddox (George Eliot, Nora Joyce, Rosalind Franklin), Janet Malcolm (Gertrude Stein and Alice Toklas, Sylvia Plath), Diana Souhami (Gertrude Stein and Alice Toklas, the artist known as Gluck, Violet Trefusis, Radclyffe Hall, Natalie Barney and Romaine Brooks, among others), Hilary Spurling (Ivy Compton-Burnett, Pearl Buck), and Claire Tomalin (Katherine Mansfield, Mary Wollstonecraft).

The story of Gisèle d'Estoc, or Marie Paule Alice Courbe, takes its place alongside these narratives. Her life, as I hope to show, was not without interest in its own right (like Nadaud's), but it also offers insight into the roles and accomplishments of women in a time and place where we often assume they are far more circumscribed than they apparently were. Women may have faced many limitations in nineteenth-century France, but not everyone played by the rules and Gisèle d'Estoc seems to have broken most of them at one time or another in her colorful life. She was not the typical French woman of her time, hardly an Everywoman, except in the sense that she was not born to riches or greatness but had a go at seizing them with her own two hands all the same, as it is given to all of us in some way to make a similar effort and see where it lands us. D'Estoc pursued her art to the point of exhibiting at the Paris Salon. She took up both the sword and the pen (and this book will have something to say about the relationship between those two artifacts). She disguised herself as a schoolboy and took both men and women as lovers (and yes, sometimes disguised herself in order to do so). And if, finally, she was not the anarchist bomber she was believed by some to be (as I shall argue), the fact that the accusation was credible testifies to her reputation for action and conflict.

Despite these attributes, d'Estoc represents the ordinary in that her real name is all but forgotten today. Thus, the story of Gisèle d'Estoc is a fascinating exercise in resurrection, an illustration à la Corbin of what can be discovered about a particular existence from records that have lasted more than a century after the disappearance of the person.[10] That these records endure is a testimony to the humble mayors, clerks, and other minor state officials who did their job and carried out their duties; that the records can still be located in the face not only of benign neglect but of denial amounting to almost willful suppression is cause for optimism. Reanimating Gisèle also provides a pretext for bringing back to life the daily reality of Paris more than a century ago, an exercise in microhistory that echoes the work of Tindall at its best.[11] And, like Linda Colley, I hope to suggest that the life of an otherwise mediocre person can illuminate broader trends at work in the period under consideration (which we will inevitably compare to our own day). We know a great deal about the circumscribed existence of the average nineteenth-century bourgeois French woman, the wife and mother who suffered and was still,[12] and we know there were also pioneering exceptions who broke down the doors to institutions of learning, to professional enclaves, and to political houses, but Gisèle d'Estoc shows the ways these paths crisscrossed, rather than running along parallel lines. The accomplishments of the famous were facilitated by the minor infractions of the forgotten, and the path of the respectable middle-class woman was perhaps not always as straight and narrow as the history manual can acknowledge.

The sheer improbability of d'Estoc's life also connects this biography to the impish work of Spanish novelist Javier Marías, who delights in exhuming lives (or aspects of lives) that are so bizarre, his readers often conclude (wrongly) that he has invented them (1). As we shall see, readers have sometimes reached similar conclusions about d'Estoc, who would be a good candidate for one of Marías's "unique tales" (the title—in translation—of the original Spanish anthology that inspired his *Written Lives*), though my purpose here is to demonstrate that she *did* exist rather than perpetuate the doubt about her.

It is, finally, the process of rediscovering the existence of Gisèle d'Estoc against the odds that provides the most important justification for this book. In retelling the story of this exhumation from the dead (or at least the disappeared), I have two goals. The first is to demystify aspects of research practices in the humanities. What do people do in libraries and archives and why do they do it? In part, I want to show that archival research is not a matter of waiting for divine inspiration that provides clear and coherent answers that spring from the mind onto the page ready formed. Indeed, often, the researcher does not even know what the questions are. Research is frequently a messy business, more like a fishing expedition subject to all the vagaries of chance that determine what will land in the net. But chance (like the odds of landing the big one) can be shaped, wrangled, and sometimes tamed by intellectual effort, and the other part of what I want to demonstrate is that successful research involves real work: intellectual work, to be sure (involving complex thought and mental application), but work in the sense of effort nonetheless (and sometimes physical effort, as the next chapter will show). It's not rocket science, though as I shall argue in the final chapter it shares some properties with that, but it's not magic either. Humanities research involves skills, skills that can be formalized (up to a point), taught and transmitted, and applied to fields both within and without the humanities per se. These skills are what people refer to when they talk about critical thinking. Critical thinking is a valuable aspect of the humanities, and why they are worth preserving and teaching, both because such thinking skills are valuable in themselves and because they can be applied in other fields. In the competition for resources that often pits the humanities against other intellectual endeavors (rocket science, but also biomedical research, social science, and just about anything else), the humanities sometimes seem to suffer from the comparison. Other fields lead to applications that cure illness, prolong life, and—not to be underestimated—keep us warm in winter. Just how warm will a good book keep you (unless you burn it)? Humanities research often feels like the luxury, the extra that you can afford once you have taken care of the basics, the fancy wallpaper in the house of intellectual effort. Why worry about the wallpaper if the walls and other fundamental structures are not sound? This book offers two answers. The first is a pedagogical answer: the same intellectual processes are at work no matter what the discipline, and training in the humanities offers a good and practical way to acquire them.

The second is more of an ontological argument: Why do we want so desperately to prolong life? What are we living *for*, exactly? What's the point of staying healthy (and warm), or living a long life? One reason is to contribute in turn to the health and longevity of others, but even then, one has to have something to do of an evening after a long day in the lab. Einstein played the violin. The humanities offer consolation. No matter how well we may succeed in prolonging life (our own as well as that of others), being human remains a terminal condition, and we will always need comforting—or seek distraction—whenever we confront that fact. The reason the humanities were so valuable to our ancestors, the reason they invested so much time in these activities, even though their lives were so much shorter, uncertain, and filled with pain than ours—indeed, precisely *because* this was the case—is that good stories are either enlightening or entertaining, and sometimes both. Whether you are wracked with pain or blissfully comfortable, you must have something to do to pass the time, since passing time is what, as human beings, we are condemned to do. Whether you are waiting for God or Godot, as Samuel Beckett helps us to see, life is both a joy and a trial, something we are constantly being forced to experience. You can try to stay busy or you can distract yourself with television, but every now and again the angel of history pays a visit to remind you we are all being propelled into a future we cannot see while being forced to watch the disasters that pile up behind us that we cannot fix, as though experiencing life through the rear window of a car when you were a child (in the days before seat belts) except that now you are expected to drive blindly at the same time. In these exhilarating, terrible conditions, a good story provides a viable alternative to hibernating and thus spending even more of our always-too-short lives unconscious (more than the third we already spend asleep). For no matter how long a life is, it is somehow never quite long enough. I believe that the humanities will continue to be of very practical use to a large number of people who, when all is said and done, still want something to occupy their thoughts. Although that is not an impact that lends itself to measurement, its pull can be felt just as surely as the forces of gravity.

Structurally, as stated above, this is a backward book in that I tell the story of Gisèle d'Estoc's life in reverse order. After an opening chapter that introduces "the story of the story" and explains the value of approaching biography in a self-consciously metabiographical way, chapters 2 and 3 take on the question of whether Gisèle d'Estoc ever really existed, a question that has dogged the search for d'Estoc since the 1930s. This debate began long after d'Estoc's death, on the eve of World War II, when the received wisdom was that she was no more than a hoax. Chapter 3, however, shows how confirmation of d'Estoc's existence may be found in contemporary newspaper accounts of anarchist attacks in Paris in the 1890s. The press coverage leads to the location of d'Estoc's death certificate, a chronological end point that becomes the starting point for the biography itself. D'Estoc became embroiled in conflict through her literary involvement, and so this chapter also recounts how she entered literary circles through her affair with the writer Guy de Maupassant in the 1880s.

Having established d'Estoc's existence, there follows an interlude that steps away from the trajectory of the (reverse) chronological narrative to consider what we know of what d'Estoc looked like. There are many surviving photos and other representations of her, but chapter 4 playfully considers that there is more to how she is depicted than just what she looked like.

Returning to the biographical narrative, chapters 5 and 6 deal with who d'Estoc really was and the controversy surrounding her identification. D'Estoc's ties to the visual arts are tracked in chapter 5, which traces her own career as an artist. She exhibited both under her married name (Madame Desbarres) and her unmarried name (Marie Paule Courbe), a double life that creates its own set of confusions, but the greatest confusion about her identity has stemmed from trying to establish her date of birth in her home town of Nancy (in Lorraine, eastern France), a story retold in chapter 6 that assesses both who she was and who she wasn't. An afterword suggests that although this may be the end of the book, the story of Gisèle d'Estoc is far from over, and it returns to the theme of the lessons that can be learned from the enterprise of her biography.

1 To Hell and Back (the Present)

Lesson #1: The story of the story sometimes makes a good story too.

To hear Margaret Atwood tell it, in order to have a story, you have to go to the underworld. Most people don't think of academic pursuits as entailing much risk, let alone as involving the life-or-death kinds of adventures associated with such journeys, and they are right for the most part. But academics have their own versions of a trip to hell, and they come in many forms. If people often imagine that academics don't live in the "real world," they have a point. But the ivory tower is always built on top of a dungeon, and for many academics, dungeons often take the form of libraries. Not that all libraries are dark, ill-lit, labyrinthine underworlds (though some are), but the business of libraries is nearly always the preservation of otherwise forgotten, cast-off things that are best kept in the dark.[1]

In classical mythology, traveling to the underworld of Hades involves negotiating the river Lethe, whose "lethal" waters make you forget things.[2] Hades is like a black hole that allows no enlightenment to escape: people arrive knowing things, but if they ever leave (emphasis on *if*), by the time they get home they have forgotten what they know—they have left it all behind in Hades, the realm of the dead. So the trick of Atwood's mythic hero who negotiates with the dead to get a story is not just that you have to go to hell and back to get it, but also that you have to remember it, somehow, after you get back from the underworld.

15

The result, according to Atwood, is that when you get back you have two stories to tell: the story you went for, and the story of how you got it, "the story of the story." In most academic research, this second story is suppressed in the final product. As Carolyn Steedman puts it in her cultural history of the archive, *Dust*, while historians are still in training as students, "They are sternly told that an entrancing story is quite a different thing from the historical analysis that deploys it" (x). Part of what I aim to show in this book, however, is that the story of the story is sometimes essential to understanding and evaluating the story itself. It is not only entertaining to know how the story was obtained (the subject of many author lectures, the intellectual equivalent of "making of" bonus video features), but it helps you assess the result.[3] The "story of the story" is the analogue in the humanities world of the "methodology" section of science and social science research, the part that allows your reader to know how you went about doing what you did. One of the recurrent themes in this book, then, will be *how* information (in this case, about Gisèle d'Estoc) has been sought, circulated, and evaluated.

It is not uncommon for researchers in my field to think of the big national libraries as a kind of underworld where you can extract information from the dead, information that might provide a story when you return to the world of the living. The process of recovering the story of Gisèle d'Estoc involved many trips to such necropolises. When (in the circumstances to be described below) the name of Gisèle d'Estoc resurfaced in the twentieth century, for example, one of the easiest ways to have begun to track her existence would have been to turn to the great French national library, the Bibliothèque nationale. Until relatively recently, this library occupied the space on the rue de Richelieu in central Paris that had been set aside when its functions were centralized by the finance minister Colbert in 1666. A huge public reading room was added in the nineteenth century to accommodate more patrons, but the palatial buildings of the original library were also retained, and even to this day, to work in parts of this library (such as the manuscript room) is to travel back in time to an era when libraries were made from hand-turned wood, were lined with leather-bound books, and contained hidden chambers and passages on upper levels accessed by precarious-looking wrought-iron spiral staircases. But the Bibliothèque nationale is the *dépôt légal*, meaning that in theory at least one copy of every publication that appears in France is to be deposited and preserved there. The original premises simply were not big enough, either to store all these documents or to accommodate all those who wanted to consult them, and at the end of the twentieth century, France proudly moved the published collections of the national library to a new site on the Left Bank of the Seine. (Some collections, including manuscripts, coins, and prints, remain at the more aristocratic site referred to as "Richelieu.") This new site of the Bibliothèque nationale was one of the first places a person might look for traces of Gisèle d'Estoc. In fact, when I first came across the name Gisèle d'Estoc (I was working on a different project about another author at the time), the library had not yet undergone this transformation, and so I began my research at Richelieu, in a place that seemed unchanged since the end of the nineteenth century, one that might have looked just the same to d'Estoc herself. I would go to the "old" Bibliothèque nationale (Bn) in the heart of Haussmann's Paris, not far from Charles Garnier's magnificent Second Empire opera building, the stock market (bourse), and the classical and historic square of the Palais-Royal. To enter the Bn's venerable public reading room was to feel oneself become part of history. Virginia Woolf (in *A Room of One's Own*) once compared being in the reading room of the British Museum to sitting in the bald domed head of a very erudite man. The reading room of the old Bibliothèque nationale gave the reader less the impression of being a thought fixed in someone's head and more the impression of being a passing thought in a grandiose waiting room at an urban train station. The neo-Gothic pillars, the vaulted ceilings high above, and especially the huge skylight with its hundreds of opaque glass panes that admitted a homogenized gray daylight remind one of nothing so much as a nineteenth-century train station. Once you crossed into this underworld, however, you forgot any sense of urgency, of time keeping, of arrivals and departures. Instead, you happily lost yourself in conversations with the dead. Under the dome of the cavernous reading room, the studious atmosphere derived partly from the constant sound of whispered conversations and of pages being turned, so that it was like standing in a forest in autumn, with a steady light breeze rustling dry leaves.

In retrospect, the reading room of the old Bibliothèque nationale seems like a scholar's paradise, but working there could be hell. The long waits to get in, the number of books that were "missing" or "withdrawn from circulation," the unhelpfulness of certain librarians whose favorite word was "non," all these factors were well known to regular patrons. In addition, this underworld actually had its own special hell, an area of the library that bore this specific name: the reserve reading room for censored books. In the catalog the call number of such books indicated that they were shelved in *l'enfer*, "in hell" (presumably that's where your immortal soul was headed, too, after you read these damnable works), and apocryphal academic rumor held that certain researchers—the name of Michel Foucault always seemed foremost among them—could always have been found working in this section of the library. Thus there were those who could honestly claim that their work took them to hell, that they had been to hell and back in order to get their story, and it was, in a way, quite true.[4]

With the widespread availability of computer technology, it is increasingly common today to think that the researcher can escape going to hell. It is true that a trip to the library may not be necessary to obtain basic information. Thanks to computers, huge amounts of information are free and available to all. But if in general "information wants to be free," some information still puts a high price on itself.[5] Cheap information may be plentiful precisely because it is relatively useless, but quality information still costs, and knowing the difference is where scholarship comes in. What is on the Internet is only what is already known (in the state and form that it is known); new knowledge does not spontaneously form there on its own. The point is illustrated by a review that appeared of A. S. Byatt's metabiographical novel *The Biographer's Tale*. In a typically arch and postmodern quest, Byatt's novel follows the sleuthing of a graduate student who gets distracted into writing the biography of a biographer with the wonderful name of Scholes Destry-Scholes. A reviewer of Byatt's book for the *New York Times* concluded that the student was "a thoroughly inept researcher" because (among other things) he made "no effort at all to use the Internet or other resources to try to find more information" (Kakutani). Moreover, complains the author of the review, the information the student does find "prove[s] to be more perplexing than helpful." This review made me laugh out loud (and Byatt, too, I suspect) for what it revealed about the reviewer's (and thus perhaps the general public's) assumptions about biography. The twin ideas that the information one needs is on the Internet and that what one discovers clarifies rather than mystifies are easily dismissed by anyone who has ever attempted biography, though I suspect that those who do not have firsthand experience understandably still cling to these notions. The story of Gisèle d'Estoc should rectify on both counts. To begin with, none of the information about Gisèle d'Estoc contained in this book was available on the Internet when I began this research (though of course I hope that this book changes that, and I know that it has already begun to do so). I did, of course, check the Internet early in my research just to be sure, but there were few details and even sources that might be assumed to be authoritative were, it turned out, usually wrong. The layperson might assume, for example, that the information in an online library catalog compiled by a source as authoritative as the Bibliothèque nationale de France would be reliable, and in general the assumption is not wrong. But in fact the information available in such a resource reflects an overworked librarian's best guess at the time the catalog was written (or updated), which means in the case of d'Estoc that dates of birth and death are wildly wrong (at least, this was still the case in 2008), and the true identity of the person still listed as "unknown" (even though by that point information about d'Estoc's true identity had appeared in print). Unfortunately, there is no index of reliability of the information on the Internet, no way for experts to signal conveniently the degree of certainty about what they report (other than a lengthy explanation that is unwieldy for things like library catalogs).

As for the second proposition—that more information should clarify rather than perplex—anyone who researches a subject seriously knows that the ratio of information to understanding when plotted resembles a bell curve. Too little information is indeed perplexing, and more does help enlighten, but after a certain point, clarity decreases as information increases. It's the same when looking at anything: words on a page are a blur from far away, come into focus when approached, but disintegrate into something that resembles the cratered surface of the moon when scrutinized under a microscope. Thus, I began my project on Gisèle d'Estoc with questions about who she was, and I was able to answer these initial questions with details gleaned from archives that revealed basic facts about her life—when she was born, when she married and whom, for example—but when all the details are assembled what emerges is even more of a mystery, in the end, than when I began (so caveat lector!). Any serious attempt to grapple with the inner person can only raise more questions than it can answer; the result will be perplexing, but I would argue that such perplexity is not unwelcome—most of life's interesting questions have no definitive answers.[6]

Using basic resources that are generally available (library catalogs, even the Internet), it is relatively easy, then, to confirm that someone named Gisèle d'Estoc existed (though it was apparently not always so obvious for some, and this is the subject of the next chapter). Moreover, one can establish that this name is generally accepted as referring to an author to whom some published works may be attributed. But such resources are merely a starting point and still require periodic independent verification. I have already mentioned that facts can be misstated (dates of birth, identities), but there are all sorts of reasons why such compilations of knowledge may mislead. Here is an example of how this can happen, drawn from the case of

Gisèle d'Estoc. Someone who turns to the Bn catalog would learn, for example, that she is listed as the author of a publication titled "Ad Maximam Gloriam Dei." It's an intriguing title, its apparent theological theme and liturgical veneer differing markedly from d'Estoc's other listed publications; as a result, it has been suggested that this is a misattribution.[7] But any attempt to learn more about this publication was stymied for several years by the fact that it was listed as missing ("manque en place"). That is, it was not just too fragile to circulate without restrictions or otherwise embargoed ("incommunicable")—in which case one could apply for an exemption or special permission—but lost altogether.[8] But none of this—neither the fact that the authorship is in question nor the fact that the document was lost and therefore there was no way to advance the discussion in any useful way—is recorded in the catalog. Someone who consults only this catalog would assume that Gisèle d'Estoc is reliably accepted as the author of this work. Information is seldom aware of its own limitations; it never thinks to warn you that it might be wrong, outdated, or the result of tiny human errors such as typos. Mere facts are like the evil sprites and demons who guard the underworld by deceiving you into thinking they are real in order to misdirect you, whether by seducing you into thinking you already have the information you came for, or by appearing so irrepressibly intractable that you give up your quest. In the end there is no way around it: you must go to hell itself and try not to be sidetracked by what seems obvious (at one end of the spectrum) or impossible (at the other). In other words, in order to satisfy my curiosity about Gisèle d'Estoc I had to make my own trip to the underworld of the Bibliothèque nationale (and more than once, it turned out).

By the time I began seriously to focus on Gisèle d'Estoc (long after I first came across the name), the institution had changed quite a bit. The old quarters were picturesque but increasingly cramped—the reading room could accommodate only so many patrons (one had to have an assigned place), and there was regularly a queue to get in. Also, the task of cataloging, storing, and preserving all published materials strained the resources of the old Bibliothèque nationale on the rue de Richelieu. Consequently, a new site and building were planned, a new monument to French culture that opened in the 1990s. The new site is in a previously underused area of central Paris, on the Left Bank of the Seine to the east of the zoo in a neighborhood previously dominated by railway depots, a neighborhood with little else in the way of monuments or other cultural sites that attract tourists. It therefore presumably offered room to grow, relatively affordable property, and the opportunity to bring culture and attention to a neglected area. The new library, known as the Bibliothèque nationale de France, or BnF, to distinguish it from the old Bn that still remains in use (scholars wanting to consult manuscripts, as opposed to printed materials such as books, still go there), is often referred to merely by its site: Tolbiac. Although Tolbiac is also the name of a métro stop, the closest métro stop to the BnF when it first opened was then Quai de la Gare, not Tolbiac; it is as though the need to mystify the use of libraries, to hide the way to Hades, somehow still asserts itself. All but the most determined would at first be deterred from finding it, despite its monumental size. The matter has since been resolved by the construction of the new number 14 métro line with a stop at "Bibliothèque François Mitterand" (yet another alias), but for a long time the entrance to hell was a hidden one.

Being an aspiring French monument, of course the library is also architecturally controversial. One would expect nothing less from the country that turned a building inside out to create the Pompidou Center art museum, matched the classical architecture of the Louvre Palace (now museum) with postmodern glass pyramids, and built, as a companion to the Arc de Triomphe, a huge "arch of peace" covered in white ceramic tiles that looks like a giant cross-section of métro tunnel re-created aboveground to finish off the vista. The BnF, named to preserve the memory of another innovative president, François Mitterand, does not fail to make a bold statement. Aboveground, it looks like a ziggurat topped by four towers, one at each corner so that it resembles a modern, steel and glass version of a nineteenth-century industrial power station (or the modern ruins of a Norman keep).[9] The books are stored in the glass towers (poor

1. Trees in cages outside the Bibliothèque nationale de France. (Photo by author)

planning, as many have pointed out, since they have to be protected from heat and light there), but most of the library proper is below-ground, just where you would expect the underworld to be.

From the point where the number 89 bus used to drop me off in front of the library to the top of the ziggurat there are fifty steps. The steps are made of wood and a notice warns that they are slippery when wet. It is often wet in Paris. (The physically handicapped, a class you risk joining thanks to wet steps, are invited to present themselves at the rear entrance, a block away.) Once you get to the top, you walk across a plateau, passing one of the towers on the way. The towers have cabalistic designations such as "the Tower of Letters" and "the Tower of Numbers" that make them sound as though they belong in *Lord of the Rings* (only there are fours towers here, not two), but in fact they look just like any tall glass office building. Just as corporate is the fact that at regular intervals around the top of the ziggurat are metal cages containing trees. France is famous for its pollarded trees, a legacy from the days of the monarchy when nature itself was subjected to regimentation in order to prove the absolute authority of the king and even trees lost their heads. In a postmodern echo of that landscaping philosophy, the trees on top of the BnF grow inside cages, and any limb or leaf that dares extend beyond the confining bars is simply lopped off to preserve the boxy shape of these well-disciplined trees. I always think that Michel Foucault must have learned everything he needed to know about discipline, and resistance to it, just from looking around himself as he went about his daily life in Paris, even though he did not know the new BnF (he died in 1984).

At the center of the ziggurat, but visible only once you have made your ascent, is a huge pit, a chasm, an abyss that reveals the library. Having scaled the slippery steps on the outside of the ziggurat, you must now descend into its depths to find its treasures. A large rubberized magic carpet (a moving walkway, or *tapis roulant* in French, though it seldom in fact moves and is mostly switched off) will convey you to an entrance about halfway down the inside of the abyss, where you can enter the magic mountain. At the center of this forbidding mythical structure is both heaven and hell, both an Edenic garden court and the *enfer* of the library itself. To enter, you may choose one of two entrances: at the east, where the sun rises, or at the west, where it sets (the literary cognoscenti congregate at this occident, the closest entrance to the halls designated for literature, book history, and art). Before being allowed to proceed further, the first-time visitor must now submit to an interview with one of the gatekeepers who will provide (or not) a library ID card. For academics with legitimate credentials (a letter from one's home institution on impressive letterhead usually suffices), getting the ID card is mostly a matter of paying the requisite fee (which depends on the number of visits one wishes to make), but though perfunctory, this is not a step that can be skipped, and it has its own protocols. Once you have the card, duly paid for, you may proceed into the library proper. But first is the ritual of the coat check (regardless of whether you actually have a coat).

In addition to storing coats, the BnF at first demanded that all visitors relinquish their bags (briefcases, backpacks, computer cases, and so on). This rule was most rigidly enforced when the library first opened, though I note it has been relaxed in recent years, and now seems more or less optional. In return for depositing your bag, you are provided with a transparent plastic carry case on a black webbed shoulder strap into which you must decant all the magical artifacts you wish to take with you on your journey to the underworld, as though preparing for a real-time version of "Dungeons and Dragons." If that sounds a little fantastic, let us not forget that genres such as history have a lot in common with genres of fiction such as magic realism, since, as Carolyn Steedman points out, "A text of social history is very closely connected to those novels in which a girl flies, a mountain moves, the clocks run backwards, and where [. . .] the dead walk among the living" (150). After all, if you can bring the dead back to life, as some might claim historians do, it seems perfectly credible that you may also have the power to turn back time, fly, and perform other normally impossible feats.

The result of this process of transfusion of goods is an interesting transparency, almost as though everyone suddenly became see-through themselves and were forced to walk around baring their soul, a new sort of panopticon. Everything you take to the underworld with you can be seen—and consequently appraised—by others, a constant reminder of the regulatory power of the gaze. I have since heard of school districts in the United States requiring pupils to carry see-through backpacks in order to ensure that no one is bringing guns to school. In such a scheme, the transparency seems clearly intended as a form of disciplinary control, but one founded on shame: the subject is made naked and subjected to the gaze of others. Though this rule of revelation at the BnF has become more relaxed (small bags of personal items are allowed), it was strictly enforced for a while, and the resulting transparency became the occasion for proud self-display leading to a certain minimalist chic ("Here are the items I absolutely cannot do without"), as though the hallways of the library were the catwalk of an academic fashion show. The BnF is a happy place to indulge in some people watching while one is waiting for one's books to be delivered, and I have spent some thoughtful moments observing what people carry around in their transparent carry cases. Of course, there are always those whose case is jammed with the latest in computer equipment or other serious work tools that are bigger (or smaller), better, faster — ostentation of one sort to be sure; but the most powerful statement is understatement, and thus the dull scholar who frets about being without a pencil is forced to admire the insouciance of someone who walks around with a plastic carry case containing nothing but a cell phone and a packet of up-market brand Rothmans cigarettes, for example, or a half-consumed bottle of brand-name spring water and some keys, or, as I once observed, nothing but a toothbrush and toothpaste (lest being carried away by one's research make one forget the insistent demands of oral hygiene).

So, you have a library card (a little ID card the size of a credit card with a photo — taken at the library and usually capturing you at your most wild-eyed and harried), and you have your belongings stowed in a special case that marks you as an elite intellectual warrior destined for the underworld of the BnF (do people steal the cases, I wonder, as a status symbol in ordinary life?), and now you are ready to undergo the tests of entry. Every reader of folktales knows that the hero has to perform certain tasks or overcome obstacles in order to enter the underworld. The first test of the BnF is to pass through a huge set of forbidding, reinforced steel double doors that look like an imagined entrance to Fort Knox. Various library guards stand around observing casually. Provided that you remain protected by library magic, they leave you alone, like enchanted mythical beasts that slumber and seem not to see you as long as you have the protection of your library invisibility cloak. You wave your library card in front of the scanner attached to a series of turnstiles, and if all is well, the gate to the magic kingdom will open to you and the turnstile will let you proceed. You advance through a sort of airlock (one huge set of steel doors followed almost immediately by another set with nothing but air and more steel in between). If you look back (yes, looking back is allowed on this journey), you will see the heavy doors to the outer world slowly whoosh shut behind you, entirely blocking out the sights, sounds, and sense of bustling activity around the coat check. You are silently alone on the other side, where everything is suddenly on a huge scale, as though you have taken your first step into Wonderland or up the beanstalk.

If truth be told, this first gateway is a bit of an anticlimax, since you are still not in the library proper. It is a lot like the imposing but overwrought entrance at the beginning of the American '60s sitcom TV show *Get Smart*: much ado about nothing. But now you are ready to begin your descent into the underworld. You are in the hall of the mountain king, in a vast chamber that stretches away above and below you. Everything is made of stainless steel (or something that looks just like it). Everything seems to be covered in rivets. The walls are hung with what look like sheets of futuristic chain mail. You are inside the Death Star. I always half expect that I will look up and see Luke Skywalker and Darth Vader battling it out with their light sabers on one of the catwalks far above me, but I attribute this to the kind of hallucinations that often beset the traveler to the underworld. You must know it for an illusion and not allow it to distract you from your quest.

The next stage is the slow descent into the inner core. You stand on an escalator that conveys you at a stately pace down, down, down into the bowels of the earth. Around you is nothing but stainless steel; it's a dizzying trip, so hold tight onto the handrail and take care not to get lightheaded and fall. At the bottom of the escalator is another turnstile, but be careful! It's a trick one! You need only scan your card when *leaving* (to confirm that you are relinquishing your seat), but you do not need to do so when arriving, otherwise you look like a rube, a first-time visitor who does not know the protocols yet (not to mention the literal falls that await the uncoordinated who attempt this maneuver just as they step off an escalator and have to adjust to being on terra firma once again while the residual impetus of the escalator fairly throws them into the turnstile). Simply pass through and you are in the company of humans once again. The steel seems to soften and is mitigated by some carpeting the color of congealed blood (or perhaps of wine, if you are French) and some warm wood accents. This antechamber is purgatory if you have not secured a designated seat before this point. Only those with designated seats can enter the library (you can request and reserve a seat assignment ahead of time, either over the phone—though the number is nearly always busy—or on the library computer system; first-time visitors nearly always have to spend a little time in purgatory). Here you must bide a little and contemplate your sins (mainly the sin of not having foreseen the need to make a reservation). A librarian angel may intercede for you and assign you a seat if there are any available, but even this takes a little time while the computer system digests the librarian's request. No one knows quite how much time. You must sit abjectly and wait, then try to scan your card at the next turnstile. If the card is rejected—oh, the humiliation!—it means the computer has not yet registered your seat assignment. If accepted, you have completed your expiation and may proceed.

Of course, those who venture to the underworld on a regular basis have made a reservation ahead of time and advance confidently to the last turnstile and the second airlock of double steel doors. *Poussez, tirez.* In each airlock, you must *push* the first set of doors, but *pull* the second set. Being able to maneuver smoothly through these airlocks, the nonchalance of remembering when to pull and when to push, separates the regulars from the mere visitors who pull when they should push, then stop abruptly, causing you to bump into them, then look around helplessly at the unyielding door before they realize that it is clearly marked "poussez" (or "tirez": the second set makes you do the *opposite* of the first just to make sure you are paying attention).[10] For those who have proved their worthiness, however, the doors to the magic kingdom will open smoothly and one may proceed into the inner sanctum where the wonders, and stories, of the underworld await.

As is often the case in hell, heaven is visible to taunt you, but you may not visit there, and this is also the case at the BnF. The vaulted halls of the library are several stories belowground and on a level with a central courtyard known as the "garden." The garden is in the open air but is closed off to those inside the library by huge panes of glass (you may see the promised land, but not enter it). The garden contains a large number of mature trees, the tops of which are at eye level to those on top of the ziggurat, so that when you stand beside the four towers ready to descend the first elevator, it is as though you are in the clouds, face-to-face with the tops of the trees. These trees grow freely; they are not pruned, pollarded, or otherwise constrained. Except in one rather bizarre way: because these trees, representing years of growth, did not actually grow on this spot but rather were transported here for effect, they have no established natural root system to hold them up. Thus, all the trees are attached to huge steel cables, guy ropes that anchor them to the ground and prevent them from simply toppling over. Occasionally, when there are high winds, one falls anyway, but the rest stand majestically swaying in the breeze, home to colorful and not-so-colorful birds that flit in and out of their branches or browse in the green grass at their feet, among ferns and giant mushrooms, all of this visible through huge sheets of plate glass but otherwise inaccessible to the serious souls imprisoned in the halls of the library within. No wonder some prankster introduced a colony of rabbits into the garden, so that the high-minded seriousness of scholars might sometimes be punctured by the whispered announcement of a rabbit sighting: "Lapin!" (The "lapin de la BnF" now even has his own Facebook page.)

Those condemned to see the garden (and its occasional rabbits) but not to enter it are invited to think of themselves as being not in hell but in a secular cathedral dedicated to the worship of learning. They are surrounded by space of almost gothic proportions: generously sized wooden work tables, wide passages, tall ceilings three stories high, and all around the *hortus conclusus*, or enclosed garden, a *deambulatory*, to give it its official title, so named for the space in a cathedral on either side of the nave where one walks (*ambulare*). One can circulate around the cloister of the library freely in this tall, airy hallway, always with the view of the garden to one side and entrance bays to different sections of the library on the other, sounds echoing yet muffled by the thick carpet that absorbs the footsteps. At each bay one can climb a few steps onto the elevated wooden floors of the workrooms and open shelves as though one were stepping onto the platform of a merry-go-round.

Each of the bays or halls is designated by a letter of the alphabet (Hall V is for French literature), and one takes one's chair at the numbered place in the appropriate hall. There is a small techno panel for each user set into the long table: a light switch to turn on the individual reading light, a socket to plug in computers, a red light that illuminates to indicate that the place has been reserved (redundant, surely, since no one gets in without a reservation), and a green light that blinks to let you know when an item you have requested via computer has now arrived and is available for checkout at the main desk. (Of course, since the library has been open for a few years now, a number of these lights no longer work. Since there is no reliable way to test whether they are working, they are mostly useless, their unlit status no longer a reliable indicator of anything.)

If you have not been able, for whatever reason, to request materials ahead of time so that they are waiting for you when you arrive, you will have a significant wait between the time you place the request for them and the time they are retrieved from the stacks and the green bulb lights up (or not) to signal you that they are ready for pick up. The librarians who perform this retrieval function (or at least the human ones, known as *magasiniers*; others are in fact robot drones) have been on strike on and off pretty much since the library first opened, so you never quite know how long this part of the process is going to take, but it can be several hours on a bad day. While you wait you are free to consult books on the open shelves, though these seem to be mostly the books you already have at home.

Of course, when spending a whole day in a library, certain human needs have to be met. The library is generously supplied with restroom facilities at ground-floor level in each of the four towers. The only snag with this is that, since the library is so vast, a trip to the bathroom can entail walking the equivalent of the length of a city block. It's as though, sitting in your apartment working, you must take a walk to the café at the end of the road when you feel a call of nature. You'd better not have any emergencies. The bathrooms themselves are well maintained, but they are marvels of technology in miniature, with all the boons and glitches appertaining thereto. Take the wash basins (please! take the wash basins). When the library first opened, these stainless steel wonders operated on sensors. Yes, that's right, no more unsanitary hands turning on or off faucets, no faucets left to run and waste water, no contamination, a miracle of modern science. I am convinced these faucets were designed as part of the set of a Jacques Tati film, something left over from the kitchen in *Mon oncle*, perhaps. You simply stuck your hand under the protruding faucet and . . . nothing happened! You waved your hand around for a minute, flailing randomly, trying to get the sensor's attention, then you realized that the problem was that you were too far away from the actual sensor (set in the neck of the faucet) and so it didn't, in fact, "sense" you. (Perhaps the library changed you from being a warm-blooded creature capable of being sensed into some sort of zombie with no heat signature.) No problem, just move your hand closer and presto, fresh water gushed from the faucet . . . straight onto your sleeve that was right below it now that you had moved your hand into range of the sensor. Brilliant! I don't know what it meant that I didn't see more people walking around with soaked sleeves in the first years of the library's operation (had everyone else in the world figured out this trick except me?), but it used to lead to a kind of Zen of hand washing. Your hand could not be near enough to activate the sensor and at the same time be under the faucet being rinsed, so one hand could never wash, or rinse, the other. What is the sound of one hand rinsing? I will never find out, because the library has since removed the sensors and returned to faucets that are activated by pressing down on top.

But such trials as these are relatively minor compared to what some must endure when traveling to the library underworld. I am always fascinated by the details others supply about the conditions of their research. Simone André-Maurois describes the library where she worked with her husband (André Maurois) on George Sand in the early post–World War II period. At that time, an important collection of literary documents that had been assembled and bequeathed by the eccentric bibliophile Vincent de Spoelberch de Lovenjoul was still kept in what had once been a convent just outside Paris in Chantilly. That name is likely to conjure up associations with the lightness and delicacy of lace for many North American readers, or sweet, light cream for Francophones, but either way it is a contrast to the reality, which is that the library was both cold and dark. "It is well known that the foundation on the rue du Connétable is neither heated nor lit," writes Simone André-Maurois (194). True, the reading room overlooked a beautiful garden, so working conditions were aesthetically pleasant on some level, but on the material side, when André-Maurois made a special visit there one day in glacial conditions, she had to make do with a little wood-burning stove as the sole source of warmth. (She fared better than the curator. There was no provision made to heat his office at all.) For physical refreshment, André-Maurois brought sandwiches and a thermos. Normally, the library was only open three times a year, Easter, July, and the end of October (195), so presumably one could save one's visits for July when the cold was not such an issue, but the lack of lighting must have strained many an eye at any time of year, and it is clear that the library was never intended to be "user friendly."

Of course, not all libraries are without heat. Recently the biographer Michael Holroyd has described the conditions at Britain's Somerset House, where he was researching his own family history: "No one who searches for a Will was allowed to take off his or her overcoat in winter lest it contain high explosives. The central heating was kept high, very high, and all staff worked in shirtsleeves" (38–39). Thus the conditions in libraries often do match those attributed to the underworld, a place of extreme heat or cold, depending on whether you are imagining a Judeo-Christian inferno or an icy realm of cold death.

The material conditions in which one works in the library thus take on an important dimension, a perspective that can come to dominate more elevated concerns. In *Le goût de l'archive* (The Taste for/

of Archives), historian Arlette Farge describes the all-out war that breaks out among researchers to commandeer what is perceived to be the best seat in the library and the petty strategies that end up dwarfing all other daily concerns (27–32). Elsewhere she retells a rumor about a reader who used to wear lots of rings to the library just so that the reflections of light bouncing off the jewelry would keep her awake during the long hours of reading (21).

Of course there is a trade-off. As Farge points out, the enforced slowness of libraries fosters creativity: "On ne dira jamais assez à quel point le travail en archives est lent, et combien cette lenteur des mains et de l'esprit peut être créatrice" (It's impossible to overstate how slow archival work is, and to what extent this slowness of the hands and mind can be creative) (71). There is a case to be made for a "slow work" movement analogous to the "slow food" movement, perhaps.

Coldness, boredom, long periods of waiting—these are the sort of conditions you must contend with to get your story, yet few readers of the resulting narrative are ever aware of just what physical (and psychological) trials must be endured by the story seekers.[11] What could possibly he hard about going to the library and copying some stuff out of old books? is probably how most people think about it, if they think about it at all. Better yet, stay at home and do the research online.

There is a cartoon that I keep pinned to my wall. It is by Shannon Wheeler and features his "superhero" character Too Much Coffee Man; it is called "Things you can't complain about."[12] It depicts people whining about "problems" that most of us would love to have: "I'm so busy I don't have time to enjoy the money I make" or "My girlfriend wants sex *all* the time." One of the complaints in the cartoon (and the reason it stays on my wall) is, "I have to go to France *again* for my high paying job!" Yeah, right! You don't get to complain about *that*. Family, friends, colleagues—everybody, it seems—get to tease me when I say I am going to France to do research. If you get to go to France to do it, it's not something you can complain about, no matter what "it" is. Well, there's some truth to that. I would be the last person to suggest that the hardships of research ever make me wish I could quit my lousy job, for example. And yet, and yet . . . there is real *work* involved in mining stories from the rocks of hell.[13] It may be true that not every library is too cold or too hot. Some, and I have been fortunate to know them, are delightful and gracious Renaissance residences with well-furnished work rooms and French windows that open onto beautifully maintained gardens where roses fragrantly bloom and birds chirp while you read quietly and contemplate your good fortune. But the point is that for better or worse, few people who are not themselves researchers know the practical difficulties and the range of unpredictable eventualities that research can entail. We all understand that scientists put in long, exacting hours in laboratories doing sometimes repetitive unglamorous work; that physical laborers perform hard, demanding work that tires the body and the mind; that farmers plow and reap. But what do researchers in the humanities do? They go to France for their high-paying jobs and they don't get to complain about it.

This book, then, is partly about what researchers in the humanities really do when they do research. It is about demystifying what research is. It is the story of the story. It is also about why what researchers do in the humanities matters. Going to hell and back for a story is one part of it. You get some good stories that way. But just as important are the skills you learn along the way, skills that are not specific to the humanities but are about reasoning, truth, discovery, puzzles, and the complicated ways these are negotiated, assessed, brought into being, and even lost.

The research for this book has led me to the old Bibliothèque nationale, the new Bibliothèque nationale de France, the archives of the Musée d'Orsay, the Archives de Paris, the Archives départementales de Meurthe-et-Moselle in Nancy (eastern France), the Grolier Club in New York, and the Family Research Center in London. These are a few of the underworlds I have visited. Some were more hellish than others. Now, it is heaven to be able to tell the story I extracted from the dead—as well as from the living—I encountered there, along with the story of the story.

2 Gisèle d'Estoc and World War II (the 1930s)

Lesson #2: Some people just love to argue.

It is hard to imagine why anyone would pay much attention to a literary spat in the Paris of June 1939, either then or today. In Paris, as elsewhere in France at the time, everyone was far more likely to be preoccupied by what they realized was an inevitable war with Germany. No one yet knew quite how devastating this war would be, of course—the average person couldn't foresee the concentration camps, the Occupation of France, the fact that the conflict would eventually draw in virtually the whole world and would require the unprecedented use of an atomic bomb to end it. It's probably just as well that they didn't know these things yet, but even without knowing the full extent of what was in store, the prospect of war was surely an important enough concern to dominate everyone's attention and drive out other matters. Yet it seems that there is always room in human society for the insignificant and gossipy but interesting thing as well as the more obviously important thing, and the way that Gisèle d'Estoc resurfaces from the depths of history in the twentieth century illustrates the willingness of people to be distracted—and thankfully so, sometimes—from what they "ought," more rationally, to be doing and thinking about.

So despite the lengthening shadows of war, some people still noticed when a review ironically (in light of the Occupation shortly to follow) called *Les oeuvres libres* (literally, "Free Works," though free in the sense of freethinking rather than cost free) published some new information about the love life of the French novelist Guy de Maupassant in its June 1939 issue.

Les oeuvres libres was a monthly literary magazine (a "revue mensuelle") masquerading as a paperback book. Each volume was numbered like a serial publication (the June issue was number 216), but the visual appearance was that of a cheap paperback and the publisher's name (Arthème Fayard) featured prominently on the cover like a title or brand name. The specialty of the review was making available previously unpublished literary materials, whether fictional, such as short stories, or biographical, such as correspondence, journals, and diaries. In the June 1939 issue, for example, there were four previously unpublished works of fiction (a complete novel, a play, and two short stories, including one by Aldous Huxley) along with a diary about Maupassant.

Although the raison d'être of the review was nominally literary, then, *Les oeuvres libres* appealed to a broader audience through its inexpensive paperback appearance and through its invocation of novelty, as well as its sometimes racy content. It offered light reading with a veneer of quality. It is perhaps no coincidence that I came across a copy of one of the issues I will be discussing here not in Paris, the literary capital, but in a used bookstore in the seaside town of Cabourg, the fashionable turn-of-the-century Normandy coast resort made famous by Proust under the name of Balbec. The review made for perfect beach reading (for me as well as for its original readers): most pieces were short and could be assimilated in one sitting; given the emphasis on previously unpublished work, there was little risk of buying something only to find you already had read it; and the biographical materials might include gossip along with some mildly titillating copy. Such was the case in the June 1939 issue, for example, which, in addition to the literary works, proposed some previously unpublished confessions ("confidences inédites") with the tantalizing title "A Female Adorer of Maupassant: The Love Diary" ("Une adoratrice de Maupassant: Le cahier d'amour"). Those looking for summer beach reading on the eve of World War II must have been delighted.

The erotic lure of the title was sure to attract attention even from people who had never heard of Maupassant, but it would also pique the curiosity of those who had, surely a vast potential readership. During his lifetime and even for a while afterward, Maupassant's public image had been carefully cultivated and protected.[1] Though adhering superficially to the conventions of his class, which required the appearance of good moral conduct, Maupassant was a rake and a playboy, and the venereal disease he contracted early in life (and presumably continued to pass on liberally) eventually killed him after destroying his mind. This was not his public image, however. He was known to enjoy life's pleasures—hunting in his native Normandy, boating on the Seine, and even the convivial company of women—but he was seen as basically a harmless, avuncular figure, no particular threat to married women, young girls, and solid bourgeois values.

One measure of the degree of public acceptance he enjoyed is the widespread use of his work to teach French language and culture to children and adolescents in other countries. Until late in the twentieth century, short stories by Guy de Maupassant were a staple of the high school French curriculum in England and elsewhere. The length of the stories was ideal, ranging from a few pages to short novels suitable for the more linguistically advanced; the language of his work was accessible yet authentic; and the themes were deemed compatible with what today we might call "family values," since cruelty and vice, if depicted, were roundly condemned. Everyone, it was thought, could enjoy stories about the pleasures of boating and flirting with pretty girls. Stories that brought out the darker side of family life (a woman who lies to or cheats on her husband, the mistreatment of the elderly, the nasty greed of inheritors) bolstered a certain claim to realism and served indirectly as ideologically charged lessons in morality (some people are very wicked). And stories that sent a shiver down your spine, like the vampire story "Le Horla," known to many generations of students of French, would be sure to appeal to bored teenagers and help motivate them to do their French reading homework. The literary hand met the pedagogical glove.

Maupassant's popularity has dwindled today, but check the foreign languages section of any used bookstore and you are likely to find several old, clothbound editions of short stories by Maupassant edited for schoolroom use—if you don't still have your own copy somewhere on the shelf, that is.

Maupassant's private life would not stand up to much scrutiny today, however, and many school textbook selection committees would have a hard time defending his work as having a wholesome influence as judged by today's standards if they knew much about his background. Even in 1939, the existence of a diary by an ex-lover that purported to reveal certain details of his personal life would have come as news to almost everyone. That he had admirers, even adorers, would not come as a surprise, but the provocative "Love Diary" subtitle, suggesting that it was not his work or literary talent that was being adored, must have raised many eyebrows (and sold many copies). Those who cared to could turn to the introduction to the diary, written by a journalist with pretensions to literary history who went by the name of Pierre Borel to find out more. Borel begins by reminding the reader that "the sometimes harmful role that certain women played in the life of Guy de Maupassant is well known" but goes on to claim that what makes this particular woman—referred to here only as "Mlle X"—special is that she was at once "the most important" and yet has remained "totally unseen" by Maupassant's historiographers (71). Intrigued, the reader learns that Mlle X was a writer, painter, sculptor, and journalist. "An androgyne, her adventures in lesbian society were often the subject of the scandal sheets of the time." The introduction continues in this mode, assuring readers that the diary offers confessions about a "devastating passion" that destroyed the poor Maupassant, who ended up "deranged by the excesses of pleasure and by the poison of drugs." The introduction promises hot stuff, and as the diary begins, the reader gets the sense that this is not an exaggeration. The first line reads: "I come away from that crazy, intoxicating, exhausting struggle with my thighs still on fire and full of desire" (73).

Those who bought *Les oeuvres libres* that month certainly got their money's worth, but there are always skeptics, so it is not surprising that more serious critics focused on some of the more substantial claims about Maupassant being made in this unexpected publication. During the next couple of months (July and August), the veracity of the love diary came under close scrutiny. The attacks were launched almost immediately, beginning in mid-July in what was essentially the literary gossip column of the *Mercure de France* (a widely read but serious literary review), where a well-known literary critic who went by the single name Auriant challenged the authenticity of the diary by pointing out certain factual errors in the narrative.[2] For example, Mlle X claimed that Maupassant was superstitious and believed in premonitions. In one instance she writes that Maupassant dreamed that his friend Harry Allis [*sic*] drowned, only to receive a message the next day that his friend had indeed died (74). Auriant scornfully noted that Maupassant died in 1893, whereas Alis (the correct spelling, he added) did not die until 1895 (and then in a duel, not from drowning), so that Mlle X's claim was patently wrong, from superficial details such as the spelling right down to all the substantive facts (490). As if that weren't enough, the memoirs were badly written, complained Auriant, and were "painfully banal" ("d'une banalité affligeante") (492). Finally, they bore more than a passing resemblance to another, earlier "confession," also by an anonymous X (though this one was a madame rather than a mademoiselle), published back in 1912 and 1913 (494). Auriant evidently relished the opportunity to denounce the diary as a fake.

This forceful attack on the "Love Diary" would seem at first glance to put an end to the matter, but Auriant succeeded in muddying the waters in ways that would in fact complicate and prolong the debate. For example, he argued that the "Love Diary" was a hoax, but at the same time he breathed life into speculations about the anonymous author of the diary by revealing her name. In the original publication (in *Les oeuvres libres*) she had been named only as the anonymous Mlle X, but Auriant reports that a third party, Léon Deffoux, had revealed to him the "nom de guerre" of Maupassant's admirer, Gisèle d'Estoc (490–91).[3] Yet, having named her, Auriant denied knowing the name himself. Despite Borel's claim that she was much talked about in the press, Auriant himself had never come across her even though he had been researching the courtesan Valtesse de la Bigne and the lesbian demimonde of the period (he was interested in the sources of Zola's novel *Nana*). He concludes (not surprisingly, given his skepticism), "The Love Diary by Mlle X looks to me just like a mystification, if not a hoax" (500), but at the same time he appears to be dismissing it, he raises new questions that prolong the interest of the story. Auriant thus gives (after)life to Gisèle d'Estoc even as he tries to take it away. "Who on earth is Gisèle d'Estoc?" asks Auriant. She is the woman who did not exist.

There is a further paradox in what Auriant contributes to the unfolding story, too: he does not explain how Deffoux could creditably supply the name of d'Estoc while managing not to know that she existed. Deffoux's own published contribution to the debate is no less enigmatic. It appeared shortly after Auriant's article, in a brief column in the newspaper *L'oeuvre* on July 23, 1939. There, he summarizes Auriant's reservations and concludes: "Souvenons-nous de nous méfier des carnets d'amour et des 'Gisèle d'Estoc'" (Let us remember to be skeptical of love diaries and "Gisèle d'Estocs") (7). The nonexistent women proliferate: they are now "des" (plural!) Gisèle d'Estocs, their growing number an index of the threat they represent, the threat of which we must guard against ("nous méfier"). Ironically, though, Deffoux's injunction is not to *forget*, but to *remember* ("Souvenons-nous") these proliferating harpies. If Gisèle d'Estoc will not stay dead and buried—and nameless—we must be vigilant, he implies. And part of the vigilance is to talk constantly about this threat to the order of things.

It is already evident, even from these first few critical exchanges, then, that one of the features that marks this debate about the existence of a woman named Gisèle d'Estoc is the extent to which the clique of critics are conscious of reading one another, citing one another, and bringing into their published interventions the conversations that take place behind the scenes, off the pages of the press.

Auriant cites Deffoux to attack Borel, the journalist who brought the love diary to light. Deffoux summarizes fellow professional critic Auriant, and the two close ranks.

The pattern continued the following month (August 1939), when the *Mercure de France* felt obliged to carry a response to Auriant's critique by the man who had written the introduction to the "Love Diary" in *Les oeuvres libres*, Pierre Borel. Curiously, this name too was a pseudonym, that of Frédéric Viborel, a journalist who had already tried to break the story of the mysterious Mlle X in a book in 1927, *Le destin tragique de Guy de Maupassant* (The Tragic Destiny of Guy de Maupassant).[4] The book had been based on information passed on to Borel by Léon Fontaine, one of Maupassant's boating buddies, whom Borel thought a pretty credible source, though not everyone agreed. But the book *Le destin tragique* did not attract attention in 1927 the way the publication of the "Love Diary" did when published in the more attention-getting format of *Les oeuvres libres* twelve years later.

Now, in 1939, Pierre Borel had finally succeeded in getting some of the limelight he sought (thanks in part to a catchier title), but the attention was not all positive. As a result, Borel felt the need—and desire—to defend himself before the literary establishment. He went on the counterattack against his detractors in a letter to the editor of the *Mercure*. Borel's rebuttal was strongly worded (the editors of the *Mercure* admitted they cut out from his response a few lines that went too far when they published his letter [240]), but the essential demand was that Auriant offer some *proof* that the diary was not authentic, as he claimed. Borel reasoned that the fact that Mlle X (or Gisèle d'Estoc, as she had now been publicly identified by Auriant and Deffoux) had made a mistake about which friend's death Maupassant had foreseen could be taken as evidence of the credibility of the document, rather than its falsity. Only a sincere person would allow such inaccuracy to stand; a forger would have taken care to check such details. Borel summed up Auriant's objections in a stinging, one-line criticism: *"Puisqu'il ne la connaît pas, cette femme n'existe pas"* (Since he has never heard of her, this woman does not exist) (241). When the name of Gisèle d'Estoc is revived in the twentieth century, then, what is at stake is her very existence. The debate quickly shifted from whether the diary was a fake to whether its author ever existed. Was *she* a real person or merely a hoax?

To drive home the point that d'Estoc was a real person, Borel proceeded in his reply to Auriant to name some of the people — well known in literary circles — who knew of and associated with Gisèle d'Estoc, and to cite a book published by Mercure de France itself (the publishing side of the operation was a direct outgrowth of the literary review) in which she is mentioned. Borel does not miss the chance to point out that Auriant seems to be ignorant of all these facts. Ignorant, too, because he does not seem to be aware of the latest explanation of the 1912 "Souvenirs de Mme X." Recall that Auriant had claimed that the "Love Diary" — published only in 1939 but recounting events from the 1880s — was cribbed from this anonymous memoir about Maupassant. He had published selected passages from both documents alongside each other, noting what he perceived to be the similarities. In response, Borel claimed to know that the "Souvenirs" were themselves indeed a hoax (unlike the diary), the work of third-rate novelist Adrien Le Corbeau, according to a friend of said Le Corbeau who revealed the hoax after the author's death. This was now common knowledge. Really, concluded Borel, how could one take seriously the reservations of such an ignorant hack ("scribe") as Auriant!

Borel was not allowed to have the last word, however, for the same issue of the *Mercure* (August 15, 1939) that published his letter to the editor also carried a rejoinder by the put-upon Auriant. The latter listed all the questions that remained unanswered: If d'Estoc had been a model for Manet (as Borel had claimed), how come the Manet scholar Adolphe Tabarant had never heard of her? (He reproduced a letter from Tabarant to this effect as evidence.) For which painting(s), exactly, did she serve as model? If so many people associated with her (he reproduces Borel's list), where, exactly, is she mentioned in their books or in newspapers or journals? Auriant reported that he checked the one specific reference Borel had mentioned, the book published by the Mercure about the nineteenth-century symbolist movement, but on the page cited by Borel he found only a reference to a certain "Madame M.D." with no explanation of how this might be understood to refer to Gisèle d'Estoc (let alone Mlle X). Far from being ignorant of the rumor that Adrien Le Corbeau was the real author of the "Souvenirs de Mme X," Auriant showed that not only was he aware of it, he was also aware that not everyone believed it, and cited a letter in which a different theory of authorship was laid out. (According to this theory, the memoirs were actually part of a collaborative novel in progress being jointly written by Maupassant and another lover, here referred to only as Mme L. de N.)[5] In sum, suggested Auriant, Borel's feeble attempts to defend the diary only ended up convincing everyone who had not already come to that conclusion that the document was indeed inauthentic.

I have summarized the exchange that took place about the "Love Diary" in order to show how the lines that separated the two camps were drawn but also to convey something of the exuberance with which both sides argued their case. Mistakes were seized on with joy, insults traded with relish, and every detail of the argument loving-ly scrutinized for what could be squeezed out of it. The only quality missing was indifference, for had no one cared to respond, the publication of the love diary would have gone the same way as that of *Le destin tragique de Maupassant* a decade earlier, especially in light of the background of world politics in 1939, where war seemed increasingly inevitable. Indeed, it is the very fact that such a trivial exchange could mobilize such passion when such larger, more obviously important life-and-death issues loomed that makes the affair of the diary so interesting. What was at stake that made such apparent triviality so compelling? What follows will show that the means to settle the argument were in fact readily to hand, but that the parties avoided mobilizing these resources; they clearly preferred having the debate to having an answer. They chose to keep desire alive by deferring the moment when their desire for answers would be met. Not for the first or the last time in human history, the having of the desire itself turns out to be the thing we perhaps all value most (as so many stories about love that vanishes once it is satisfied would seem to testify).

In the case of the claims about Gisèle d'Estoc and her sensational love diary, it would be nice to think that scrupulous scholarship would allow the reader to evaluate one side as more credible than the other. After all, that is usually the claim about the power of reason. Auriant, too, would like to think so, as he tried to make much of his own scholarly background and paint Borel as sloppy and unreliable. He never seemed to miss the chance to point out Borel's mistakes. When Borel misspelled the name of Laurent Tailhade (one of the figures in this debate), Auriant was quick to seize on it, especially as Borel misspelled it in no fewer than two different ways (Tailhaude and Tailhande), and the second reference was meant to be the correction of the first but still got it wrong (243)! But Auriant was just as capable of carelessness, even if Borel did not always catch the mistakes. For example, Borel referred Auriant to Ernest Raynaud's "book on symbolism published by the Mercure de France" (241), which Auriant subsequently identified as *La mêlée symboliste* (243). But this was a three-volume work that appeared in 1918–22, whereas the reference to Gisèle d'Estoc as Madame M.D. was in a later book (though with a similar title), *En marge de la mêlée symboliste*, a volume of supplemental memoirs that had just been published by Mercure de France in 1936. If Borel is less credible because he slips up once in a while, the same logic dictates that Auriant, too, be held accountable. In the end, it may not be the most "scholarly" critic who is right, and the veneer of learning does not enable the reader to decide who is more reliable in this literary duel. Good scholarship is generally thought to be scrupulous, but one lesson of the debate between Borel and Auriant seems to be that everyone makes mistakes once in a while, and it is not enough to point out such slips in order to refute an argument. The rhetoric of casting your opponent as careless may serve to imply a carelessness about facts in general, but humans are just sloppy about details.

Borel and Auriant continued to slog it out in print over the summer, but by September of 1939, it had become impossible to ignore the more urgent business of war, and the exchange in the literary periodicals abated, without resolution. But the diary affair of summer 1939 was far from over. The debate succeeded in staking out the two positions that would be maintained in scholarly backwaters, on and off, for the next thirty years until it would be asserted, in 1967, that Gisèle d'Estoc had finally been "found" (though wrongly, it turns out). Over the decades, Pierre Borel quietly continued to press his claims about d'Estoc, and his critics continued to resist being persuaded. In part, the hiatuses in the debate had to do with external factors such as war: the materials Borel published during the World War II years were overlooked for a long time. For example, some of Maupassant's letters to d'Estoc appeared under the title "Une amie inconnue de Guy de Maupassant" (An Unknown Friend of Guy de Maupassant) in *Le mois suisse* in November 1941, but perhaps received little attention because the neutral territory of Switzerland was out of the literary mainstream during (and even after) the war years. It did not help matters that Borel so loved alliteration that almost all his articles appear to have the same title: "Une *adoratrice* de Maupassant" (1939), "Une *amie* inconnue de Maupassant" (1941), and "Une *amoureuse* inconnue de Maupassant" (1958).[6] Readers could be forgiven for thinking that he was merely publishing the same thing over and over again (as indeed he sometimes was).

Somewhat more puzzling is why an entire book with a more distinctive title (though still with the letter *A*)—*Maupassant et l'androgyne* (Maupassant and the Androgyne), published in 1944—was not more widely noticed by those who took an interest in the affair. This volume contained a reprint of the "Love Diary" but also much, much more, as will become apparent in later chapters of this book. For those who still wanted proof of d'Estoc's existence, Borel's book contained plenty of detail, not to mention photographs. Yet those who responded to Borel's postwar attempts to keep beating the drum seem unaware of it. They continued to insist on the prewar questions: How can we be sure this is not a hoax? Where is the proof that Mlle X/Gisèle d'Estoc ever existed?

Of course, one person observing the debate from the sidelines must have thought that the evidence was obvious. A large part of the debate (the exchange between Auriant and Borel) took place in the pages of the literary review *Mercure de France*. This review had been founded (in 1889) by a group of writers affiliated with the symbolist movement, and it had become famous for — among other things — "discovering" the symbolist poet Arthur Rimbaud. Moreover, as Borel pointed out, the publishing branch of the review published books about symbolism such as Ernest Raynaud's memoirs *En marge de la mêlée symboliste* (in which d'Estoc was supposedly mentioned), and it was this fin-de-siècle crowd that had personal knowledge of Gisèle d'Estoc — not the poets who called themselves symbolists, necessarily, but a wide-ranging group of writers both in the center and on the fringes of the literary scene in the late nineteenth century. Though they are not household names today, they are well known to specialists in the period, as Borel's list that appeared in his first, defensive letter to the *Mercure* illustrates: "Catulle Mendès, le Sâr Péladan, Octave Mirbeau, Jean Lorrain, le Père Didon, Jean de Bonnefon, Rachilde, Séverine, René Maizeroy, Richard O'Monroy" (241). Nonspecialists would not be expected to know them, but right in the middle was a name that jumped off the page at me because when I first read it, I was working on a biography of that very person: the "decadent" writer Rachilde (Marguerite Eymery Vallette, 1860–1953).

More to the point for *this* story, that name might have jumped off the page to any contemporary reader of the *Mercure* (where the article was published, remember?) because Rachilde was so closely associated with the review itself. Her husband, Alfred Vallette, had been one of its founders, its editor for many years, its guiding hand. Vallette had only recently *stopped* being editor when the squabble about d'Estoc began (he had died on the job in 1936, just three years previously). Rachilde had published much of her work — well known at the fin de siècle — in the pages of the review, and had served as a regular book reviewer until the 1920s. And, at the time the diary affair was unfolding, she continued to live in a small apartment on the premises of the review and publishing offices (located on the rue de Condé in the center of Paris, less than a stone's throw from the Luxembourg Gardens). So why, I found myself wanting to ask, didn't Auriant just hop up the stairs and confront Rachilde: "That fellow Borel says you know this mysterious d'Estoc—is that true?" It is not as though Rachilde was a stranger to Auriant—he published a series of his memoirs of her in 1953–54 (when Rachilde had just died and the debate about d'Estoc was in its second go-round). Why, for that matter, didn't Rachilde write a letter to the editor of the *Mercure* (as other interested parties did) and throw in her two cents: "I can't say if Gisèle d'Estoc is really the author of the diary attributed to her, but I can tell you she really existed." It would have been so easy! Ah, but therein lies a tale of human passion and revenge that it took me the better part of a decade to understand.

For Rachilde might well have "fessed up" to knowing d'Estoc, but such an admission might have brought out the fact that Rachilde and d'Estoc had briefly been lovers in the 1880s. And then it might be necessary to confess that when Rachilde had rejected her, d'Estoc had turned round and written a nasty, hurtful, tell-all book about Rachilde under a thinly veiled disguise, a book denouncing Rachilde's literary aspirations, a book that mercifully (for Rachilde) was all but forgotten in the 1930s (*La vierge-réclame*, about which more later). And, really, which would you rather do: spill your guts and relive a painful past or hold your counsel while others write your nemesis out of existence? This was not a revenge Rachilde worked to bring about, it was simply a windfall that required only that she say nothing, the very tactic she had once recommended to others for dealing with d'Estoc when the woman had been such a thorn in everyone's side.[7] Some fifty years after d'Estoc's denunciation of her, it must have been sweet vindication for Rachilde to sit on the sidelines and watch as someone who had sought to ruin her reputation was instead dealt her comeuppance ("nothing more than a hoax") while Rachilde reigned as the matron saint of new literary generations.

So those who knew did not tell. Those who did not know did not ask. And in this manner (don't tell, don't ask), the debate continued. After World War II, Borel began publicizing the relationship between Maupassant and d'Estoc once again. He reprinted the letters from Maupassant that had appeared in Switzerland in 1941 in a French review, the *Revue des deux mondes* in 1950, reviving interest in Maupassant's "unknown friend," and followed up with a book, *Le vrai Maupassant* (The Real Maupassant) in 1951. This time, he got a reaction from a new postwar generation of scholars. Artine Artinian, a professor at Bard College in the United States, responded in *Modern Language Notes* with a "warning" for Anglophone readers that summarized the debate from the first salvo in 1939 to the then present (though mysteriously ignoring the book *Maupassant and the Androgyne*). Artinian quoted with sympathy Auriant's conclusion that the "Love Diary" was a hoax, but conceded that at the time, the conclusion had lacked direct evidence. Cued, perhaps, by Borel's tendency to repeat himself, Artinian compared the words ascribed to d'Estoc in the cahier with the words ascribed to Maupassant's close friend Léon Fontaine in Borel's first (also largely ignored) publication, *Le destin tragique de Maupassant*, concluding that there was a striking similarity that called into question Borel's credibility. Who was the real author of the words, Artinian wanted to know: Fontaine? D'Estoc? Or even Borel himself? The implication was that the diary was a forgery (perhaps also the letters attributed to Maupassant), but there was a concurrent implication that if d'Estoc was not the true author of the diary then she had no other independent existence either. The two issues were treated as inseparable, since, so long as no one mentioned the book *Maupassant et l'androgyne*, the only proof of d'Estoc's existence that figured in these debates was the "Love Diary." (Later chapters of this book will return to the importance of *Maupassant et l'androgyne* and what it can teach us.) Weighing the evidence as he knew it, Artinian came down on the side of the d'Estoc deniers.

Borel was not to be outdone, however, and took one more stab at convincing the world in "Une amoureuse inconnue de Maupassant" in yet another issue of *Les oeuvres libres*. This time he went into greater detail. Much of the research that his claims about d'Estoc were based on had appeared in *Maupassant et l'androgyne*, but the book had been caught up in the politics of the war and was never properly disseminated. Borel later explained (in a letter to Armand Lanoux) that he had given the manuscript to "G. N." to publish, unaware that this person had usurped the publisher Ferenczi's business with Nazi approval. Just as the book was about to go on sale, the war ended, Ferenczi returned to reclaim his business, and G. N. was arrested. Tainted by its association with the Nazi collaborator G. N., Borel's book was pulped (Lanoux 374).[8] Which would explain why most of Borel's midcentury critics seemed unaware of it.

Since the book never made it into wide circulation, the critics' ignorance is understandable, but the work remained in both manuscript and printed form, and word of it might have made the rounds of those who professed an interest in Maupassant and his circle. In this manner, the materials might have reached (but apparently did not) Artine Artinian, an American bibliophile and scholar who took a lively interest in French publishing (his collection of rare books and manuscripts became part of the world-renowned holdings of the Humanities Research Center at the University of Texas at Austin). As a serious collector of French literature, he was presumably well connected to scholars and bibliophiles in France. Yet it was clear from reactions like his that even critics who followed the debate remained unaware of *Maupassant et l'androgyne*. If Borel was to retain any credibility, then, he had to repeat the information for an international audience, placing his material in chunks in reviews that seemed to circulate well and would get attention.

It is regrettable that more critics did not know about *Maupassant et l'androgyne* in the immediate postwar period, for it contained much compelling information, and the lack of attention to it set the inquiry into d'Estoc's identity back by half a century. Apart from anything else, the book made it perfectly clear that d'Estoc had a well-defined existence other than merely as the author of the "Love Diary," and it contained references that could be verified, along with photographs purportedly of d'Estoc, all of which made her seem much more than Artinian's caricatural "siren identified as 'Gisèle'" (251).

But the way this published evidence was overlooked mirrors a pattern already noted. There were those still alive who had known d'Estoc; they were not questioned. There were references to d'Estoc's publications; the critics stayed away from the libraries where they might have found copies of them. If they had bothered to go to the Bibliothèque nationale, for example, they would have been able to consult the *Catalogue générale des livres imprimés de la bibliothèque nationale*, which had begun to appear as early as 1897 under the aegis of the Ministère de l'instruction publique et des beaux-arts, and which contained a list of the library's holdings alphabetically by author. (The last volume, number 231 [Zimmerman–Zyzkin], appeared in 1959.) The volume of authors from Eschine to Ezziani (vol. 48) had already appeared in 1912, and so was available for consultation. In this volume, in column 497 (there are two columns to a page), it is easy to locate Estoc (G d') and see the three publications then ascribed to her. The first name is given only as an initial, so the sex of the writer is not evident to someone who does not already know, but that fact was not in question. The neophyte researcher would have no way to know that one of the publications attributed to her was probably done so in error (as already discussed in chapter 1). Nor would it be clear that the catalog's listing is not her complete bibliography (it lists only two "bona fide" publications, *Les gloires malsaines*—aka *La vierge-réclame*—and *Psychologie de Jeanne d'Arc*). But the listing is more than enough to establish that someone named G. d'Estoc existed, and it offers a starting place to find out more. However, it was not a resource that experts of the 1930s chose to pursue.

It is almost as though these experts *avoided* finding proof of d'Estoc's existence, and one has to ask why. If scholars are primarily concerned with the search for truth, why would one avoid anything that could lead to its discovery? One answer to this conundrum is to complicate the very notion of truth in biography. The work of Janet Malcolm, a justifiably celebrated journalist and biographer, has continually foregrounded the complicated relationship between truth and narrative. Time and again, her work demonstrates that what readers find credible are narratives that present coherent explanations of things, even (especially) when the reality is messy. This is most obvious in the context of the legal system (as Malcolm examines in works such as *The Journalist and the Murderer* and *Iphigenia in Forest Hills*), where juries essentially vote on which version of the truth they find most persuasive, but Malcolm shows the same dynamic at work in biographical narrative (in her work on Sylvia Plath, for example). This insight leads to a paradox: because of this bias toward coherence, we judge that narrative to be truest that is in fact the most artfully and artificially constructed. When it comes down to it, we prefer verisimilitude to actual truth. Thus Borel's narrative, with its incompetent misspellings and unreliable dates, may seem less true, upon reflection, than the confident dismissals of critics, even though it may contain more truth (Gisèle d'Estoc existed).

In the case of the debate about d'Estoc's existence, the critics demanded coherence from a narrative that could not supply it: Borel was like a bad defense lawyer who could not persuade the jury of history that he was telling the truth. The critics of the 1930s also wanted something else more badly than they wanted truth. Jurors have an incentive to reach a verdict (their pronouncement on the truth of the matter), but critics—professional and amateur alike—are under no such pressure to conclude, especially if a final judgment puts an end to the pleasure of debate. Perhaps especially insofar as the exchange presented a welcome distraction from wartime troubles, these authors seem to have relished the displaced confrontation offered by academic debate. They traded insults with gusto (A mere scribe! A hack!) and never seemed to be lost for a response. If the question of d'Estoc's existence had been settled once and for all, there would have been nothing more to talk about, but so long as the question remained alive, there was always something more to say, a pretext for another round. And so the pleasure of debate trumped the pleasure of truth, a lesson for all of us about the limits of scholarly disinterest. Being disinterested and being uninterested are surely two different things, as any high school English teacher will be prompt to explain, and supposedly being disinterested is the prerequisite for an evenhanded scholarly approach. But it's a fine line, and the debate over d'Estoc's existence as it first surfaced illustrates that if one is entirely disinterested, one may also be sadly uninterested. To be interested enough in a question to bother to debate it means one cannot be entirely disinterested, whatever one might argue to the contrary.

When the name of d'Estoc first resurfaces in the twentieth century, then, it is to dismiss her as a hoax. This chapter has traced the diary affair and looked at how the various experts of the period managed to remain ignorant, and it speculates about their stake in remaining so. The next chapter considers another important topic they managed *not* to know about: her alleged involvement in an anarchist bomb plot. Telling this story entails talking about d'Estoc's death, which will thus be the starting point for telling the story of d'Estoc's life. Last things first.

3 A Storm in a Teacup and a Bomb in a Flowerpot (the 1890s)

Lesson #3: Think hard before taking someone else's word for it.

The fact that the literary critics of the 1930s could not establish once and for all that Gisèle d'Estoc was indisputably the author of the "Love Diary" seems understandable. Questions on that score still linger today. To begin with, the manuscript mysteriously disappeared after it left Pierre Borel's possession. When questioned in November 1960 by critic Armand Lanoux, who had taken up the cause of investigating d'Estoc's existence, Borel claimed that he sold the cache of manuscripts to someone in the United States through a dealer in Lyon after World War II (Lanoux 394). In France, in the 1960s, this was apparently as good as saying that the materials were irretrievably lost to civilization.[1] Borel forgot the details of the sale and Lanoux seems to have made no attempt to trace the whereabouts of the collection.

Even were the manuscript of the cahier to be located and made available for inspection today, there might still be questions as to its authenticity. So the critics' skepticism about Gisèle d'Estoc's role as author might be justified in the case of this particular work. What is harder to understand now is why the self-styled experts of the 1930s dismissed d'Estoc's existence altogether, why they did not recognize d'Estoc's name from another context, and why they were unable to join up the dots, as it were, that would offer a picture of her existence.

As the previous chapter about the diary affair showed, the re-tired cop Ernest Raynaud (1864–1936) had offered a helpful key to d'Estoc's identity in his book *En marge de la mêlée symboliste*, which

Borel had cited in response to Auriant's skepticism. In this loose collection of memoirs, Raynaud reported the rumors surrounding a (presumed) anarchist bomb attack that came to be known as the "attentat Foyot" (the attack on the Foyot), named for the restaurant where it took place. At one point, a certain "Mme M.D." had been thought to be responsible, Raynaud reported. Critics such as Auriant were mystified as to how to connect the name of Mme M.D. with that of Gisèle d'Estoc, but the reference was really not so hard to decode, as this chapter will show. If Auriant and his contemporaries had followed the links, they would have discovered that Gisèle d'Estoc was the pseudonym of Madame Marie Paule Parent Desbarres, a person whose existence was well documented through other sources in the nineteenth century. Knowing her married name was still not quite the end of the road in the search for her existence, but it would have been an important stepping-stone to other information.

Anyone who has studied the 1890s — whether in the United States, France, or any number of other European countries — knows that it was an era marked by shocking levels of political violence. The anarchists were the terrorists of their day. We have today perhaps lost sight of just how widespread the political attacks were at the turn of the nineteenth century, but historian Alex von Tunzelmann has recently reminded us of both the extent and the intensity of the violence. In the years leading up to the assassination in Sarajevo that would ignite the First World War, anarchist attacks not only took the lives of notable victims, including heads of state from around the world ("the presidents of Mexico, France and the United States, the empresses of Korea and Austria, a Persian shah and the kings of Italy, Greece and Serbia") but struck with a frequency and intensity that would be shocking today. Portugal, for example, lost two kings to assassination *on the same day* in 1908 (Tunzelmann 36). The public reaction in the United States to fin-de-siècle events such as the assassination of President McKinley on September 6, 1901, or to the Haymarket riot in Chicago a little earlier, in 1886, was no less intense at the time than the reaction to the events of September 11,

2001, a century later (we always think we'll never forget, but we always seem to manage to do so). France was no different, since the anarchist violence would similarly lead to the assassination of the country's leader, President Sadi Carnot. Just as we might think today that it will be impossible to forget the events of September 11, it must have seemed inconceivable that public memory would ever be able to erase the trauma of the anarchist attacks that peaked in the years 1892–94. But the way the experts of the 1930s reacted to the claims about Gisèle d'Estoc's terrorist connections suggests that memory can be very fickle.

France was not the only country to suffer a veritable wave of anarchist violence in the last decade of the nineteenth century (in Britain, for example, it quickly became the stuff of literature, spawning such well-known novels as Joseph Conrad's *The Secret Agent* and G. K. Chesterton's *The Man Who Was Thursday*), but events in France were particularly spectacular. In addition to the assassination of a sitting president, they included a bomb in the national assembly and the execution by guillotine of an anarchist who had become a folk hero.[2] This is the stuff of mainstream public history. Even a superficial familiarity with the period would surely touch on the "revenge" killing of President Sadi Carnot in Lyon on June 24, 1894, which in turn would alert one to the wave of anarchist attacks that led up to this moment of national trauma. Anyone less than an expert might be forgiven for not knowing by heart all the names of all the suspects in every bomb plot, but one would not have to be a specialized historian in order to know the general picture and to have an inkling of where to find such details if one wanted to check. There was no shortage of plots, after all, as a cursory review of events illustrates.[3]

As the capital city, Paris was understandably at the center of the happenings that dominated the political scene of the 1890s. The decade began with anarchist riots in Paris on May 1, 1891. Then, in 1892, a series of bomb attacks targeted the homes of those involved in the ensuing legal trials. That same year—1892—saw the beginning of the trial of Ravachol, the most famous French anarchist, who became a household name and something of a martyr to some (he

claimed that his terrorism was intended to draw attention to the suf-
fering of the poor, and he was condemned to death even though in
the specific case for which he was tried he had killed no one). His execution was carried out the following year (1893), just before a bomb
went off in the Chamber of Deputies in December. The culprit in that
attack, Auguste Vaillant, was similarly executed in February 1894.
Two weeks later, a bomb went off in the Terminus Café at the Gare
Saint-Lazare in central Paris. Later in the year, President Carnot
was stabbed to death in Lyon by an anarchist shouting, "Vive la
Révolution! Vive l'Anarchie!"

This is but a brief summary, yet it is enough to illustrate the impact of these events on the entire population: the profile of the victims
of the attacks ran the gamut from ordinary people—the kind who
might patronize a railway café such as the Terminus—to the most
prominent (the leader of the Republic), which means that these events
affected just about everybody and were front-page news. Indeed, the
daily press quickly established a special rubric for reporting the latest
news on this topic: "dynamite."[4] Whether you feared for your own
life or for the leadership of the country, anarchism touched everyone.
The tenor of these political times—the social unrest that produced
assassins, their grievances, and the context for their actions—these
things have become part of the historical record in myriad ways,
from the daily press to the history books. As one critic has recently
written, "There was no ignoring anarchist terrorism in fin-de-siècle France" (Lay 80). Except, apparently, among the critics of the
1930s.[5]

The attack (or "attentat") on the swanky Left Bank Foyot restaurant that took place on April 4, 1894, was another spectacular chapter
in the history of fin-de-siècle anarchism. The restaurant was located at 33 rue de Tournon, just across the street from the Luxembourg
Gardens, the location of the Senate, and hence it was a popular eat-
ing place for important politicians.[6] A bomb explosion so close to
the heart of government was a reminder of how vulnerable the leading political institutions of the country still were. There had been a
bomb in the Chamber of Deputies just a few months earlier, for ex-

2. A police reconstruction of how the Foyot restaurant bomb must have been made. (Photo by Christian Laucou, reproduced with permission)

ample, so the Foyot attack served as a warning that anarchists could still strike at the heart of power, that no one was safe.

In the Foyot attack, however, it was not in the end political leaders who were hurt; rather the main victim was the journalist and writer Laurent Tailhade, who lost an eye as a result of the explosion. (Tailhade had lived at the Hotel Foyot from 1883 to 1890 and continued to frequent its restaurant.) The irony was that Tailhade was an anarchist sympathizer who only a few weeks before the bomb attack had publicly expressed sympathy for the anarchists in a much-quoted (and much-misunderstood) quip: "Qu'importe les victimes si le geste est beau?" (What do the victims matter as long as it's a fine gesture?)[7]

The perpetrators of the attack have never been identified with certainty, but there have been plenty of theories, most of them blaming anarchists in one way or another. One hypothesis focused on the anarchist oddball Félix Fénéon, the guy with the goatee famously captured on canvas by pointillist Paul Signac in the psychedelically colorful painting that now hangs in the Museum of Modern Art in New York (though Fénéon's guilt is far from being universally accepted, despite the way it is sometimes treated).[8] Who was really responsible is not the important question here, however, since that concern would lead us away from our pursuit of Gisèle d'Estoc; what matters for our purposes is the fact that the contemporary press was full of speculation about the matter, and one popular theory that emerged was that the attack was the work of a woman. The police had determined that the bomb had been hidden in a flowerpot (containing a hyacinth, no less; see the police reconstruction in fig. 2), and the popular imagination saw this as a definitive sign of a female hand at work.[9] This purported determination of sex, plus the injury to Tailhade, seemed to point to a woman who had a personal score to settle (rather than to male terrorists with a political agenda), and attention turned to Gisèle d'Estoc, whose combative tendencies and feud with Tailhade were well known in literary circles at the time. The rumor of d'Estoc's guilt, begun by Gabriel Randon (alias Jehan Rictus), was fueled by Ernest Raynaud, a participant observer of the symbolists and their times and a personal friend of Tailhade, who chronicled the events in his memoirs. These were the materials that Borel pointed to in his defense of d'Estoc's existence when challenged by Auriant. But the latter had been unable to make head or tail of the reference because Raynaud referred to "Madame M.D." rather than d'Estoc (the name by then known to Auriant and his fellow critics). To those who remembered the anarchist days, however, the reference was perfectly clear. Here is what Raynaud has to say:

On a parlé d'une vengeance personnelle de femme: Madame M.D., qui en voulait à mort à Tailhade, paraît-il, d'avoir médit d'elle. L'idée du pot de fleurs est en effet assez féminine. Madame M.D. qui ne s'habillait qu'en homme avait déjà, dans certaines circonstances, fait preuve de décisions viriles, mais comment ne pas hésiter à la croire capable d'une machination aussi diabolique?

(There has been talk of personal revenge by a woman: Madame M.D., who held a mortal grudge against Tailhade, apparently, because he spoke badly of her. The idea of the flowerpot is rather feminine, after all. Madame M.D., who wore only men's clothing, had already displayed a certain virile thinking in certain circumstances, but how can one without hesitation imagine her capable of such a diabolical plot?) (*En marge* 130–31)

The accusation is not without its internal contradictions—the femininity of the flowerpot clashes with d'Estoc's notably "virile" tendencies, for example—but Raynaud's reported speculation enjoyed credibility for several reasons. To begin with, he was a cop (a "commissaire de police") with a policeman's hunches ("flair de policier") (Borel, "Une amoureuse inconnue" 141). But the main reason was that everyone at the time who followed the vicissitudes of the literary subculture had witnessed the developing feud between Tailhade and d'Estoc in the pages of the press, where partisans followed each new accusation and counteraccusation.

The details of the feud boil down to this. Back in the fall of September 1888, Laurent Tailhade published a review essay about the poet Charles Cros in a literary review, *Le décadent*. The rather mundane title of the article—"Notes sur Charles Cros"—gave no hint of the explosive consequences its publication would have (metaphorically speaking!). It would earn jail time for its author, and it would be invoked as the pretext for the Foyot explosion, but at first it garnered little attention except among a small coterie of writers.

The interest Tailhade's article generated was not on account of its ostensible subject (Charles Cros) but stemmed from what Tailhade wrote about other people. For in this article Tailhade did two things related to naming names (though neither had to do with naming Cros). The first thing he did was to give away the sex of a person who had hitherto been known to the public of the 1880s only by the gender-neutral name of "G. d'Estoc." This person, he revealed, was a woman. And the second thing he did was to link the name of said G. d'Estoc to that of the novelist Rachilde, the darling of the decadents, who had won instant notoriety with the publication of her novel *Monsieur Vénus* four years earlier in 1884. Both disclosures were incidental to Tailhade's main purpose: he was intent on introducing his readers to another woman poet, Marie Krysinska. He commended Krysinska as an "excellent girl," one who would supply the stuff of passionate daydreams for a generation "ignorant encore Mlle Rachilde et Mme G. d'Estoc" (3), a generation that had not yet heard of Rachilde and d'Estoc. It was this casual remark that would set off a firestorm.

The juxtaposition of these two names does not seem so inflammatory today, but to understand what was at stake in the linking of these names at the time the modern reader needs to know the backstory that would have been familiar to readers of the literary press in 1880s Paris. It is a story that makes it clear why the critics of the 1930s need only have asked Rachilde to confirm d'Estoc's existence, but one that also makes it perfectly clear why Rachilde was not about to volunteer such information.

Rachilde was a popular novelist who in the 1880s hitched her wagon to the rising star of the decadent movement to make a literary name for herself. She flirted with scandal in order to create publicity for herself and her work, and created an eccentric public persona that positioned her as a unique figure (along with everyone else). Her most famous novel, *Monsieur Vénus*, is often linked with *A rebours* by Joris-Karl Huysmans, which appeared the same year (1884), as representing the apotheosis of decadent writing. What is less well known is that at some time in the mid-1880s Rachilde and d'Estoc had a brief affair. According to Pierre Borel, "Gisèle est rapidement devenue la maîtresse d'une jeune femme de lettres qui, à cette époque, obtient un très vif succès avec des romans et des nouvelles fantastiques dans le goût d'Edgar Poe et de Barbey d'Aurevilly" (Gisèle quickly became the mistress of a young woman writer who, at the time, was enjoying marked success with fantastic novels and novellas in the style of Edgar Poe and Barbey d'Aurevilly) (*Maupassant et l'androgyne* 53). Every day, continues Borel, Gisèle writes "des lettres de folle passion impossible à reproduire" (letters of mad passion impossible to reproduce), but the young writer upon whom she lavishes this epistolary "mad passion" shies away from commitment

(she is only interested in brief affairs, "des passades"), and dismisses Gisèle abruptly ("elle la congédie brutalement"). Gisèle does not
give up easily, however, so much so that she earns the nickname "la
ventouse" (leech or bloodsucker).

In his book *Maupassant et l'androgyne* (published while Rachilde
was still alive), Borel refers to this woman writer only by the initial
letter *R*, but by the time Armand Lanoux comes to retell the story in
1967, he refers openly to this person by her full name: Rachilde (she
had died in 1953). It is also now known that Rachilde's affair with
d'Estoc ended badly in mutual recriminations that took shape in
print, a paper trail that testifies to the course of events. It is not clear
when or how they met (though the interlude of the next chapter offers
a theory that they might have been already acquainted by 1884), but
we know that by 1887 it was all over. In that year d'Estoc published
a tell-all roman à clef about Rachilde titled *La vierge-réclame*.[10] The
"novel" takes a young writer named "Raclife" to task for hypocrisy:
she pretends to be virtuous, but she is really a slut; she leads men on
through her sexually suggestive fiction but heartlessly allows them
to kill themselves over her; she pretends to care about literary values but is interested only in self-promotion. The text is summed up
in the accompanying illustrations by Fernand Fau. The front cover,
for example, shows a young woman whose general features indeed
seem to resemble those of Rachilde, here depicted wearing a low-
cut circus costume with hearts all over it and beating a drum. The
sign behind her is only partially legible, but it advertises an attraction "visible pour hermaphrodites seulement" (for hermaphrodites
only), a fairly transparent reference to *Monsieur Vénus*, which featured a heterosexual couple who traded gender roles. In other words,
d'Estoc presents Rachilde as a cheap sideshow performer drumming
up business in the streets for a freak show.[11] It is hard to avoid the
conclusion that d'Estoc, too, used sensationalism to sell, except that
La vierge-réclame does not seem to have sold particularly well. The
only remaining copies appear to be in the Bibliothèque nationale and
its annex, the Arsenal (though the book is now available in digital
form, making it accessible to everyone). As a literary work, it has

not stood the test of time very well, and anyone who reads the work without knowing its status as a roman à clef seems simply baffled by it; nevertheless, one understands why its author would not want her name to be linked with that of its (covert) subject.

Rachilde published her own version of d'Estoc in a novel that appeared the year after *La vierge-réclame*. *Madame Adonis* (1888) was evidently intended to echo the title of the successful if scandalous *Monsieur Vénus* of 1884. Rachilde may have enjoyed the flirtatious stage of the relationship with d'Estoc, but she found her hard to shake off once the charm wore off, and the nickname she gave her ("la ventouse") evokes not only the way d'Estoc clung on but also an unpleasant propensity to vampirism or bloodsucking.[12] Rachilde's depiction of her former lover in *Madame Adonis* is not nearly as vitriolic as the portrait offered in *La vierge-réclame*, suggesting that the hard feelings did not run quite as deep (or that *Madame Adonis* was written before *La vierge-réclame* appeared). Still, it is not hard to imagine that Rachilde was in no hurry to correct the critics who doubted d'Estoc's reality in 1939. If, after all these years, history had chosen to erase the very existence of her former rival and consign her work to oblivion, which is where it seemed headed, Rachilde must have enjoyed a little smug pleasure that kept her from hurrying to set the record straight.

But back in 1888, while Tailhade's linking of the names of Rachilde and d'Estoc in print may have seemed innocent enough to those outside the circle, to insiders it was bound to lead to trouble, given d'Estoc's touchy nature. And indeed things escalated quickly. The editor of the review, Anatole Baju, received a threatening letter from d'Estoc. Its exact contents were never disclosed, but it was described as a "lettre grossière" (crude letter) and deemed too rude to print by the editors, who nevertheless acknowledged receiving it in the pages of the review.[13] Feeling provoked, Tailhade responded on his own behalf in a letter that *was* printed in the journal later the same month (September 15–30). Even a second letter was drafted, but never published (Tailhade referred to it in *Lettres à sa mère*

[177–78]). Denied satisfaction in print, d'Estoc invoked the law and brought suit against Baju as the publisher and Tailhade as the author of the original offense. They were acquitted at first, on February 27, 1889, but d'Estoc won on appeal and the men were fined. Tailhade found himself unable to pay, though, and as a result was arrested and served some time in the Sainte-Pélagie prison in May 1890. He was released on May 17, after a friend paid the fine for him. The bad feelings continued to fester through the following years, pitting d'Estoc and then her new champion Léo Pillard d'Arkaï against Tailhade, Baju, Rachilde, and others affiliated with the *Décadent* journal, so that the rivalry seemed still fresh and unresolved when the bomb exploded at the Foyot restaurant in 1894 with the result we have seen above: d'Estoc was a prime suspect and therefore her name (and existence) are recorded for posterity in the popular press.[14]

The nature of the relationships takes some unraveling, but the publications that documented them were there in public libraries in the 1930s for those who looked in earnest. In other words, the "experts" of 1939 either were unaware of this chapter of literary history (in which case, their reputation as experts suffers) or they chose to ignore it. Either way, when it was brought to their attention by Borel's reference that Gisèle d'Estoc was Madame M.D., thought to be the perpetrator of the attentat Foyot, they expended no energy following up. Explaining the link would have required a little more research, it is true, but Borel basically told them where to look, as we shall see. Had they pursued the connection even a short way, they would have been forced to admit that the person of Gisèle d'Estoc—whatever else she was—was not a hoax invented by Pierre Borel in the 1930s.

They might also have discovered, too, that not everyone was equally convinced of d'Estoc's guilt in the matter of the Foyot explosion in 1894. She had a faithful defender in journalist Léo Pillard d'Arkaï, who leaped to her defense (and his own, as he had been jointly accused with her). He published a broadside in Nice on April 20/25, 1894, defending both himself and d'Estoc, claiming that on the evening of the attack he had been miles away, and that d'Estoc had not been in Paris for several years. Moreover, he added, at the time of the attack, she was too ill to have been involved, being "en sa retraite, alitée, gravement malade" (retired, bedridden, seriously ill). This broadside would have confirmed the link from the name Gisèle d'Estoc to the name "Madame M.D.," since the person defended by d'Arkaï under the name d'Estoc was clearly the same person accused by Raynaud under the latter name.

Armand Lanoux set forth this link in his book on Maupassant in 1967. He cites Raynaud's reference, the one that had been made available to Auriant, and notes that a colleague, Pierre Cogny, had recently investigated the Foyot affair, coming across a copy of Pillard d'Arakaï's broadside in the process. Arnoux helpfully provides the Bibliothèque nationale call number for the newspaper (379), but fails to grasp how it might provide a clue to more information about d'Estoc, concluding only, "Non seulement Gisèle d'Estoc avait existé, non seulement Pillard d'Arkaï avait existé, mais leur collusion était établie" (Not only did d'Estoc exist, not only did Pillard d'Arkaï exist, but their collusion was established) (379–80).

The broadside eventually allowed subsequent biographers to trace what happened to the "gravely ill" Gisèle d'Estoc and to confirm the last link in the search for her identity. To find a death certificate in France, one needs to know where the person died, in whose jurisdiction, in what administrative unit (*département*). Some thirty years after Cogny and Lanoux became aware of the broadside, the information provided by Pillard d'Arkaï that d'Estoc was at death's door in Nice in 1894 enabled literary scholar Gilles Picq to locate her death certificate. This official document (not without its problems, as we shall see) confirms that the person known to literary (and anarchist) history as Gisèle d'Estoc died in Nice on May 8, 1894.

When exactly d'Estoc moved from Paris to Nice is hard to trace with certainty. Some speculate that it might have been as early as 1890 (Picq, *Laurent Tailhade* 260). Another libel case that involved d'Estoc in 1892 establishes a link between Pillard d'Arkaï and Nice by that date.[15] On the other hand, *Tout Paris*, the annual listing of the names and addresses of "la société parisienne," continued to list Madame Desbarres of 2 and 4 rue Caroline in 1892 (giving also the name d'Estoc), but that is the last time she is listed.[16] It would seem, then, that d'Estoc had left Paris by 1893. In retrospect, the information provided by the death certificate—that she died in Nice a year later (1894)—lends credence to d'Arkaï's claims that she was too ill to have been planting bombs in Paris just a month beforehand (especially if, as Pierre Borel claims, she died of leprosy).[17] But even without the confirmation of the death certificate that is now available to us, thanks to Pillard d'Arkaï, there were traces of d'Estoc's existence in the public record that were available to scholars. Pierre Cogny and Armand Lanoux found them, and earlier critics too might have come across the information if they had dug a little deeper.

To begin with, the name of the journalist Léo Pillard d'Arkaï, who had defended d'Estoc (and himself) against charges of involvement in the Foyot affair, was, if obscure, not unknown. It was he who sold the dossier on d'Estoc to Pierre Borel in the first place (on May 12, 1928, according to Borel; see Lanoux 394). Most likely d'Arkaï inherited the papers directly from d'Estoc herself. We now know from the death certificate that he was the one who notified the authorities when d'Estoc passed away, giving his name as Louis (his legal birth name) Pillard d'Arkaï and stating that he was no relation to the deceased. Louis/Léo was at that time a journalist of twenty-five, a fact that may be confirmed from his own birth certificate. Like d'Estoc (as we shall see), d'Arkaï, too, was from Nancy, where he was born on April 26, 1869, the son of Nicolas Pillard, a tinker or "ferblantier" (the suffix "d'Arkaï" was an affectation to make himself sound more interesting).[18]

According to scholar Gilles Picq, the up-and-coming journalist moved to Paris in 1886 after completing his *baccalauréat* high school diploma and lodged for a while with his compatriot Mme Desbarres (who would also introduce him to Rachilde).[19] His first volume of poetry (*Les fleurs du Dom****) was published by A. Voirin in Nancy in 1887. The following year he spent a year in Sainte-Pélagie prison after the book caused a scandal and he was embroiled in a duel.[20] D'Estoc tried to defend him in a review that she founded in late 1887, the *Revue caudine*. After his release, he was drawn into Rachilde's orbit for a while but returned to d'Estoc's side by the early 1890s, when he found himself living nearby. He resided at 9 rue du Mont-Doré, just a street away from d'Estoc on the rue Caroline, near the place de Clichy in the heart of the Batignolles district where many impressionist and other artists had studios.[21] It was here that he visited her and interviewed her for a newspaper article. Borel quotes liberally from that interview in his book *Maupassant et l'androgyne*. The author d'Arkaï leads the reader into the peaceful garden behind the outer street wall on rue Caroline, although that retreat appears distinctly less peaceful when the narrator draws our attention to the targets and mannequins there that have been used for target practice and are riddled with holes (testimony, in hindsight perhaps, to d'Estoc's bellicose tendencies). Inside the somewhat "provincial" house, the narrator finally meets "Madame Gisèle d'Estoc" and immediately cannot help blurting out, "Jeanne d'Arc!" The Amazonian figure has the short haircut of her compatriot from Lorraine, and the effect is perfectly offset by her décor, which re-creates (if a little fancifully) the era of Charles VII (Borel, *Maupassant et l'androgyne* 40–41).

Borel states that this visit took place in 1885 (*Maupassant et l'androgyne* 40) but, as noted earlier, Borel is sometimes bad when it comes to details, especially dates: internal evidence from the interview suggests that it in fact took place several years later. For example, d'Estoc refers in the interview to her *Revue caudine*, which appeared, as she herself states, during the winter of 1887–88, as well as to her first work *Noir sur blanc* (published, like d'Arkaï's poetry, in Nancy in 1887) and to her short story publications in *Vingtième siècle* and *L'estafette* (44–45). These references make it impossible to believe that the interview really dates from 1885, before these publications had seen the light of day. Most likely, the interview dates from around 1891, since in her speech about herself d'Estoc refers to her work on Jeanne d'Arc as "nearly finished," the first installment of which "paraît en ce moment" (43). Only one installment of this work—"The Psychology of Jeanne d'Arc"—in fact ever appeared, and it was in 1891, so this is probably a more accurate guide to the date of the interview.

While Pillard d'Arkaï was a young innocent at the time of their first meeting around 1886, Gisèle had already had several lovers. Rachilde was one, but the most famous was the one already discussed: Guy de Maupassant. It was thanks to the link with Maupassant that the name of Gisèle d'Estoc would be preserved for posterity, since it was this connection that initially made her a person of interest to Borel, who capitalized on this connection in his many publications about her.

The first trace of the relationship with Maupassant dates from late 1880 or early 1881. Borel claims that the author came to d'Estoc's attention through his acclaimed publication *La maison Tellier*, which appeared in 1881. Recovering the exact chronology now seems impossible, and d'Estoc's side of the correspondence is missing, but it seems perfectly probable that Maupassant's first letter to her must be the one in which he is answering a piece of fan mail.[22] In the correspondence that has survived, Maupassant wrote to "Paule Parent Desbarres," evidently in response to a letter from her seeking to make his acquaintance based on a description of him by a third party (a "jeune homme qui vous a donné sur moi des renseignements" [a young man who gave you some information about me]) (Maupassant, *Correspondance* 1:301).[23] She is as yet an "inconnue" to him, but he declares himself willing to make her acquaintance.

Born in 1850, Guy de Maupassant was just entering his thirties and was at the start of his fame as a writer at the beginning of the 1880s. Thanks to the work of Armand Lanoux in the 1960s, there has long been some confusion about when d'Estoc was born. As we shall see, Lanoux placed her birth in the 1860s (erroneously, as we now know), and based on this apparently authoritative determination, critics have enjoyed pointing out that "Gisèle" would have been a mere seventeen or eighteen years old when she began her relationship with Maupassant.[24] In fact, d'Estoc was *older* than Maupassant at the time (though there's no evidence that he ever knew, or cared), and up to this point in her life, her main activity had been that of an artist. The decade of the 1880s, however, sees her add writing credits to her résumé, and it is tempting to speculate that her involvement with literary figures (first Maupassant, then Rachilde, and eventually Pillard d'Arkaï) led to her own literary aspirations. The first use of her pseudonym Gisèle d'Estoc dates only from this era: the first documented use of this nom de plume dates from 1884, so that her persona would seem to be a creation of this literary stage of her life.

D'Estoc's writing career would culminate in the clash with Laurent Tailhade that placed her in line for the blame for the Foyot bomb explosion, but it even began with vitriol — an acid sometimes used literally in attacks, though not by d'Estoc, who favored the metaphorical kind — when publication became a way of settling accounts with ex-lovers (she seems to have died before she could quarrel with Pillard d'Arkaï). D'Estoc's first vitriolic publication would be the attack on Rachilde in 1887, but perhaps the first of the literary figures who would steer d'Estoc toward writing would be Guy de Maupassant.[25]

After the initial contact, d'Estoc's correspondence with him continues in January 1881 (here the dating is on a somewhat more solid footing). Maupassant has already formed an impression of his correspondent based on her letters: she is "une femme un peu blessée, un peu irritée, mais très intéressante" (a woman who is a little wounded, a little irritated, but very interesting) (*Correspondance* 2:8). Maupassant may not have known d'Estoc well at this point, but in his summing up of her character, he seems to have grasped the essentials of her personality quickly (as readers will perhaps be in a position to judge for themselves by the end of this book). After further exchanges, a rendezvous was set for a Saturday later that month (or perhaps in early February), after which Maupassant wrote once again, commenting on the way he behaved perfectly during their unchaperoned, three-hour visit and asking her to wear the same dress to their next meeting (15–16). Things evidently progress quickly, however, for by the next letter Maupassant is describing himself as "plus . . . faune que jamais" (more of a satyr than ever) and offers "mille baisers . . . partout" (kisses everywhere; the hesitation in Maupassant's original suggests how this was meant to be read) (20). Despite the hints of physical intimacy, Maupassant continues to address her with the formal "vous," though this moves onto a more informal level soon after in a letter that ends with the somewhat more explicit "Mille caresses sur . . . toutes tes lèvres" (caresses on all your lips) (22), only to return to the formality of the "vous" form in the next letter and those thereafter.[26] Despite the mostly formal address, they were evidently sexual partners, but things took an even more curious turn: still in early 1881, Maupassant writes that his friend Harry Alis has a charming but somewhat naive mistress who has "une envie folle de goûter d'une femme, ce qui ne lui est jamais arrivé" (a crazy desire to try a woman, which she has never done before) (20); Maupassant wonders if Gisèle is interested ("Cela vous va-t-il?").

D'Estoc evidently *was* interested in helping to realize such fantasies, and she rapidly seems to have become not only Maupassant's mistress herself, but a sort of procurer for him, setting up lesbian sex scenes for the voyeuristic enjoyment of Maupassant and his dining companions.[27] Recruits for this amateur mise-en-scène of girls going wild were (then as now, apparently) not hard to find. In a later missive, Maupassant promises that Catulle Mendès is bringing to one such dinner "une jeune et jolie femme, son amie, ravagée par des désirs féminins . . . elle n'en dort plus" (a pretty young woman, his lady friend, ravaged by feminine desires . . . it's keeping her awake at night), so much so that during sex with him she cries out, "Une femme, une femme, donne-moi une femme!" (A woman, give me a woman!)[28] The lady in question will obviously not put up much resistance, but Maupassant warns his accomplice in seduction not to be so "(comment dirai-je) . . . prompte" as with the last one ("celle de l'Opéra") (*Correspondance* 2:25–26).

We can get an idea of the kind of scenario Maupassant, Mendès, and their friends enjoyed from what d'Estoc herself wrote (if the *Cahier d'amour* can be believed). She describes a dinner attended by one Suzanne L., a blond "hot girl" ("une fille ardente") of thirty who has nothing but love on her mind ("ne pense qu'à la joie, à l'amour"; see the account in Borel, *Maupassant et l'androgyne* 174). During the meal—d'Estoc does not specify here if this took place *chez* Maupassant, but that would fit the pattern—Suzanne is quite the party girl ("elle a été follement gaie"), flirting literally left and right:

"Tantôt, elle donnait à mon voisin ses belles lèvres rouges et charnues. Tantôt, à moitié nue, elle s'offrait à mes caresses" (One minute she gave her full red lips to her neighbor, the next, half-naked, she offered herself to my caresses) (174). On this occasion, it would seem that d'Estoc was not overly "prompt" (to use Maupassant's reproachful word), allowing her neighbor (Maupassant himself? D'Estoc does not say) his share of the action. Nevertheless she perhaps moves too fast and scares Suzanne away at a critical juncture: "Au moment où j'allais la renverser sous mon étreinte, elle s'est refusée net prétextant que son mari l'attendait." As d'Estoc moves in (when she was about to "bend her to her will"), then Suzanne gets cold feet and invokes a waiting husband as an excuse to leave, but d'Estoc wonders if her fright was sincere or if she was merely teasing them, stoking their desire ("jouait-elle la comédie pour attiser encore davantage notre désir déjà si violent de ses baisers et de sa chair"). This is but one episode, but it sheds light on the background to d'Estoc's correspondence with Maupassant in this intense early stage of their relationship.

After this early epistolary frenzy, however, the correspondence settles into a routine: Maupassant writes letters when he is away traveling (in North Africa in 1881, for example), and quick, businesslike notes to arrange rendezvous or to explain why he hasn't written in a while (illnesses and injuries, work, etc.), and by 1882 things seem to have cooled quite distinctly: he ends his letters by kissing only her hands ("Je vous baise les mains") (*Correspondance* 2:52, 53), apparently losing interest in all the other parts so coyly invoked in earlier letters. D'Estoc seems to have resented the diminished attention, for Maupassant suspects her of writing anonymous letters and has to defend himself. (Perhaps, like Rachilde, he was beginning to discover the bloodsucking side of her; his own tale of vampirism, "Le Horla," dates from 1887.) He writes from Menton on May 14, 1882, addressing her formally as "Madame," in response to a letter that he describes as "pleine d'injures brutales ou dramatiques, de tirades violentes, de colère peu dissimulée, même de menaces de mort" (full of histrionic and brutal insults, violent tirades, barely concealed anger, even death threats) (56). The long letter reads like the sort of state-

3. Gisèle d'Estoc in her schoolboy costume. (From Pierre Borel, *Maupassant et l'androngyne*)

ment made by couples who are breaking up, full of self-justification and recrimination: he reminds her that she was the one who made the first move, that he made no promises, and concludes that she can come and pick up her stuff whenever she likes. The exchange marks an evident crisis point in the relationship, but not the end. The storm blows over, and short subsequent notes continue to make perfunctory social plans and convey gossip.

A telegram postmarked 1886 confirms that d'Estoc and Maupassant were still what would appear to be "friends with benefits" at this late date. The letter has a rather stiff and formal tone. It begins with the excessively polite language of request, of the "Would you be so kind as to?" nature ("comme vous seriez aimable de"), and (nearly) ends with a textbook example of formal epistolary style: "Croyez, Madame, à mes sentiments les plus empressés et les plus dévoués." The content is at odds with the style, however. Maupassant invites her to dinner with their old friend Catulle Mendès along with two ladies she does not know, Mesdames Barbier and Lacroix, and then in a casual postscriptum adds: "Ah! j'oubliais. Si possible, en collégien, n'est-ce pas!" (Oh! I nearly forgot. If possible, dressed as a schoolboy, of course) (*Correspondance* 2:208). There is a photo of d'Estoc "en collégien" at the beginning of Borel's *Maupassant et l'androgyne* that helps round out the picture (though the photo itself is undated). Maupassant's letter sounds like yet another seduction setup, and it would appear that part of d'Estoc's role in these encounters was to come disguised as a schoolboy and let the women fuss over her (or him). This may originally have been d'Estoc's idea, as one of Maupassant's pornographic poems, "La femme à barbe" (The Bearded Woman), suggests (included as pages 78–79 in an appendix to a reprint of the *Cahier d'amour* in 1993; the references in what follows are to this edition). The poem describes the narrator's surprise at seeing a woman he invited to dinner arrive dressed as a young man, complete with a beard (hence the title). He is surprised by his own reaction, because the woman was frankly ugly, but he finds the man rather attractive and they proceed to a "monstrous coupling" in which he finds himself drawn to "des curiosités des plaisirs que l'on tait," curiosity about pleasures that aren't usually discussed openly.[29] When the woman undresses and he sees a tall, skinny figure with none of the usual discernible roundness associated with femininity, she is like "un homme, avec un trou" (a man with a hole), but contrary to expectation he finds the spectacle extremely arousing.[30] The woman takes charge, straddling him as if he were a horse (d'Estoc liked horses, says Borel [*Maupassant et l'androgyne* 77]) and playing the active role: "Et dans son vagin sec elle enserra ma pine" (in her dry vagina she inserted my prick). Despite the perfectly calibrated meter of the alexandrine, the "poetry" (one hesitates to use the word without the distancing of quotation marks) of lines such as this illustrates the extent to which the pleasures of the flesh could cause Maupassant to betray his gifts as a writer. The verse describes the pleasure the narrator experienced when he believed that he was being "baisé par un garçon!" (fucked by a boy), and perhaps led to further encounters in which Maupassant and d'Estoc could share multiple pleasures of the kind not normally talked about by using her disguise to draw other women into the sexual games.

One of Maupassant's valets, François Tassart, left a description of such an evening, when Maupassant set up a situation for his own entertainment. François was instructed to prepare a dinner for an intimate group of four one Friday evening. The doorbell rang, and he admitted two ladies "d'un chic extraordinaire," then it rang again and he opened the door to reveal "un collégien" who appeared a little awkward at first, "comme un potache ahuri" (like a bewildered schoolboy) (qtd. in Maupassant, *A la feuille de rose* 165). The boy soon recovered his composure at the dinner table, entertaining the company with his stories of student life. The women giggled and Maupassant looked on, amused but aloof. He told François to serve the coffee and at nine thirty François had the carriage brought round for the schoolboy, who had to be home by ten o'clock. The ladies wanted to know who the charming boy was, but they never found out. François was let in on the secret, though: it was a woman. According to François, Maupassant told him:

Vous rappelez-vous la petite institutrice qui était venue l'année dernière me demander de la recommander au ministre de l'Instruction publique; c'est elle! . . . Ayant obtenu l'emploi qu'elle désirait, elle m'a écrit pour me remercier. Je me suis souvenu de son air gamin et je lui ai demandé de bien vouloir venir jouer ce petit rôle, qu'elle a, d'ailleurs, parfaitement rempli. . . . Elle habite avec sa mère; c'est une jeune fille très honnête.

(Do you remember the little schoolmistress who came last year to ask me to recommend her to the Minister of Education; that's her! . . . Having got the job she wanted, she wrote to thank me. I remembered her boyish air and I asked if she'd be willing to come and play this little game. . . . She lives with her mother; she's a very honest young woman.) (167)

The description does not seem to fit with the rest of what is known about Gisèle d'Estoc, however. François Tassart began working for Maupassant on November 1, 1883, so he could not be expected to remember his master's first encounters with d'Estoc, who entered the picture in 1881 at the latest. There's no solid evidence that d'Estoc was involved in public education, nor that she lived with her mother.[31] Perhaps when Maupassant wrote to d'Estoc and asked her to assist him in playing a trick on the ladies by coming "en collégien" she declined (perhaps not for the first time) and so he found a stand-in, someone with enough androgyny and a flair for acting, someone who owed him a favor, as a substitute in a seduction routine first perfected with Gisèle and later witnessed by Tassart. Whether or not d'Estoc agreed to reprise her role on the occasion that prompted the telegram in 1886 we do not know, but it is the last extant letter from Maupassant to this correspondent.

For Pillard d'Arkaï, meeting Gisèle d'Estoc seems to have been something of a stunning *coup de foudre*. Within a few years, both had left the capital for Nice, where Pillard d'Arkaï made a career for himself in journalism.[32] He lived at 136 rue de France and edited the *Tribun du Midi* under the name Pyart d'Arkaï. If they found happiness together it was to be short lived, for just a few years later his name was publicly linked to that of d'Estoc at the time of the Foyot bomb in 1894 when he came to her defense invoking her terminal illness as alibi. When she died shortly afterward he was the one to notify the authorities, and he seems to have inherited (or at least taken possession of) her papers and manuscripts after her death, papers he kept until passing them on to Pierre Borel.

Intimate they may have been, but d'Estoc evidently did not reveal everything about herself to her young lover (if lover he indeed was), beginning with her true age. Pillard, born in 1869, would have been a mere teenager when (if) they first met in 1886. D'Estoc was older, considerably older, but she may never have let on quite how much older she was. When she died and it was time to notify the authorities, he gave her age as thirty-five, ten years older than his own twenty-five.[33] This meant that "Courbe, Paule, veuve de Parent Desbarres" (as she was identified on her death certificate) would have been born in 1859. As you will read in a later chapter, this date of birth is wrong by a long shot, but no one realized quite how badly wrong for some time. And whether Pillard d'Arkaï knew it was wrong, and by how much, we shall never know. At the time it made little difference.

The death certificate of Gisèle d'Estoc was rediscovered only at the end of the twentieth century and its contents published in 1998 (Picq, "On destocke" 118). During most of the discussion about d'Estoc in the twentieth century, it was assumed that she died in the early twentieth century, around 1906. In part this was because Borel claimed that she was between forty-two and forty-four when she died (Lanoux 396), and once Lanoux established (or thought he had established) that d'Estoc was born in 1863, simple mathematics meant that death would have caught up with her in the first decade of the twentieth century.

At the end of her life, d'Estoc's aggressive nature also caught up with her, and her reputation for tenacious feuding caused her to be a suspect in a high-profile bomb attack. Though by this time she had made her creative mark in both artistic and literary circles, it was not these efforts that would ensure that her name remained written in the history books. But written it was. In the end, what matters in this chapter is not whether d'Estoc was guilty or innocent in the Foyot affair (though she was almost certainly innocent), but the simple fact that her name was recorded. What matters is the fact that she was accused, that her name was linked to this attack. Because it means that there was a record of her existence: her name was part of the history of the period, it was included in journals, it was part of the record for anyone who goes back and reads the press of the period. It is hard to imagine a future in which historians who claim to be experts in the beginning of the twentieth century will not be familiar with the events of September 11, 2001, for example, or even other cases such as the Oklahoma City bombings, the Unabomber, or the work of Eric Rudolph, who was involved, among other things, with placing bombs at the Olympic Games in Atlanta (though what does it mean that I already have to add an explanation of who he is?). And it is hard to imagine that just a generation or so after d'Estoc's death, the bomb attacks of the 1890s went unremembered, yet this seems to be what is required in order to understand how d'Estoc was "disappeared." When her name came up in the late 1930s in Paris, the voices of scholarship could find no reason to believe she had ever been real.

Laurent Tailhade set in motion a series of events when he wrote, in his article about Charles Cros, of a younger generation "ignorant encore Mlle Rachilde et Mme G. d'Estoc," a generation that had not yet heard of Rachilde and d'Estoc. His wording ("ignorant encore") suggests that he thought it was only a matter of time until the younger generation caught up and learned about this pair. From the fact that d'Estoc took him to court over it, we might infer that she thought so too. But several generations have come and gone that—sadly, I think—never did come to hear of them. The Rachilde-d'Estoc couple never really figured in the public's consciousness. In the end, d'Estoc's fears were groundless.

"In the end . . ." To retrace the existence of Gisèle d'Estoc it is necessary to begin at the end, the end of her life and the end of a thread that will lead back to the person who became Gisèle d'Estoc in the first place. This chapter has shown that the doubts about her existence voiced in the 1930s can be put to rest once and for all — indeed, the evidence was there all along to silence her critics if only they had bothered, wanted, to look for it. In exhuming that evidence, it has also been shown that through a series of affairs with literary figures in the decade of the 1880s, d'Estoc gradually transformed herself into a writer, too, if not necessarily one very memorable for her own talents. These facts alone cannot tell us who d'Estoc was, however; they cannot remove the mask of the pseudonym and reveal the face behind it. But they establish a starting point, they provide some hints, and working backward from d'Estoc's death (from leprosy?) in 1894 and through the 1880s will eventually lead to that discovery, as the next chapters will show. But first, an interlude.

4 An Interlude (No Time in Particular)

Lesson #4: How you appear isn't always the same thing as how you look.

This interlude interrupts the otherwise backward narrative account of d'Estoc's life in order to pause and consider what we know about what she looked like and the larger cultural connections between identity and appearance. An interlude typically comes between two parts of a game or play (inter + ludus) and may also have its own playful qualities. It may even take the form of a play, or at least possess a performative element. This interlude aspires to a certain playfulness, and also has games as its theme, since it will focus on two representations, each with a sporting motif (fencing and tennis). More specifically, it focuses on the ways d'Estoc has been portrayed, especially in ludic contexts. It will show how depictions of d'Estoc have contributed to her continued mystery rather than serving to clarify her identity, while nevertheless staging something about the way identity in general works in our culture.

The one thing that has survived all the doubt and obfuscation about d'Estoc is that name, her pseudonym. Even when we have not been able to say much else about her (such as who she really was), we have had that one piece of her identity. There have been various iterations of the pseudonym (G. d'Estoc, Gisèle d'Estoc, J. d'Estoc, and so on), but the "d'Estoc" has been a constant. *Estoc* is an old French word for a sword, the kind a medieval knight might have wielded (think Excalibur, Charlemagne's Joyeuse, or, if you are so inclined, the sword of Gryffindor). Such swords might have been

79

blessed by the pope, so the holder of such a weapon might have felt a certain sense of self-righteousness, which may explain why "d'Estoc" was such a popular pseudonym to begin with. In the case of Gisèle d'Estoc, the one thing we have known about her all along, even when we did not know who she really was, is that she chose to present herself to the public by her righteous relationship to the sword. The epithet fits her combative nature and crusading spirit, but there may be a more specific reason that she came to be known under this name.

One of the persistent rumors attached to Gisèle d'Estoc is that she fought a duel—with swords—with an ex-lover, Emma Rouër. Such "petticoat duels" (or *duels en jupon* in French) were not unknown (despite being illegal), both in life and in fiction, and in the 1880s fencing was an increasingly popular sport in general, and one that attracted a number of women.[1]

In a survey of *salles d'armes* (fencing galleries) published around 1887 (to judge from the preface), Albert de Saint-Albin noted how the Franco-Prussian War had highlighted the need for more attention to physical fitness in France, which in turn led to an explosion of interest in fencing, starting around 1880. To belong to a fencing club was increasingly fashionable, and Saint-Albin lists some of the more famous ones to be found in Paris around this time. Each *salle* had its own characteristics. For example, the Salle Caïn in the passage de l'Opéra was favored by artists and writers such as Guy de Maupassant and René Maizeroy (141). What is perhaps surprising, given "modern" views of nineteenth-century misogyny, was that many clubs also admitted women. Saint-Albin notes that the painter Louise Abbéma, for example, was an expert ("une escrimeuse des plus alertes et des plus habiles") (67) and had even illustrated a book on the subject. The Salle Chazalet on the chaussée d'Antin boasted "une clientèle spéciale et choisie de jeunes Américaines, qui font des armes par ordonnance du médecin" (151), but in addition to the American young ladies who fenced for their health, there were women who appealed to no pretext other than love of the sport. Fencing was so popular among women that it even made its way into theater, writes Saint-

Albin (226), noting that the actress Marguerite Ugalde, who played d'Artagnan in *The Three Musketeers*, frequented the Salle Caïn along with the artists and writers.[2] And no doubt Gisèle d'Estoc, too, was a member of one such club (perhaps Maupassant introduced her to the Salle Caïn), though she was not famous enough for her name to have made it into Saint-Albin's "who's where."

The rumor that d'Estoc fought a duel with another woman can thus be seen against this backdrop of public interest in fencing in general and the spectacle of women fencing in particular. But this particular story was rumored to be behind a specific painting that capitalized on the fencing craze, a painting that had a lively reception when it first appeared and went on to have an afterlife that continues into the present day. The painting was exhibited in 1884, the year in which the pseudonym Gisèle d'Estoc first appeared.

Do you know the work of Emile Antoine Bayard (1837–91)? You probably do, though you may not realize it. Can you picture that moon-faced waif with the wild hair who has come to represent the Broadway musical now referred to by its abbreviated title, *Les Mis?*[3] Cosette is her name, a little scrap of a thing. That image was created by Bayard, at least originally. He is not a household name today, but he was well known in his own time, and his illustrations captured the popular imagination well enough that he created a face still known to millions today. He worked in various visual media but became best known as an engraver of illustrations in novels. He gave visual form to the imaginary inventions of Jules Verne, for example, but his most enduring legacy has proved to be his renderings of scenes from Victor Hugo's novel *Les misérables*. In particular, an adaptation of his version of the character Cosette has become the poster child—literally—for this work.

Before finding his niche as an illustrator, however, Bayard produced paintings of a rather stodgy academic style. One such work, *Une affaire d'honneur*, was exhibited at the Paris Salon that opened on May 1, 1884, alongside works by mainstream academic painters such as Pierre Puvis de Chavannes and William-Adolphe Bouguereau.[4] Bayard's painting reached an even wider French audience when it was

4. Emile Bayard's *Une affaire d'honneur*. (By permission of Swordsmen Appraisals)

reproduced as a black-and-white engraving in the large-format, popular illustrated newspaper *L'illustration* on Saturday, May 3, 1884.[5]

The painting (and subsequent engraving) depicts two women fencing. Both are stripped to the waist, though the woman facing the viewer retains her hat with decorum, and each fights with one hand behind her back (holding her skirts out of the way?); both appear to be right-handed. The understanding of this encounter as a duel, a matter of honor, is shaped by the title of the painting (*Une affaire d'honneur*) as well as by the presence of four onlookers, presumably the two seconds for each party. Two women huddle together behind the duelists, leaning in for a better look, perhaps in consternation. A third woman, wearing just one black glove, stands (leans?) against a tree with her arms crossed in a pose of aloof detachment.

Gilles Picq, the specialist on d'Estoc's nemesis Laurent Tailhade (the victim of the Foyot bombing), has suggested that this last witness looks a bit like Rachilde ("On destocke" 121). As we have already seen, Rachilde would have a brief affair with d'Estoc that would end badly (with a literary if not literal duel), though probably not until well after the time this picture was painted and displayed. In May 1884, when it first appeared in the Salon, Rachilde was busy writing her shock novel *Monsieur Vénus* and her affair with d'Estoc was still in the future.

Parenthetically, *Monsieur Vénus* reminds us of Rachilde's own fencing connections. In addition to being an accomplished horsewoman, Rachilde was an avid fencer, as the fencing scenes in *Monsieur Vénus* attest. Moreover, Rachilde originally published *Monsieur Vénus* with a coauthor, Francis Talman, a young man she claimed she met at a fencing gallery. The purpose, she maintained, of listing him as a coauthor was that if there were challenges to a duel as a result of the publication of the novel, he would be the one to provide the defense. He was the insurance policy, as it were. Rachilde herself, apparently, while as happy to wield the sword as the pen, found that the former was in fact mightier, even if only as a threat. To carry Picq's speculation further, perhaps Rachilde and d'Estoc first met through their mutual interest in fencing, and it may have been her service as a second in a duel that drew Rachilde into d'Estoc's orbit and led to their affair. If indeed Rachilde appears in Bayard's painting, this helps establish the fact that she and d'Estoc were acquainted at least by 1884.

The fourth and last onlooker in Bayard's painting stands back among the trees and is barely more than a silhouette, though we can see that with her right hand she appears to be lifting her dress as she picks her way through the undergrowth. She holds what looks like a handkerchief (a white, blobby object) to her mouth with her left hand, like a member of the Greek chorus commenting on the drama that unfolds before her.

In the foreground of the painting, clothes are strewn around, presumably the garments shed by the fighters, and in the bottom left-hand corner lie a hat and what looks like a riding whip. The whip is a visual link to a chain of semantic associations that increased the titillation of the painting: the whip can be seen first of all as alluding to horseback riding, and hence serves initially to evoke Rouër's claim to fame as a trick pony rider. But the allusion to riding also reminds the viewer of the sidesaddle position that "proper" women typically adopted when riding in the nineteenth century. This position was known, paradoxically, as riding "à l'amazone" (in the Amazon position), a mode more suitable for ladies because it did not entail an undignified spreading of the legs as in the normal (masculine) riding position astride the horse. Its name appears to be a paradox because the figure of the Amazon (as understood through classical sources such as Herodotus) was the antithesis of the proper woman in the nineteenth century. Amazons were first and foremost rebels in the popular imagination, warrior women who declared war on men and were therefore sometimes used to hint at lesbianism. Thus the presence of the whip in the painting serves to bring out sexual undertones and suggests the deviant sexuality of the women who duel. Even those viewers who did not know that the women in the painting were ex-lovers might nevertheless gather something of this sexual history from the Amazonian reference of the whip. Amazons were also reputedly skilled horseback riders (not unlike Rouër), and in order to perform better as archers, they supposedly cut off their right breast, a shocking form of voluntary sacrifice but one that fits in with the late nineteenth-century preoccupation with how women were unsexing themselves in their quest for equality with men. The undress of the two duelists reassures the viewer that these women are not in fact Amazons — they proudly display *both* breasts! — but even as the image reassures, the whip unsettles because of the associations it puts into play. And this is without mentioning the hint of sadomasochism that the whip further allows.

The dark clothing of the well-covered onlookers contrasts sharply with the lighter colors of the exposed flesh and petticoats of the duelists *en déshabillé*. A brief comment on the painting accompanying its publication as an engraving in *L'illustration* referred to "cette délicieuse *Affaire d'honneur*, de notre collaborateur et ami M. Emile Bayard, qui a mis dans ce duel de femmes, avec tout son esprit et son entrain, toutes les élégances de la grace la plus raffinée" (this delicious *Matter of Honor* by our friend and colleague Mr. Emile Bayard, who, with all his wit and enthusiasm, has put into this duel between women all the elegance of the most refinèd grace) (290).

The wording in *L'illustration* does not explicitly tell us that there is a connection between the painting and any real-life event, but it is entirely possible that such a connection was well known unofficially and in literary circles. Whether the painting is connected to any event in her life or not, it has become part of the story of d'Estoc that she is one of the duelists in this painting, and the afterlife of Bayard's depiction of the event has taken on a life of its own.[6]

Gisèle d'Estoc thus appears to have adopted this pseudonym at the same time that she appeared publicly in a painting of a duel; she took up the literal and figurative swords at the same time. Both the duel and the pseudonym were codified choices with their own rituals and rhetoric. When it came to dueling, for example, there was little risk that such an encounter would prove dangerous to either party; French dueling in the late nineteenth century was well known for its ritual rather than its actual danger (Hopton 341–44).[7] In any case, the duel was to be fought with swords, not pistols, thereby reducing the likelihood of fatal injury. Moreover, both d'Estoc and Rouër had studied fencing with an expert, Arsène Vigeant (1844–1916), who among other things had served as Napoleon III's personal fencing master. A native of Metz, he also published books about fencing, such as *La bibliographie de l'escrime ancienne et moderne*. Having studied with the best, then, d'Estoc and Rouër were not simply posturing for a painting when they agreed to a duel, they were engaging in a ritual whose codes they understood. The duel supposedly took place in the bois de Vincennes to the east of central Paris. D'Estoc was the winner when Rouër was wounded in the left breast in the fourth round (Borel, *Maupassant et l'androgyne* 55).

Bayard's depiction of an affair of honor thus would seem to enable us to date the end of d'Estoc's (love) affair with Rouër, since we know that the painting was exhibited in the Salon of 1884. Certain problems arise, however, when trying to reconcile this date with the more extended account of the love affair given by Pierre Borel in *Maupassant et l'androgyne*. Not for the first time we are forced to reflect that Borel is consistently unreliable when it comes to dates, yet it may be possible to fit the gist of what he recounts into the timeframe of Bayard's work.

The confusion begins even with the simplest of facts. Borel states, for example, that Rouër was a trick horse rider and trapeze artist at the cirque Medrano in Paris, but the cirque Medrano did not yet exist in 1884. (This famous troupe would not come into being until 1897.) Perhaps Borel was thinking of the cirque Fernando or some other popular venue with horse acts; perhaps Rouër later did find a place in the cirque Medrano, so Borel conflates the two moments; whatever the explanation, the discrepancy remains. Borel furthermore suggests that d'Estoc turned to Rouër *after* Rachilde sent her packing (*Maupassant et l'androgyne* 53), but Bayard places the end of the affair in 1884, when the affair with Rachilde was still to come.

The exact timing of d'Estoc's affair with Rouër remains vague, then, but Borel nevertheless re-creates the stages of the relationship in great narrative detail. For d'Estoc, the first glimpse of Rouër as she pulled off her latest acrobatic stunts at the circus (a circus that was not yet the Medrano) was a *coup de foudre*. The whole crowd went wild with applause, and d'Estoc threw a bouquet of Parma violets.[8] That same night the two women dined together in a private room and d'Estoc wrote to Rouër the next day about how their encounter had imprinted itself literally on her body memory: "Ton image est dans mon coeur, ta caresse est dans ma chair. Je garde sur mes lèvres le goût âpre de tes baisers" (Your image is in my heart, your touch is on my flesh. I retain the sharp taste of your kisses on my lips) (Borel, *Maupassant et l'androgyne* 54).

The course of this love did not run smooth, however. At one point, Rouër ran off to Hamburg with a German sailor who beat her up. When she returned d'Estoc took her back, so there was evidently more than one breakup and reconciliation when the affair is taken as a whole. Borel quotes from a letter that he frames as one of reconciliation after the Hamburg incident, but a reference that d'Estoc makes in the letter to trailing Laurent Tailhade in order to administer a punishment means that the correspondence dates from around the end of the decade (1888–91) when d'Estoc was feuding with Tailhade. And, according to Borel, it was *after* the Foyot explosion that Rouër abandoned her friend and began spreading rumors about her, rumors that led to the duel. Yet the Foyot affair was not until 1894 and was swiftly followed by d'Estoc's death. Clearly Borel's chronology cannot be sustained by the evidence: Bayard's painting and the Foyot explosion were a decade apart. Once again, Borel proves himself to be unreliable about dates. But if the specifics of the timeline are not borne out, the general picture may nevertheless have some truth to it. The on-again, off-again affair with Rouër may have extended over a long period of time (before and after her elopement with a German sailor), and perhaps it was an earlier stage of the affair that ended—though not definitively, as it would turn out—with an acrimonious duel captured in paint by Bayard. (We shall see that Bayard himself envisages a "reconciliation," too.)

Bayard's painting has a long afterlife which, like his portrait of Cosette, is still with us today, though in a form that has undergone transformations. Tracing some of these reworkings (as the next few paragraphs will do) serves to highlight an instructive paradox. In a sense, if indeed Gisèle d'Estoc is one of the duelists, then she is all over the place even today. Yet at the same time that she is visible everywhere, she is identifiable nowhere. Her image remains even as her identity is lost, showing how visibility is entirely compatible with obscurity. It is not enough for the future to see you for the future to know who you are. In other words, the survival of identity relies on more than a visual tradition; it requires a sense of history. But to explain this, let us return to the afterlife of *Une affaire d'honneur.*

The story of a duel fought between two women over a third woman was quickly taken up in a novel just a few years after the 1884 Salon in terms, moreover, that made explicit reference to Bayard's painting. The novel, *Zé'boïm* by Maurice de Souillac (the pseudonym of one Madame Lefèbvre), is barely remembered today but was first published by Alphonse Piaget in 1887. Zé'boïm, the author claims, is another Gomorrah, and this long (322 pages) and mainly trashy novel tells the story of Madeleine, who attracts all the wrong kinds of attention. The plot is complicated but easily summarized: other people are always falling in love with Madeleine, beginning with her schoolgirl friend Hermance, who is rapidly displaced by Mlle Dufaut, one of their teachers, followed in the holidays by Cécile (Madeleine's cousin), Pierre Gardot (Cécile's husband), and Louis Gardot (Madeleine's cousin's husband's brother). To the relief of the reader (who by now is exhausted from trying to keep track of these characters), Madeleine eventually escapes this predatory milieu when she marries a baron and minor politician, an alliance that places her in different social circles. Naturally, however, all the old crew turn up sooner or later, and Madeleine, unable to continue resisting the advances her seductive effect elicits in others, is sucked back into her life of vice. After another series of adventures in Algeria (where Madeleine meets Hélène, aka the comtesse de Terville, and the two women survive abduction and shockingly bad treatment by Algerian rebels), the baron eventually catches the women in flagrante and finally grasps what is going on (he is a little slow on this score). The women flee to Italy, where they pass as a young married couple, the Count and Countess d'Eon (Hélène passes as the man). Of course the name "Eon" should be a clue, since it recalls the name of the French diplomat the Chevalier d'Eon (1728–1810), who spent the first half of his life as a man and the second half as a woman, but no one seems to pick up on it. The "honeymoon" ends only when the women spend the winter back in France in Pau, where they run into Cécile (Madeleine's cousin, remember her?). After recognizing her old acquaintances, Cécile calls on them and insists on fighting a duel with Hélène over Madeleine. It is at this point that Bayard's painting is invoked, and a more leisurely consideration of this part of the novel will show how Souillac's work capitalizes on Bayard's image while pretending to repudiate it.

Cécile is a purposeful girl, so when she calls on Hélène she comes prepared for the duel to take place right away. When Hélène asks if they don't need seconds, Cécile scornfully dismisses the idea (the only reason to have witnesses would be so that Hélène could pick out her next lover, she says). Also, the duel will take place indoors, privately. Cécile criticizes the impulse to play to the gallery by settling a private dispute in public, by offering a catfight as a spectacle.

On the one hand, Cécile's summary judgment may appear an implied critique of the way the d'Estoc-Rouër duel became fodder for journalistic (and even artistic) exploitation through Bayard's painting. On the other hand, Souillac is also contributing to that same dynamic. Although there are no *diegetic* witnesses to this fictional indoor duel within the novel itself, the *reader* is a willing—indeed, perhaps eager—witness to what transpires, and Souillac is clearly using the risqué content as a bid for publicity for the novel (just as Bayard had exploited the women in his painting). The reader is offered a kind of striptease as the two women prepare their "toilette de combat": Cécile removes her hat and coat, the upper part (the "corsage") of her dress, followed by her corset and blouse, until she appears a "singulière vision, le buste nu jusqu'à la ceinture" (a singular vision, her upper body naked to the waist). Hélène follows suit, and both pick up a fencing sword. It is at this point that the author explicitly compares the scene to Bayard's painting with the words "Alors s'entama cette fameuse *affaire d'honneur*" (And so this famous *matter of honor* got under way) (234).

Lest there be any confusion about the reference, it is followed by a more explicit comparison:

Est-ce qu'on se rappelle? Il y a quelques années figurait, au Salon, parmi les toiles à succès, un tableau de ce genre: deux femmes impudiques sirènes, les mamelles au vent, ferraillant ensemble. La reproduction — en photographie ou en chromo-gravure — de cette toile affriolante s'exhibe à mainte vitrine des passages, à la grande satisfaction des *potaches*, qui s'arrêtent immanquablement pour dévorer ce plat égrillard de leurs yeux en boules de loto.

(Does anyone remember? A few years ago, among the successful canvasses in the Salon, there was a painting of this kind: two women, shameless sirens with their mammaries to the wind, crossed swords. The reproduction of this savory canvas—a photograph or a chromo-engraving—is on display in many a shop window in the passages, to the great satisfaction of schoolboys, who never fail to stop and devour this tasty dish with eyes the size of lottery balls.) (234)

The author goes on to suggest that Cécile and Hélène could have been the models for this painting (is Cécile, then, as winner of the duel, perhaps a literary portrait of d'Estoc?) before concluding that "la vie a de ces drames, de ces drames vrais, invraisemblables parfois" (life has these dramas, true dramas, improbable sometimes) (235). In presenting Bayard's painting, originally displayed among "toiles à succès" (as though Bayard's painting was not one of these successful canvases), then displayed in reproduction in shop windows as merely eye candy for hungry schoolboys, the author appears to be condemning such objectification of women. Souillac is at pains to emphasize that Cécile and Hélène's duel takes place in private, not in public. But in *describing* the duel, particularly in such a lurid manner, Souillac presents the events once more to the public in the same sensationalizing way—though in words rather than pictures—as Bayard's painting. Once again, d'Estoc is made into a spectacle.

For there can be no doubt that *Zé'boïm* is a sensationalist novel, bordering on the pornographic, despite the de rigueur claim in the preface that the work is realist in its principles and merely describes what already exists. The novel, whose plot has already been sketched above, presents one lascivious scene after another, and while many things are only hinted at (unspeakable things done by Algerian rebels), the avid reader, like the *potache* schoolboys with their eyes the size of lottery balls, finds plenty to stimulate the imagination. For example, the novel follows the trajectory of classic fin-de-siècle plots in that, after allowing the protagonists full rein for several hundred pages, the author punishes the deviants in the closing pages to satisfy bourgeois morality. But the punishments themselves add to the spectacle. Thus, Cécile is raped and then murdered and then mutilated by burglars who break into her house, and as if that were not bad enough, she winds up posthumously exposed to public humiliation in the morgue.[9] Madeleine ends up destitute and in a brothel about to become a prostitute. As the (mostly) passive victim of others' lust, she is spared the final dishonor of selling herself, however: she is eventually rescued by her devoted husband, Albert, and is reformed by true (heterosexual) love, marriage, and maternity in an epilogue lifted straight out of George Sand's novel *Indiana*.

While Souillac's work might still bear a connection to d'Estoc, even if it is a connection we have lost sight of today,[10] subsequent invocations of Bayard's painting gradually shed their association with the women it was reputed to depict as it made its voyage around the world and through time. The image was quickly plagiarized to sell cigars in the United States, for example. Already by 1887 a cigar box produced by L. Newburger and Bro. of Cincinnati, Ohio, offered a gaudy reproduction of the painting with the title "For honor," while a trade card advertising D. Buchner and Co. with an 1887 calendar on the reverse side cropped the picture to fit a portrait-shaped frame (rather than landscape), eliminating some elements of Bayard's original composition while adding a pair of fighting roosters and modestly placing camisoles on the dueling women to encourage consumers to "smoke Victory tobacco."[11] There is no sense that American smokers had any idea about who these women were meant to be or that the images did any more than call up well-established stereotypes about the virility of smoking and perhaps the volatile Latin temperament of women associated with cigar manufacture — familiar from stories such as Prosper Mérimée's *Carmen*. The "affaire d'honneur" was also re-created with live models for a series of erotic turn-of-the-century postcards and for stereoscope cards.

A decade later, Bayard's painting had given rise to a racy theatrical adaptation of the duel (as well as two early film adaptations), but again the interest was more in the excuse to depict half-naked women than in any historical reality that might have underlain the picture.[12] In a "pantomime" version of the spectacle that retained the French title of *Une affaire d'honneur* when it was performed in New York at

Maupassant au tennis (tableau de Fournier).

Georges Legrand

Hélène Lecomte du Nouy

Maupassant

Gisèle d'Estoc

(Coll. Pierre Borel)

Comtesse Potocka

5. Reproduction of a painting (by Fournier) of Maupassant playing tennis as it appears in Pierre Borel's *Maupassant et l'androgyne*, where the identity of the players is indicated.

Koster and Bial's in December of 1898, the pretext for the duel was a quarrel between the women over a French officer, and the main interest of the reviewer for the *New York Times* was whether the police censor in attendance was going to shut the performance down (he did not). The reporter noted that the "startling sensation" was based on two paintings by Bayard—the *Affaire d'honneur* already discussed and a second, *Réconciliation*, that was understood to show the aftermath of the duel—and commented that "the portrayal of the artist was faithfully carried out," which seems to be a coded reference to the fact that the women performed a striptease onstage in order to fight in the same state of undress as in the painting rather than a reference to faithfulness to the pretext of the fight or to any other details about its history ("New Music Hall Sketch").[13]

Most recently, Bayard's painting has served as inspiration for plays on the theme of "Babes with Blades," again invoking the theme of women fighting in general without reference to d'Estoc explicitly. Babes with Blades is a professional organization based in the United States that exists to promote acting action for women, and the group decided to sponsor a play-writing competition that would provide more such roles for women. Its website explains the inspiration for the competition: "The inaugural theme was proposed by Fight Master David Woolley, inspired by the print of Emile Bayard's 'An Affair of Honor' that hung on his living room wall."[14] Bayard's painting has thus become almost as well known as his depiction of Cosette, although no one (or almost no one) today would connect the image of two women dueling with the story of Gisèle d'Estoc. Although the image survives, the name has been lost.

In some way, then, both Bayard's painting and Souillac's novel are about the problem of identifying Gisèle d'Estoc, but not simply because they depict her. The point is not to suggest in some simplistic way that *Une affaire d'honneur* offers a portrait of d'Estoc or that the character Cécile in *Zé'boïm is* d'Estoc; rather, it is to suggest that there is something about the dynamics of dueling in both the painting and the novel that evokes the problem of d'Estoc's identity. A second visual representation of d'Estoc, again involving a competitive sport (this time tennis) and the erosion of names that is characteristic of biographical entropy, may facilitate thinking more about what that "something else" might be. This second image appeared in Borel's 1944 book about d'Estoc, *Maupassant et l'androgyne*. It was subsequently reprinted in the *Album Maupassant*, one of the authoritative iconographies of canonical authors published in the prestigious Pléiade series, in 1987. The illustration is a black-and-white reproduction of a painting by Louis Edouard Fournier, taken (the Pléiade volume's notes tell us) from Borel's book (Réda 322). This picture once again depicts a sporting exchange. The painting is horizontally bisected in the middle from left to right by a tennis net, with a dog lying in front of it, perhaps ready to act as "ball boy." On the left half of the painting, a group of three tennis players stands on the far side of the net in the background. There appear to be two men, both in light-colored suits (perhaps a version of tennis whites?). One stands casually with a hand on his hip and one ankle crossed over the other.

Both men are holding racquets, but neither seems ready to play. A woman in a long dress, holding her racquet out as though to receive the ball, completes the trio. In the foreground, and occupying the right-hand side of the picture, are three women: one seems clearly poised to launch an underarm serve. The wind catches her skirt as she moves to pull back her racquet with her right hand and throw up the ball with her left. (The ball is nowhere in sight; the picture resembles those newspaper competitions where the readers are invited to guess the position of the ball based on the posture of those in the picture.) Next to her, another woman stands listlessly in a shawl holding a racquet but with no apparent intention of engaging in play, while a third woman bends daintily from the waist and holds her racquet stiffly out of the way of her serving partner. As in Bayard's painting of the duel, the women are decorously (if casually) hatted despite their exertions, while garments lie strewn in the bottom left-hand corner.

For those who turn to the *Album Maupassant* hoping to find out something about d'Estoc, though, this painting only adds to the enigma. The caption provided in the album tells the reader that the title of the painting is *Maupassant au tennis* and helpfully names the players "from left to right": Georges Legrand, Guy de Maupassant, Hélène Lecomte de Nouÿ [*sic*], Gisèle d'Estoc, Emmanuela Potockà (240). The viewer begins to match the names to the figures. From left to right . . . but there are four women in the picture and only three women's names. The identity of the men is clear, but which woman is which? Gisèle d'Estoc is one of the two women in the middle, but which one? The one facing the viewer or the one with her back to us?

This problem of identification does not arise in the reproduction of the image in Borel's original text. Here, the players are identified by lines pointing to each one. Whether the identifications are correct or not, at least there is no confusion about who they purport to refer to. According to Borel, Gisèle d'Estoc is the active player with her back to us.

Of course part of the identification problem relates to class: the woman who remains unidentified is a maid and therefore "has" no name, since domestic staff are always invisible, especially when behaving as they should.[15] But even after we register how attitudes to class have evolved (servants may now be expected to have names), the larger point about the general degradation of information remains. The loss of information that occurs when Borel's book is "reproduced" echoes what happens when books are copied, whether by hand, by photocopier, or by digital scanner. Although the Pléiade volume takes the image directly from Borel's book and explicitly acknowledges the fact, for some reason it omits the identifying lines that link each name to a player, thereby reducing the amount of information passed on to the reader.

This apparently trivial example illustrates a broader trend with very significant consequences. The very attempts we make to preserve (and improve) information entail a loss. Medieval scribes make mistakes, repeatedly photocopying a document eventually makes it illegible, genes never quite reproduce themselves perfectly. As the laws of the universe state, things tend toward entropy, so preserving knowledge is not the natural state of things but the result of an act of will that must supplement the simple act of copying (which never simply just copies). Biography works to mitigate the degrading forces of entropy, then, but it also raises the question of what counts as information. The process of charting a life may be compared to the mapping of geographic space. Early attempts to represent space in the form of what we would call a map may appear to us now as approximate, impressionistic, even whimsical. They lack precision, but record certain beliefs about the general state of things: there is a river on the other side of those hills, this town is to the east (or west) of that one. Larissa MacFarquhar, reporting the insights of Craig Murphy, cites the example of early maps of Africa that were very imperfect in many ways but provided approximate information about features of the interior, such as rivers and towns, that were omitted from later maps because they were based on unscientific sources such as hearsay (45). As mapmaking became more precise, the resulting maps initially became less informative: the interior of the continent was simply blank because knowledge that didn't meet the standards of "a mappable fact" was simply omitted. Eventually, knowledge improved further and the interior could be recorded in ways that met the new expectations, but the initial cost of raising standards was a loss of information. Information deteriorated before it improved. In the case of geography, the land (mostly) doesn't go away and can be rediscovered, but information lost in time may be lost irrecoverably. The role of rumor in biography, then, is to preserve those traces of information that may be "unmappable" at one time but may later be verified by higher standards of scholarship. Borel's work is just such an example, and his identification of Gisèle d'Estoc in the Fournier painting is one small instance of the way his book, while far from meeting modern scholarly standards, is nevertheless essential.

But having seen how a sporty d'Estoc is shown playing tennis, let us now return to the painting of the duel. In this picture, too, one of the parties has her back to us. Some (including Gilles Picq) have proposed that Gisèle d'Estoc is the duelist who is facing us, but the picture itself suggests otherwise. The painting seems to depict the "touché" moment in which one duelist succeeds in landing a blow. While the woman facing us steps back and parries, it seems as though her assailant, on the attack, swerves and lunges to place a blow that will hit home. Indeed, the seconds seem to be leaning in precisely to see this moment, and the triumph of the attacker is aesthetically underscored by the colors of the painting: the woman with her back to us is dressed in an eye-catching vibrant red, while everyone else wears black, brown, or dark green and blue. If this interpretation that the cynosure of the painting is about to strike is correct, it would enable us to identify the purported participants, since we know that d'Estoc was the victor in the encounter. Once again, then, Gisèle d'Estoc has her back to us.

Before proceeding further with this discussion, it is necessary to acknowledge and consider the counterarguments against this identification. First is the fact reported by Borel that Rouër was wounded in the left breast, while in Bayard's picture the blow appears about to land on the woman's right side. But there is no evidence that Bayard was a witness to the duel, nor would he have felt constrained to rep-

La Réconciliation

6. Emile Bayard's *Réconciliation*. (By permission of Swordsmen Appraisals)

resent everything exactly as it happened even if he were. His business was painting, not history, and the elements of the picture are
clearly arranged for aesthetic effect, not as watertight testimony.

A second possible objection concerns the companion piece to *Une
affaire d'honneur*, the second painting titled *Réconciliation*. This supposedly twin picture depicts the end of the duel, when one party has
been injured and lies wounded on the path. All the same characters
are present, but in different poses, everyone composed into one central cluster with a single figure off to the left in dramatic counter-
point. In the main grouping the two seconds now seem to be confer-
ring off to one side, perhaps sticking to their role as witnesses. The
woman who had been off in the distance now solicitously holds the
hand of the fallen loser. The woman thought to be Rachilde is now
turning away from us and appears to be hailing with her glove a
horse-drawn carriage that is just visible in the distance. But the fall-
en woman, the victim, who languishes with one outstretched arm,

is clearly the woman in red, the one who had her back to us in *Une affaire d'honneur*. The one still hatted, then, leaning over her opponent to be reconciled, would appear to be the winner, hence Gisèle d'Estoc. Should this second painting be read as proof that the woman in red is Rouër?

Not necessarily. If you look not at the figures but at the landscape in the background of the two paintings, it is clearly not the same scenery. The continuity between the two paintings is violated. The general setting is similar: a path with trees on either side. But they are not the same trees! The birch-like trees on the right seem to have doubled in both size and number from the first painting to the second, while the tree that "Rachilde" appeared to be leaning against has receded and changed species from a sort of blighted sycamore into something resembling a species of pine. The flowering weeds that grow in the right foreground of *Une affaire d'honneur* are now in the left foreground of *Réconciliation*. These paintings are not of the same place. It could be argued that the setting has changed because the duelists moved during their encounter, but even if this were true, it does not account for the seasonal difference in tone in the two paintings: in *Une affaire d'honneur*, most of the trees have brown leaves, suggesting fall, while the trees in *Réconciliation* are a mature, summery green. In case you fail to "spot the differences" (as in the popular children's game), the victim on the ground is actually gesturing toward the tree that forms the strongest vertical element in the composition (the sycamore/pine), and the dramatic diagonal of her movement is prolonged and echoed by the woman hailing the coach, so that there are, in effect, two people in the picture pointing toward the tree. "Look at that tree," Bayard seems to be saying. "Notice anything different?" A similar diagonal in *Une affaire d'honneur* points in the same direction: the naked back of the woman in red leans to the left and her head lines up with those of the two witnesses to create a series of stepping-stones leading the eye to a coppice of trees, while the raised arm of the opponent gestures in the same direction. By directing the viewer's attention to the differences in his two paintings, Bayard seems to release the viewer from the obligation to treat them as related, as depicting two moments in the same story. When it is not read alongside *Réconciliation*, and when it is read in its own terms (the use of color and composition), *Un affaire d'honneur* shows us a woman set apart from the others by her vivid clothing—red, the color of the blood she is about to draw.

A final piece of evidence that relieves us from the obligation to read *Une affaire d'honneur* and *Réconciliation* together is the fact that there is nothing to suggest that they were conceived and painted at the same time. While *Une affaire d'honneur* was widely commented on at its appearance in 1884, the critics do not so much as mention *Réconciliation*. We know that it exists by 1898 when the events depicted in the paintings are adapted to the theater, but it is quite possible that Bayard painted his second canvas only much later and to capitalize on the success of the first (though it must have been completed before his death in 1891).[16] Given this evidence, then, it seems perfectly plausible to suppose that the person foregrounded by the color and composition of *Une affaire d'honneur* is the more dramatic and colorful of the participants, Gisèle d'Estoc, who stands with her back to us poised to deliver the winning blow.

Rather than simply depicting d'Estoc, then, both of these paintings (the duel and the tennis match) stage something about the workings of identity itself. It's not that we don't have other representations—photos, drawings, paintings—that purport to show us what Gisèle d'Estoc looked like. It's more that d'Estoc comes to represent a recurrent enigma in which identity—always hidden in plain sight, as it were—is something that is simultaneously offered and yet eclipsed (in the same way that everything about d'Estoc is always somehow in front of us and yet hard to see). The key to understanding this positioning is in the poses of the sporting exchanges. Both the duelist and the tennis player engage with their opponent. The swordswoman lunges, while the tennis player brings her right arm back and shifts her weight to her right foot, ready to swing at the ball and send it shooting across the net. Since the French word for ball and bullet are the same (*balle*), there is in some ways no difference between what tennis players and duelists (at least those with pistols) exchange across the space that separates them.[17] If identity is not just about how one labels oneself, but about how others recognize and respond to that projection of self, the engagement of the sporting exchange echoes the give-and-take of identity. The back-and-forth of the duel and the tennis volley parallels the mutual establishment of identity, in which playing the game entails a need for an Other and a recognition of the Other's role in shaping the engagement.[18]

Finally, a clue to the identity of the woman in red is encoded in Bayard's painting. The Petit Robert dictionary explains that the technical expression "frapper d'estoc" means to hit "avec la pointe de l'epée" (with the point of the sword).[19] In other words, the gesture of the figure with her back to us in Bayard's *Une affaire d'honneur* names the name of the person performing the action we see. D'Estoc is *doing* precisely what her pseudonym describes, sticking it to her opponent, hitting home with the point of the sword. This figure is giving us the key to the way d'Estoc chose to be known in public (through her choice of pseudonym) not by showing us her face, but by enacting the assumed identity. The old word for a sword is more than just a reminder of Gisèle's aggressive personality (evident in long-running and bitter feuds with people such as Laurent Tailhade) or of her volatility. It is a symbol of the lunge that calls out for a response, a gesture of identity that aggressively provokes a reaction in acknowledgment.

Similarly, the tennis player is engaged in exchange with the other player. It has been suggested that the name *tennis* is a corruption of the imperative form *tenez* (from the verb *tenir*, to have or to hold), an injunction that would announce and accompany the serve that begins each round of play. The exclamation calls out to the other ("Here! Take this!"), enjoining him or her to assume a position of readiness and prepare to receive — and return — the *balle* (or *bulle?*) that the server will send.[20]

In both representations — the duel and the tennis game — it is not given to us to see d'Estoc directly, that is, face on; we see her from behind. But in this position, we see her indirectly by seeing her effect on others. And perhaps, finally, this is how it is given to us to

7. Portrait of d'Estoc by Henri Louyot from 1891. (From Pierre Borel, *Maupassant et l'androgyne*)

see everyone. If we lack much direct information about d'Estoc, we know about her because of the way she impacted the lives of others (others such as Maupassant, Rachilde, Tailhade, Borel). But rather than being an exception, the case of d'Estoc is perhaps illustrating the rule that identity is always revealed more profoundly in interactions with others than in the full-face but static image fixed in a portrait.

There are known pictures that purport to represent Gisèle d'Estoc, and Borel published a number of them in his book *Maupassant et l'androgyne*. In addition to a reproduction of the tennis game painting (opposite page 64), which shows d'Estoc only from the back, and a problematic photograph of an adolescent Marie Paule Desbarres with her friend Marie Edmée that appears to have been "doctored" in some way (opposite page 48), Borel reproduces two images that reproduce images of a more ambiguously gendered nature. First there is a frontispiece opposite the title page that shows d'Estoc cross-dressed "en costume de collégien." Then there is what is described as a "portrait" of d'Estoc, an engraving of d'Estoc by Henri Louyot from April 1891 (opposite page 128).[21] This portrait presents a militarized d'Estoc, so that we see a beetle-browed masculine face, framed by short hair, that stares off into the distance to one side of the viewer. D'Estoc appears to be dressed in a tailored military jacket with frogging and a cross of Lorraine at the neck.[22] Her left arm crosses in front of her, foregrounding a strong forearm and a pair of no-nonsense gauntlets. Her right arm, hanging at her side, holds what appears to be a sword. A fullness at the hips suggests that the tailored jacket gives way to a flared skirt, but we do not see d'Estoc from the waist down, so it is possible to maintain the illusion that she is also cross-dressed in this portrait; the masculinizing traits detailed above certainly combine to suggest and buoy (boy?) up such a fiction. Even these portraits, then, complicate her identity rather than rendering it more accessible to the viewer.

It should come as no surprise, then, that when interest in d'Estoc returned at the beginning of the twenty-first century, one manifestation of that interest took an iconographic form. The French literary journal *Histoires littéraires* published two photographs of d'Estoc. One of the photographs was originally published by Borel in *Paris-Soir* on May 28, 1939, evidently intended as publicity to prime his publication of the "cahier d'amour" in *Les oeuvres libres* the following month. The other had not been seen publicly before. In one way, the two pictures could not be more different: one shows a seated figure tightly laced into a fussy, corseted Victorian dress that sheaths the entire body. There are provocative details — a foot that protrudes from the hem of the dress and a lace jabot that in the grainy quality of the photograph manages to suggest a revealing décolletage — but the abundance of clothing in this image could not be in more striking contrast to the accompanying image in which the person identified as Gisèle d'Estoc stands stark naked (except for a belt just below her breasts). She trails a length of patterned fabric that seems to be a cape and the explanatory note that accompanies the photos (by Philippe Chauvelot) suggests that this may be the photo that d'Estoc sent Maupassant in which she describes herself as Phryné, the celebrated Greek courtesan of the fourth century BC famous for a naked display of her body (Chauvelot 252). Especially in light of the second of these images, it would appear that we have seen literally all there is to see of Gisèle d'Estoc, and yet . . . I cannot help but be struck by the fact that in both of these photographs (from the same sitting, hypothesizes Chauvelot) d'Estoc's face is covered. In the "clothed" picture, she wears a vaguely oriental-looking head covering that allows only her eyes to be seen. The lower part of her face is veiled, and not with the gauzy kind of veil that reveals even as it conceals.[23] This veil is forbiddingly thick, the kind of thing worn by a terrorist (which is, of course, precisely what d'Estoc would come to be suspected of being after the Foyot attack). In the second, nude image, d'Estoc appears to offer her entire body to the viewer's gaze, yet even as she makes this defiant gesture, she holds her right arm up and across her face, keeping this part of herself in reserve and reversing the usual opposition between what is thought of as the public face and the private body.[24] It would seem that for d'Estoc access to her body was freely given (to sexual partners, but also to the general public through the painted representations of her), but what remains consistently shielded from view are the features of her face.[25] If d'Estoc was known for her sword, the other accessory of the warrior — the shield — was also part of her panoply, and the iconographic record shows both accoutrements at work.

D'Estoc succeeded in keeping herself hidden for over a hundred years. Even when parts of her, such as her pseudonym, were well known (at least in certain circles), more private details, such as her date of birth, would elude the general public. It would be over a century after her death until her birth certificate was published, for example. In one sense, then, d'Estoc is representative of a larger problem, which is the difficulty in really "seeing" women who yet seem to be revealing themselves. Her story offers a cautionary tale but also a positive one, for while certain things about her may never be known and will always remain veiled, she has not entirely disappeared. Previous chapters have explained how the existence of a person known as "Gisèle d'Estoc" could be confirmed, and how she could be linked, though publicly available materials, to a married woman by the name of Madame M. Desbarres. By the second half of the twentieth century, it had been established beyond a doubt that such a person existed. The remaining chapters of this book, then, explain how scholars discovered the identity of Madame Desbarres. Thanks to a hint left by a librarian and to the discovery of her death certificate, it was determined that Madame Desbarres's unmarried name was Courbe, and thanks to this discovery, the final pieces of the puzzle of her identity could be assembled. But not before a few more assumptions had to be corrected.

5 Gisèle d'Estoc When She Was Real (the 1870s)

Lesson #5: Names can be tricky things.

Of course, in some ways, Gisèle d'Estoc is *not* a real person. The name is—and was always understood to be—a pseudonym. The critics of the 1930s were right in a sense after all: "Gisèle d'Estoc" did not exist; it was just a name, a mask. But of course they also thought that the name could not be traced convincingly to someone who *did* exist in the real world, and in this respect they were and are very wrong. Gradually the connection between the pseudonym and a real person was established, but long after it came to be accepted that there was some truth to the claims of Borel, long after it was accepted that Gisèle d'Estoc was more than just a hoax, experts have continued to ask who this Gisèle d'Estoc really was. This and the next chapter address this question. Who was the person who was accused of planting a bomb in a flowerpot in 1894? Granting that Gisèle d'Estoc *was* a real person, *who* was she?

The fact that d'Estoc was accused of being a terrorist made sure that her name was preserved for posterity in the press, as the third chapter has shown. It also showed that the pseudonym Gisèle d'Estoc could be connected to a real person, a person referred to cryptically as "Madame M.D." by memoirist Ernest Raynaud and as "Paule Parent Desbarres" by Guy de Maupassant. Together, these facts can help reconstruct a life, but it has taken the better part of a century to understand how.

Even before she was accused of being a terrorist, Gisèle d'Estoc was a journalist with a reputation. She had a reputation for being combative (a wielder of the sword both figuratively in print and literally in duels), as the story of her feud with Tailhade and her duel with Emma Rouër have already illustrated. Part of the reason she got into trouble with Tailhade was her relationship with Rachilde, and here, too, she showed a vindictive side in the publication of *La vierge-réclame*. But before she tried her hand at writing, she had been an artist, and her participation in the art world left a trace, though not one that was immediately perceived.

The editors of Maupassant's correspondence note that the name Gisèle d'Estoc does not appear before about 1884. Before then, Madame Desbarres (or Des Barres, as the name was sometimes written) was known to the artistic milieus of Paris as an artist who exhibited regularly at the Salon. And sure enough, there is a dossier on her in the archives of the musée d'Orsay (the main museum of nineteenth-century art in Paris) under the name Desbarres, Mme Paule. When I consulted the dossier (in 1999), it contained a black-and-white photograph of a bust of a peasant woman (*paysanne*) dating from 1887. The information came from a 1909 catalog published by the museum of Toul (a town not far from Nancy in the eastern province of Lorraine), which lists the sculpture as a gift of the artist. Also in the dossier, a single photocopied page headed "La Lorraine au salon (1re année) (1887)" lists a plaster bust of a "paysanne Lorraine" as number 3873, giving the artist's name as "Desbarres (Mme Paule)" and adding her place of birth: Nancy. This dossier may not have been available to—and its contents certainly appear not to have been known by—researchers such as Auriant and Armand Lanoux, but it demonstrates that in the art world that paralleled the literary milieu, there were traces of such a person, and they turn out to corroborate some of Pierre Borel's claims. Indeed, the compiler of the exhaustive and scholarly reference work *Dictionnaire des peintres, sculpteurs, dessinateurs et graveurs*, Emmanuel Bénézit, lists her in his dictionary as early as 1950, giving her the following entry: "Desbarres (Paule Marie), née Courbes,

sculpteur, née à Nancy (Meurthe-et-Moselle), XIXe siècle (Ec. Fr.).
Elle fut l'élève de Chapu et Delorme" (197).

The entry accounts for the instability in her first name evident in the fact that Raynaud gives the initial M., as in Marie, while Maupassant wrote to someone called simply "Paule." Paule Marie—or rather, Marie Paule, as Borel gave it (Bénézit gets it backward)—is *both* M *and* P. It was not uncommon in nineteenth-century France for good Catholic girls to be given the first name Marie (sometimes hyphenated), and equally not uncommon for them to drop the name for the rest of their lives, so that Madame Desbarres might answer to both Paule and Marie Paule, depending on how formal she was feeling. The information that she was born in Nancy (in the administrative department of Meurthe-et-Moselle) helps confirm that we have the right person. And Bénézit supplies an all-important piece of information that nevertheless remained unknown to literary researchers for decades: her unmarried name is given as Courbes.

When Armand Lanoux went looking for Gisèle d'Estoc in the 1960s, he lacked this crucial piece of information and had to discover it through sheer good luck. He knew that he needed to search for the origins of Gisèle d'Estoc in Nancy—Borel had been clear about that much—but Lanoux looked for her under the name Desbarres. In the regional archives (Nancy is the capital of the Meurthe-et-Moselle *département* and hence where regional archives are kept), he combed birth records from 1840 to 1860 looking for this name, but came up empty-handed (393). And he would have been stuck in this dead end were it not for a chance discovery by the regional archivist M. Delcamp, evidently a party to the search, who later found a reference to a Mme Desbarres in the card catalog of the municipal library of Nancy. (This is the point in the story where fans of old-fashioned card catalogs may bemoan their loss.) The card referred to the book *Noir sur blanc: Récits lorrains*, which was published under the pseudonym Gyz-El, but on the index card, an unknown hand at some unknown time had penciled in "Mme Desbarres née Courbe" (Lanoux 393). Who wrote this "unmappable fact," when, and based on what information remains a mystery, but for those who yet remained unaware of the connection drawn by Bénézit, this was the missing piece of the puzzle: Gisèle (or Gyz-El) d'Estoc was Paule Desbarres, née Courbe. (Bénézit writes an *S* at the end of the name, but this would not have changed the pronunciation in French, so like the difference between Desbarres—all one word—and Des Barres, such variations in spelling were common and accepted inconsistencies.)

Looking for Gisèle d'Estoc under her artistic identity as Marie Paule Courbe, aka Madame Desbarres, allows us to fill in another chapter of her life—the life before she became a writer—as well as to confirm more of the details (if not the exact dates) originally provided by Borel. He wrote in *Maupassant et l'androgyne* that Marie Paule Desbarres attended the "école municipale de dessin" (drawing school) in Nancy, which had something of a reputation (19–20), but switched to the more difficult—and "virile"—art of sculpture, an interesting choice since, as the daughter of a "wealthy industrialist," she might have chosen an easy middle-class life of indolence. Even if she had shunned idleness, she might have pursued her artistic talent in more feminine ways, in drawing and in watercolors alone, for example. But somehow it seems fitting that the woman who was drawn to swordplay, the woman vitriolic enough to be credible as a bomber, should want to make a mark also in a more "virile" genre. From provincial Nancy, she moved to the capital Paris and there began to establish a reputation as a sculptor by showing her work at the annual Salon.

Art historian Mathilde Huet has traced Madame Desbarres's participation in the Paris Salons, and her research makes it possible to fill in some of the details of the life of Gisèle d'Estoc before she met Guy de Maupassant (personal communication). When artists registered for the Salon they not only gave their name, they also had to provide an address, so Salon records contain some basic facts that are retrievable today. Marie Paule Courbe first exhibited (at least under that name) in the Paris Salon in 1869, giving her address as 12 rue du Regard (in the sixth arrondissement on the Left Bank). A few years later, in 1873, she again exhibited under the same name, but now gave 47 rue Saint-Placide as her address. (The interrup-

8. The very exclusive rue Herran, where d'Estoc lived in 1880, showing the gates. (Photo by author)

tion in her career at this point may be attributable to the upheavals of the Franco-Prussian War of 1870 and the subsequent civil war of the Commune that turned Paris into a battleground in 1871, when the Salon was cancelled.) Thereafter, throughout the decade of the 1870s, she exhibited regularly, but moved around constantly, though always within the same few blocks in the sixth arrondissement: in 1875 she lived at 99 rue de Rennes; in 1876 she gave her address as 29 rue du Vieux Colombier; in 1877 she was back on the rue du Regard, but now at number 10 (though this was in fact the address of her teacher Delorme's studio). Then, in 1878–79, there was an unexplained hiatus in her career when she did not exhibit. When she returned to the Salon in 1880, she had changed neighborhoods, abandoning the Left Bank altogether. Perhaps the move was due to "Haussmannization," the nineteenth-century equivalent of gentrification named for its planner, the baron Haussmann, that swept away old neighborhoods and rebuilt Paris in the elegant manner so familiar today. Certainly, the rues de Rennes and du Regard were all rebuilt in the late 1870s and early 1880s, as dates on the buildings that stand on these locations today attest. There is no longer a number 29 in the rue du Vieux Colombier at all, for example. But there was more to the move from the Left Bank to the Right than just an address. Marie Paule Courbe also reconstructed herself.

When Mademoiselle Courbe began exhibiting again in 1880, it was under a different name: she had become, according to Salon records, Madame des Barres. She now gave her address as in the more upscale sixteenth arrondissement to the west of Paris, at 6 rue Herran. She would remain in the west and northwest of Paris, in the neighborhoods favored by other artists, such as the Batignolles district, for the remainder of her time in Paris, as we saw earlier.[1] This move to the Right Bank corresponded to the time she first met Maupassant (late 1880 or early 1881) and her gradual shift to a career as a writer, but she did not abandon the art world right away. In 1881 and 1882, she was living at 78 boulevard des Batignolles and gave her name as Madame Parent-des-Barres. She skipped the Salon in 1883–84, but according to Borel, she was still pursuing her art. She had been working on a sculpture titled *Sapho*, but was distracted from it by Maupassant. Instead of exhibiting in the Salon, she showed three drawings at the "Blanc et noir" exhibition (the "black and white" Salon for prints and drawings). These were a landscape depicting the banks of the Seine, a "superb nude" of Emma Rouër, and the interior of a painter's studio at dusk (Borel, *Maupassant et l'androgyne* 111). Alas, the catalogs

9. 1 rue de Tocqueville, where d'Estoc was living in 1885. (Photo by author)

of the "Blanc et noir" exhibitions have not survived, so we have only Borel's word to go on for these tantalizing details.

D'Estoc did return to the more prestigious venue of the academic Salon in 1885, again under the name Desbarres, giving her address as 1 rue de Tocqueville, in the seventeenth arrondissement.[2] From 1885 to 1889, as we have already seen, she lived at 2 rue Caroline (later 2

10. A bust of a peasant woman from Lorraine that d'Estoc exhibited in 1877. (Archives of the musée d'Orsay)

and 4).[3] She exhibited at the Salon for the last time in 1889 and moved to Nice, where she would meet her death just a few years later.

In other words, we can now sketch the activities of the person known as Gisèle d'Estoc more or less from the time she left her native Nancy in the late 1860s until her death in 1894. And in retrospect, we can see that one of the reasons she was so hard to keep track of, one of the reasons Auriant was baffled, was that she seemed to have so many different names. Just to look for her under her married name in an alphabetical listing, for example, one would have to check under Barres (des), Desbarres, and Parent Desbarres (B, D, and P).[4] No wonder Auriant found it difficult to connect Gisèle d'Estoc with Madame M.D. and Armand Lanoux was initially stumped when he started looking in archives for her birth records.

But what of Marie Paule Courbe's art, a preoccupation that lasted for two decades? What can be said about what kind of artist she was? Here, the record continues to defy, because the only work that remains known today is the bust of the peasant woman from Lorraine, and this can be seen only in a two-dimensional photograph; the original, in the museum at Toul, was destroyed in a fire.

We can form a broader idea from the list of works she presented at the Salon, which show an emphasis on three-dimensional portraiture. Most of the works are busts in plaster or terra-cotta and are of people identified only by their initials (her first exhibited work, for example, is a portrait of Monsieur C. S. Jr.). Occasionally the name of the sitter is given in full, suggesting that these might have been commissioned works. When names do appear, they are not without resonance. Emile Deschanel (1819–1904), for example, whose bust was shown in 1870, was a politician and a scholar at the prestigious Collège de France. He is credited in France with having introduced the modern usage of the word *lesbian* to designate female homosexuality (rather than merely an ethnic description of an inhabitant of the island of Lesbos) in an article published in 1847.[5] Mademoiselle Marie Paule Courbe also exhibited (in 1875) a bust of someone described only as the son ("fils") of Deschanel. Perhaps this was his son Paul (1855–1922), who would later become the eleventh president of the French Republic. Her last known work to be exhibited, a terra-cotta bust shown in 1889, was a portrait of Monsieur Boyer d'Agen, known for his work on Michelangelo. Is it mere coincidence that, according to Borel (*Maupassant et l'androgyne* 38–39), d'Estoc too wrote an article (now lost) about the theme of intersexuality in the work of Michelangelo? These clues, gleaned from the stark list of d'Estoc's work, show that she was extremely well connected to both the intellectual and the political elite. Moreover, the interests of her sitters often overlapped in suggestive ways with the themes to be found in her own work, both plastic and (later) written.

It is impossible to offer an assessment of the artistic merits of D'Estoc's own contribution to the plastic arts, since nothing concrete remains to evaluate, but she did not only produce work herself; she also served as a model for others. Her role in Bayard's painting has already been discussed, and the claim that she was the model for Henner's *Bara* has been mentioned in an earlier chapter.[6] Jean-Jacques Henner (1828–1905) was a somewhat stodgy academic painter, but he hailed from Alsace (he was born in Mulhouse), so he may have shared d'Estoc's perspective on patriotism (intensified by the loss of Alsace-Lorraine after the Franco-Prussian War), and perhaps this was the bond that brought the two together or created sympathy. Pierre Borel also reports that d'Estoc was the model for the character Argine (the personification of silver, and hence money) in *La dame de Trèfle* (The Queen of Clubs) by Henri de Beaulieu (37). This oil painting shows a scantily clad woman standing with her left arm defiantly raised above her head who appears to have emerged in a puff of smoke like a genie from the bottle standing by her feet. It is hard to say with any certainty whether the figure resembles d'Estoc, since the face is masked and we can see only her mouth and the tip of her nose. Once again, d'Estoc (if it is she) seems to deny us a clear view of her face, but the body of the woman in the painting casts a shadow of a heraldic lion holding a sword, so perhaps the weapon was Beaulieu's way of hinting at his model's identity: the woman famous for her duel with Emma Rouër.[7]

Borel also moots another rumor that had caused its share of problems for researchers — to wit, that d'Estoc was a model for the painter Edouard Manet. This was another of Borel's claims that Auriant undertook to explore. By the time Auriant began to inquire, however, Manet was long dead (he died in 1883), so it was impossible to ask him in person. Auriant did the next best thing and asked the Manet expert Adolphe Tabarant. In his *Manet et ses oeuvres*, published in 1947, Tabarant made public his exchange with Auriant: "En 1939, M. Auriant nous demandait s'il était vrai, comme l'écrivait M. Pierre Borel dans un fascicule des 'Oeuvres libres,' que lorsque Maupassant rencontra Gisèle d'Estoc, elle venait de servir de modèle à Manet." Tabarant denied the assertion, stating that it was "purement imaginaire" (along with the claim that Manet had done a pastel of Emma Rouër) (470). But Tabarant's denial illustrates a common problem in the philosophy of referentiality and epistemology: What if you do not know that A and B are really one and the same? It is possible to believe that statement X is true of A but not of B because one does not know that A and B refer to the same object or person. The problem is usually illustrated in philosophy with references to things like the morning star and the evening star, but one might substitute the names Gisèle d'Estoc and Marie Paule Courbe and achieve a similar effect. Auriant did not know the true identity of Gisèle d'Estoc. At best, he knew that there was a connection to a Mme M. Desbarres, but the name Courbe had not yet been linked to the person of Gisèle d'Estoc. And what of Tabarant? Did he know that the Gisèle d'Estoc who preoccupied Auriant was the same person as the sculptor Marie Paule Courbe or Madame Desbarres (assuming he had even heard of them)? Because if not, he may not have realized that the person Auriant was asking him about was this contemporary of Manet's. He might legitimately state that the name Gisèle d'Estoc was totally unknown to Manet (the pseudonym was apparently not used before 1884 and Manet died in 1883), but it does not mean that the person later known as Gisèle d'Estoc did not serve as a model for Manet, who knew her (as a fellow artist) under another name.

This mistake in referentiality is easy to make, and it is one the musée d'Orsay makes, too, for in addition to the dossier on "Desbarres, Mme Paule" there is also a dossier on "Courbe, Me Marie-Paule," but with no cross-referencing that would suggest that anyone in the art world (or this art world, at least) knew that these were two names for the same person. The dossier on Marie Paule Courbe contains a photocopy of a page identified as being from Stanislas Lami's

Dictionnaire des sculpteurs de l'école française au dix-neuvième siècle of 1914.[8] The dictionary entry reads: "Courbe (Mlle Marie-Paule), née à Nancy (Meurthe), élève de Delorme, Hiolle et Chapu, a exécuté plusieurs bustes et médaillons qu'elle a exposés au Salon, de 1869 à 1877. Cette dernière année, elle demeurait à Paris, 10, rue du Regard. Elle avait une soeur, Mathilde-Isabelle Courbe, également née à Nancy, qui a pris part au Salon en 1874 et en 1875" (Courbe [Mlle Marie Paule], born in Nancy [Meurthe], pupil of Delorme, Hiolle, and Chapu, has executed several busts and medallions that she exhibited at the Salon from 1869 to 1877. This last year she was living in Paris at 10 rue du Regard. She had a sister, Mathilde Isabelle Courbe, also from Nancy, who took part in the Salon in 1874 and 1875) (437).[9] The entry is followed by a list of fifteen works, starting with two portraits exhibited in 1869 and ending with a plaster bust shown in 1877.[10] The article then cites its sources: the "livrets" or catalogs of the yearly Salons and the supplement to the *Dictionnaire général des artistes de l'école française* by Bellier de la Chavignerie et Auvray.[11]

Lami's dictionary states that Marie Paule Courbe exhibited from 1869 to 1877. Yet, as we have seen above, her last known contribution to the Salon actually came in 1889. What accounts for the fact that the dictionary omits her work after 1877? Again, the answer lies in the problem of referentiality. After the hiatus in her career from 1878 to 1879, she began showing her work under her married name, Mme Desbarres (or des Barres or Parent Desbarres). So little is left of the person of Marie Paule Courbe in this new name that dictionaries such as Lami's are unable to make the connection between the two artists; Marie Paule Courbe has simply vanished and a new artist, Mme Desbarres, has appeared on the scene.

Since the artist formerly known as Marie Paule Courbe metamorphosed into Mme Desbarres in the interval between 1877 and 1880, it is tempting to assume that this is when her marriage—the change in her *état civil*, or civil status, that transformed her identity from being her father's daughter (Courbe) into that of her husband's wife (Desbarres)—took place. How curious, then, to discover that she was married in 1875, and even curiouser to learn that by the time she started using her married name professionally, she was in fact no longer married but a widow. The facts (gleaned from the Paris municipal archives) are these. The sculptor Marie Paule Courbe married Paul Joseph Parent Desbarres on September 22, 1875, in the sixth arrondissement, where she was living at 99 rue de Rennes with her parents (exiles from a Lorraine that now belonged to Germany). She was declared to be "sans profession" (unemployed), sculpting not being considered a profession (that is, she was not a professional sculptor; she did not make a living at it). Her spouse, Paul Joseph, was described as an industrialist ("industriel"), a native of Paris born in the tenth arrondissement on September 23, 1836—thus he was just about to turn thirty-nine when he married.

The groom's parents, François Pierre Parent Desbarres and Louise Eulalie Caffieri, also lived in Paris, in the same neighborhood as his wife, at 28 rue Cassette, but they hailed originally from Clamecy in Burgundy, where they were part of a distinguished clan.[12] François gave his profession on his son's marriage certificate as "libraire éditeur," that is, he was a bookseller who also published, a useful connection for the woman who had yet to become Gisèle d'Estoc, had she shown an interest in literature at this period of her life. His most well-known publication seems to have been his contribution to a two-volume history of China (still being cited, for example, on Wikipedia) in 1860.[13] He also wrote a short history of Spain (1839), a history of Poland (1842), a "Bulletin du zèle et de la charité" (1853), and an edition (in Greek) of the works of Saint Gregory of Nazianus. As a publisher, he seems to have produced mainly stodgy scholarly works (a history of England, for example, and things that were cited in Catholic book catalogs) from his location on the rue de Seine (in the sixth arrondissement, the heart of the Left Bank publishing district).

At the time of his marriage, Paul Joseph himself was living in the heart of Paris, at 358 rue St. Honoré. The address in the expensive first arrondissement suggests that whatever the branch of industry he was in, he was quite successful at it.[14] The specific location of

11. The corner of the rue St. Honoré and the place Vendôme, where Paul Joseph Desbarres was living at the time of his marriage to Marie Paule Courbe in 1875. (Photo by author)

this address, on the corner of the rue St. Honoré and the famously upscale place Vendôme (location of the Ritz Hotel and top jewelers such as Cartier) leaves no room for doubt about the class Marie Paule Courbe was marrying into.

Paul Joseph had several brothers and sisters. In addition to two children who died in infancy, François and his wife, Louise, produced Emile Antoine Des Barres in 1835 (who seems to be the eldest), Marie Cécile in 1839, and Jenny Marie Pauline in 1848.[15] Marie Cécile married in Paris on May 1, 1861, Jenny Marie Pauline on February 3, 1869.[16]

If a life of married bliss opened up for the aspiring artist Marie Paule Courbe in September of 1875, it quickly closed again, however. Just three months later, her husband was dead. Shortly before Christmas of that year (December 20, to be precise), the "négociant" (wholesaler) Paul Joseph Parent Desbarres died at 200 faubourg St. Denis (a medical establishment in the tenth arrondissement) on the

Right Bank of Paris. This was not his permanent address, which was given as 66 rue de Rennes (on the Left Bank), perhaps a misremembering of number 99 (his wife's residence when they married) on the part of the two informants who immediately reported the decease to the authorities (it was recorded on the same day that it happened) and who described themselves as "employees" (i.e., not family members).[17] Death records in France, as already noted, do not contain information about the cause of death, so there is no certain way to know what caused Paul Desbarres's demise: a sudden fatal accident that unexpectedly cut short a promising marital partnership or the last chapter in a prolonged illness that had already declared itself in September when a sculptor needing money or status cynically married a dying wealthy man? The latter seems more likely given that he was under medical care, but it remains an open question. From everything that can be gleaned about Gisèle d'Estoc, it seems unlikely that the woman who would cross-dress as a schoolboy to seduce women for the voyeuristic pleasure of aging writers was destined for a life of monogamous heterosexual fidelity. On the other hand, it seems equally a stretch to suppose that she was so desperate for cash that she would sell herself into matrimony, even if only for a short time. She was, if nothing else, a woman of principle — as the feud with Tailhade and the duel with Rouër attest — and however misguided the principles may have been (having a man thrown in prison for linking her name to another's), she chose the principles over the easy life on more than one occasion.

If nothing can be known, at this temporal distance, about the motives that propelled Gisèle d'Estoc into marriage, there is nevertheless something to be said about how she represented her married state publicly. The marriage came and went so suddenly that it is not surprising that at the Salon of the following year (1876), Marie Paule Courbe continued to use her unmarried name. It was the one she had been known by at this public event for several years, and her choice signaled a certain professional continuity, whatever the emotional wrenches of the past year might have wrought. What is more surprising is the re-presentation of herself in 1880, after two years away from the Salon, under her married name. Having lived as a widow for five years, and having continued to be Marie Paule Courbe for so long, to assume an identity that could be heard as that of a dead man, as Mme Paule Desbarres chose to do, appears nothing short of an extreme makeover. (Because the boy's name *Paul* and the girl's name *Paule* sound exactly the same in spoken French, the fact that she may have retained part of her own name—Paule with an *e*—in writing does not mean that she was not heard to be taking her husband's name, Paul.) Perhaps she assumed the identity of a married woman because married women were thought to be more respectable and this status served as an alibi for her sexual adventures. It was just a few months later in 1880 (or in early 1881 at the latest) that she began her liaison with Guy de Maupassant, and perhaps she did not wait for this occasion to begin her cross-dressed seductions: it does not sound as though she was experimenting on Maupassant, but rather as though she already had the routine down when he met her. It was her married name that Maupassant used when writing to her, and her married name that was still in circulation when Raynaud wrote about her, so it was not a passing whim to pass herself off as a "madame" rather than a "mademoiselle."

One final note that can be gleaned about this part of her life (again, from the official records that are all that remain): both her in-laws, Louise Eulalie and François Pierre, died within a few months of each other in 1881. Louise's death was recorded on May 7, and François survived her by only a few months, succumbing in early September (recorded on September 8). By late 1881, then, all (known) close connections to her family by marriage, the (Parent) Desbarres, were gone.[18] There was apparently nothing to remind Marie Paule Courbe of the wife she once was, nothing to constrain her to honor her husband or observe the conventions of conjugal decorum. Yet the very time when these ties were finally loosed is the time that Marie Paule Courbe becomes (and remains) Paul(e) Desbarres.

Although she turned increasingly to writing in the 1880s, when she took the name Gisèle d'Estoc, Madame Courbe Desbarres did not abandon her artistic career, and indeed she used her knowledge

of the art world as raw material for some of her fiction. Her first published work (in 1887) was a collection of short stories with a regional flavor ("récits lorrains") published in Nancy and called *Noir sur
blanc*. The title offers a play on words, since "black on white" is how
artists often depict the world, sketching in charcoal or pen and ink
on white paper, so that the author suggests a parallel between writing and drawing. Her writing is thus an organic extension of her visual art (though in two dimensions rather than the three of sculpture). At the same time, to tell something "noir sur blanc" is to state
something clearly, without nuances or shades (of meaning). When
everything is black and white, there are no gray areas. So the title
also announces d'Estoc's aesthetic: the stark truth, no compromises.

The stories in *Noir sur blanc* range across various topics and include depictions of other well-known figures of the day such as the
novelist Gyp, but they also draw on (pun intended) d'Estoc's knowledge of the art world.[19] Thus, in "Un mariage manqué" (A Missed
Marriage), the narrator sets off with the recalcitrant donkey Achille
and a group of artist friends for a day of painting and picnicking "en
plein air" (the characteristic of the impressionists, who distinguished
themselves from the stuffy academic painters who stayed indoors in
studios).[20] It is early on a Sunday morning in July in Lorraine, and
the artists enjoy the landscape until they break at noon to eat. After a
postprandial cigar, the artists fall asleep, and when they awaken they
are surrounded by local children who want to know what sort of a
show they put on. Realizing that they have been taken for a traveling circus, the artists decide to use their talents as clowns, jugglers,
acrobats, and musicians to offer such an entertainment in the town
square. Even Achille is roped in, as the "âne savant," the clever ass.
The narrator asks him to pick out the most lovelorn member of the
audience, then steers him adroitly to a buxom red-cheeked girl. As
the narrator observes, it wasn't hard to tell that she was obviously in
love with somebody, and he gets Achille to repeat the trick several
times, to great hilarity all round. After a good supper at the inn, the
artists return home at ten at night, with good memories of an innocent day of fun. One morning the following winter, the narrator is

roused by his friend Tancrède, who had been the star acrobat of the "circus," who announces he is getting married—in part to please his mother—and asks his friend to accompany him that evening to an official interview. The narrator deems it a tragedy that his friend is settling down but acquiesces and thus finds himself that evening at a very serious-minded reception where down-at-heel but earnest musicians play an interminable trio. Then Tancrède's intended sings, and her song about the birds causes the narrator and Tancrède to exchange a look: they are both transported back to the carefree day they spent hamming it up last summer. They exchange a smile, and a week later the marriage is off.

The message of the story is that the settled bourgeois life is not for the artist, who prefers freedom and spontaneity to stuffy interiors, even if it means being poorer in a material sense. The theme reveals the author's disdain for the comforts of the settled life, a message echoed elsewhere in d'Estoc's affective life. Writing to an admirer who was a little too assiduous, she claimed not to believe in love, which was no more than "dangerous madness," and cited her "personal motto": "Tout passe, tout lasse, tout casse" (Everything passes, everything tires, everything breaks). She was not interested in feelings or sentiment, preferring by far what she called "complicated adventures."[21]

On this occasion it was the lover who was too clingy, too much of an unwelcome hanger-on, so it is ironic to recall that from Rachilde's point of view, it was d'Estoc who appeared to cling with the determination of a leech (earning the nickname "la ventouse"). D'Estoc would appear to be the kind of person who is only interested in those who are not interested in her, those who offer the challenge of seduction; once the person becomes equally invested in the relationship, it becomes tiresome ("tout lasse"). In other words—the words of Bizet's Carmen (words formulated by librettists Henri Meilhac and Ludovic Halévy)—"If you don't love me, I love you, and if I love you, look out!" D'Estoc was thus in some ways the classic femme fatale, though her bead was not always drawn on naive young men like Don José.

This unwillingness to commit does suggest, though, that her marriage was never intended to be permanent (unless she was seriously self-deluded when she entered in to it). Whether she knew it would end so soon after being contracted, or whether there was from the beginning an understanding that it would be what is today called an "open" marriage, it seems unlikely that d'Estoc intended to settle down in 1875 as the wife of a successful businessman. Nothing in her life up to this point suggests that she envisaged such a conventional life for herself.

It is hard to know what propelled Marie Paule Alice Courbe into matrimony in 1875, and without more information it is hard to know if the untimely end of Paul Joseph Desbarres came as a shock or a relief, but one fictional source offers some intriguing hints. Rachilde was one of the people who could have confirmed the existence of Gisèle d'Estoc in the 1930s, but she chose to remain silent. One of the reasons for her silence was no doubt a desire to leave an unpleasant past behind, but Rachilde had not always been so silent about her onetime lover, and in the mid-1880s she had written a novel that, in hindsight, may be read as offering some insight into d'Estoc and her marriage.

Stripped of its subplots, the core of Rachilde's novel *Madame Adonis* (1888) consists of one central conceit: the recently married couple Louis and Louise Bartau cheat on each other with another couple, this one a brother and sister pair, Marcel and Marcelle Désambres (note the echoes of Paul and Paule); what Louis and Louise don't realize (until the dramatic dénouement) is that Marcel and Marcelle are the same person.[22] There are plenty of clues to alert the reader along the way—Marcel and Marcelle are never seen together at the same time or in the same place, Marcelle drops plenty of hints (she gives Louise a copy of Théophile Gautier's racy novel about a cross-dressing woman, *Mademoiselle de Maupin*, to read, but Louise is too naive to understand it), and of course there is the fact that the brother and sister look identical—but Louis and Louise are slow to make the connection (they are provincials, not wily Parisians).[23]

As the pairing of the names suggests, Louis and Louise might also be viewed as the masculine and feminine aspects of the same person, mirroring the "twins" Marcel and Marcelle. The novel presents Louis and Louise as two distinct people (unlike the Marcel[le]s), but the story can also be read as a mise-en-scène of how an androgynous woman such as Rachilde (who, among other things, presented herself as an "*homme* de lettres" and played up her cross-dressing) may have experienced an attraction to another woman. In other words, in creating the character of Marcel(le) Désambres, Rachilde may have drawn upon her acquaintance with Gisèle d'Estoc and the affair the two were reputed to have had.

To begin with, there is the name of the novel's main character, the "Madam Adonis" of the title. Marcelle's full name is Marcelle Carini Désambres, the initials of which (M.C.D.) could also stand for Marie Paule Courbe Desbarres (not to mention the fact that the names Désambres and Desbarres are virtual anagrams). This might be no more than coincidence, but Rachilde's novel draws attention to the oddness of the name in various ways. In most families, siblings have the same *last* (family) name and different *first* (or given) names. In Marcel and Marcelle's family, this custom is inverted: the brother and sister Marcel and Marcelle share the same first name, but have oddly different last names. When Louise first meets Marcel (the cross-dressed Marcelle, as we later learn), he is accompanied by his brother, an artist who introduces himself as Hector *Carini*. (Marie Paule *Desbarres*, let us not forget, also had a sibling who was an artist, though a *sister*, not a brother.) But we learn that Marcel's last name is *Désambres*. Hector and Marcel are brothers, but do not use the same family name. Hector refers to his brother as Désambres, then explains that "c'est un frère que j'ai qu'on appelle ainsi pour le distinguer" (he is a brother of mine who is called that as a distinction) (18), as though having different *first* names (Hector/Marcel) were not sufficient for people to be able to tell them apart. In most families, brothers share the same last name with no confusion; this is obviously not most families.

The mystery around naming increases when Louise meets the brothers' sister, Marcelle. Unlike Hector and Marcel, who apparently cannot be told apart even though they have different names (Hector's reason for the different last name), we are expected (though not really) to tell Marcel and Marcelle apart even though they have the same first *and* last names (Marcel[le] Désambres). When Louise sees Marcelle's full name on her business card—Marcelle Carini Désambres (173)—she notes with some surprise (though no insight) that both brother and sister (Marcel and Marcelle) thus have exactly the same name. Marcelle's name can be explained by the fact that she has been married (Carini would thus be her unmarried name and Désambres her married name, like Paule Courbe Desbarres), but it does not explain why her brother Marcel would go by the same name, his sister's married name. Marcelle feels a need to explain, telling Louise that Marcel is "celui qui s'appelait comme elle and qui ajoutait son nom de dame à son nom d'homme par plaisanterie" (196). That Marcel is (in this explanation) teasing Marcelle and joking by yoking their names is clear if unconvincing, but who is adding which name to whose is obscured by the working of French pronominal adjectives. "Son nom" can be translated as either "his" or "her" name. The most obvious reading is thus that Marcel is taking her (Marcelle's) "nom de dame" (her married name, Désambres) and linking it to his "nom d'homme" (Carini), but what makes Carini a man's name ("nom d'homme") in the first place when it was Marcelle's legal (unmarried) name to begin with remains unclear.[24] All this could be attributed to the fact that Rachilde wrote the novel in haste and only later realized she had given her heroine and her brother different last names, which somehow had to be accounted for.[25] But Rachilde clearly wants us to know there is something "funny" about Marcelle Carini, or rather something louche about Louise's inability to see identity and sameness even when it jumps out at her. (Rachilde herself evidently thought one name was plenty.)

The hypothesis that Marcelle Désambres is indeed based on Gisèle d'Estoc derives further support from the fact that much of the description of Marcelle is consistent with what is known about Gisèle from other sources, beginning with her general physical appearance. When Louise first sees Marcel (which is to say the cross-dressed Marcelle) at the château d'Amboise where he is helping with some restoration work, "he" is dressed as a hunter (more about the hunting connotations in a moment) in clothes that signal gender-ambiguous codes: the hunter wears a short brown velvet jacket and leans on a gun (22). Louise thinks him a "*joli* garçon" (21; emphasis added), a "pretty" boy, a somewhat unusual though not unheard of way to describe a man but one that often connotes femininity. Dressed as a hunter in his velvet jacket, he has something of the Henri III *mignon* in his attitude (22). The favorites, or *mignons*, of Henri III have long been a code for sexual inversion. *Mignon* is usually translated as "cute," but it also gives us the word "minion," which often carries a more sinister connotation. When used of men (as opposed to, say, steak) it suggests femininity and homosexuality.

The first appearance of Marcelle as herself (as a woman) is also marked by gender ambiguity: she first shows up as a black speck ("un point noir") that could be taken for either a lady or a priest ("Dame ou curé") with a "démarche virile" and "quelque chose de bizarre [qui] se dégageait de son costume" (something strange that emanated from her clothes) (164). Physically, she is tall and slim (165), and she looks like "une couleuvre dans un lierre" (202), a snake wrapped up in ivy.

Her facial appearance is also consistent with the portraits of d'Estoc (both verbal and visual): "Elle se couronnait de fourrure avec une crânerie féline qui lui faisait pardonner son nez, en bec d'aigle, sa lèvre relevée par un rictus mauvais, ses yeux mi clos et sombres, ressemblant à des yeux de chatte hystérique" (165). This feline, sneering look with its aquiline nose is hardly the stuff of traditional feminine beauty, but d'Estoc was hardly known for her seductive looks. Interestingly, there is also the veiling we have come to associate with d'Estoc. One scene in particular evokes the kind of sexual play that took place at the dinner parties in which d'Estoc would flirt with women for the pleasure of Maupassant and his guests. On one occasion when Louise dines with Marcel, she suddenly finds

herself ("se trouva") half-undressed, "le buste épanoui hors du corset sans savoir comment ce mystère s'était accompli." Louise does
not quite understand how this uncorseting came about, but Marcel,
to reassure her, offers to cover his eyes ("je vais me voiler la face")
(223).

The truth about Marcel(le) emerges slowly as her (female) body is
gradually revealed, but the descriptions of this physique as it emerges from its clothing also match the representations of d'Estoc's body.
Since she could model for the portrait of a boy such as Bara, it is not
surprising to learn that when Louis sees Marcelle naked, he thinks
she has the body of a fifteen-year-old boy (240, 252), with sex-inde-
terminate breasts ("seins d'éphèbe") (239). Louis learns that she has
to wear fake hips ("paniers") to give herself a feminine outline when
she is dressed (240). No wonder Maupassant thought that having sex
with her was like having sex with a boy (only different), and perhaps
this was part of d'Estoc's attraction for Rachilde (who was also attracted to young men such as Maurice Barrès, whom she once compared to a "houri," or dancing girl).

While Marcelle's breasts may be small, they are what give her
away in the climax of the novel. Louis, finding his wife in flagrante
with Marcel, stabs his rival, and when Louise removes Marcel's shirt
to render assistance, she discovers that Marcel has "une poitrine de
femme" (290). Louis realizes that he has stabbed his own mistress,
while Louise is still trying to grapple with the fact that her lover was
a woman (Marcelle, not Marcel) all along (291).

The reading of *Madame Adonis* that I am proposing here is a ret-
rospective one. It is because I believe that the character of Marcelle
may have been based on d'Estoc that I am looking for the evidence in
the text that would support such a reading. None of Rachilde's contemporaries seem to have been aware that the novel could be read
this way, that it was a sort of roman à clef, nor that it could serve to
help identify Gisèle d'Estoc as Marie Paule Courbe. But if I am right,
then accepting that Rachilde was offering such a portrait may teach
us other things about d'Estoc.

Others might have started putting two and two together when

it became clear that d'Estoc was a sculptor, because Marcel—and Hector—are also sculptors, but according to Rachilde's depiction, sculpting is not Marcelle's only talent. She taunts Louis that he doesn't know the half of her skills, and she enumerates them for him. She mentions painting, and shows him "une nymphe de Henner"; sculpture, and shows him a plaster hand; literature, and taps her head (206). These are all skills that d'Estoc would claim, and Rachilde offers tangible evidence: d'Estoc modeled for Henner, sculpted in plaster, and in the mid-1880s her literary works were starting to germinate in her head. It is interesting, therefore, that the list of Marcelle's skills in fact begins with music, not a skill that d'Estoc is recorded to have had by any other sources. Perhaps Rachilde is telling us here of an aspect of d'Estoc that others did not record, or perhaps Rachilde is having a joke at our expense. The "evidence" of Marcelle's musical talent is that "elle touchait du doigt la lyre de Sapho" (she touched Sapho's lyre with her fingers) (206). Perhaps d'Estoc really did play a stringed instrument, even though no one thought to record that fact, but perhaps she was just good at playing Sappho. For this, we do have corroboration.

Then there are the allusions to hunting (a theme that had played a role in *Monsieur Vénus*, too). The title *Madame Adonis* seems to be an attempt on Rachilde's part (or that of her publisher) to cash in on the success of *Monsieur Vénus* by using the same formula: a title (Monsieur/Madame) plus a gender-mismatched classical allusion (Venus/Adonis) promising something of beauty. If Monsieur Vénus was about an effeminate man, as readers might reasonably have been expected to know by the mid-1880s, Madame Adonis would bring them more of the same (mutatis mutandis), the prospect of a beautiful man in the body of a woman. Adonis was a paragon of (young) male beauty known popularly through the work of Ovid. He was killed by the tusks of a wild boar, which provides a link to the hunting theme in Rachilde's novel and to Marcelle's cross-dressing costume. Marcel first appears dressed as a hunter (22), and it is in this guise that Louise finds him most seductive. The décor of Marcelle's house features hunting trophies (along with panoplies of arms that recall d'Estoc's dueling reputation) (193). In *La vierge-réclame*, d'Estoc would present Rachilde as Diana the huntress—in other words as a vindictive woman who would not hesitate to destroy men who got too close, just as Diana punished Actaeon, who violated her sanctuary (Diana turned him into a stag who was then torn apart by his own pack of hounds). Perhaps Rachilde, in *Madame Adonis*, was offering a preemptive warning: if Gisèle d'Estoc was a vengeful huntress, hunting men had better watch out. Although Adonis was not Diana's target, he had a nasty hunting accident all the same, and Marcel/Marcelle comes to a bad end (ultimately self-inflicted, so Louis and Louise are spared the brunt of the guilt).

If Rachilde did indeed offer a portrait of Gisèle d'Estoc in *Madame Adonis*, then perhaps the most interesting information comes from the details supplied about Marcelle's marriage. When Marcel(le) and Louise meet, Marcelle is already a widow, just as d'Estoc was by the 1880s, but in the course of the novel we learn a little about her unsuccessful marriage. "Marcel" tells Louise about his "Parisian sister" (which is to say, him/herself), "qui avait souffert d'un mariage désassorti" (who suffered from an ill-matched marriage) (53). Perhaps d'Estoc told Rachilde about her marriage, and how it turned out to be a mistake. Marcelle goes into further detail in words that might originally have belonged to d'Estoc: "Je n'ai jamais aimé les hommes, ils sont si bêtes et si brutaux. Mon mari m'en a dégoûtée pour le reste de ma vie. On m'avait fait épouser un vieux tout plein d'idées baroques, je fus complaisante, m'imaginant que la complaisance était un des prinicpaux devoirs conjugaux et . . . mon cher ami mourut au bout de quelques semaines de lune de miel" (I never loved men, they are so stupid and brutal. My husband turned me off them for the rest of my life. I was made to marry an old man with baroque ideas, I was obedient, thinking that obedience was one of the main conjugal obligations and . . . my dear friend died after a few weeks of honeymoon) (205). It is hard to imagine, given what we know of her belligerence, that d'Estoc was forced into marriage, or that she felt obliged to please her husband ("je fus complaisante"), but her "dear friend" did indeed die only a short time before the honeymoon ended, and d'Estoc certainly avoided entering into matrimony for the rest of her life.

Another detail about Marcelle that would turn out to be true of d'Estoc, too, was her age. Marcelle is, rather surprisingly, in her forties (even though she can pass for twenty-five when she is dressed in her man's hunting clothes) (22). As the final chapter of this book will make clear, d'Estoc would indeed have been in her forties when Rachilde knew her and wrote *Madame Adonis*. She could pass for younger, and many people chose to believe for a long time that she was born in the 1860s and was thus still a naive young woman when she first met Maupassant,[26] but the records will show that they were mistaken. If anyone had paid attention to Rachilde's disguised portrait of d'Estoc, then, they might have realized the error sooner.

6 Gisèle d'Estoc and Who She Wasn't (the 1960s)

Lesson #6: It often turns out that you find (only) what you expect.

Despite the protests of the willfully ignorant critics who insisted that d'Estoc was no more than a hoax, that such a person simply didn't exist, this book has demonstrated that someone known as Gisèle d'Estoc not only can be shown to have existed, but that quite a great deal can be discovered about her, even today when the trail has gone somewhat cold. Thanks to records of all kinds (historical records, catalogs, books and manuscripts), it is possible to trace her life back from the time of her death to her hometown of Nancy with relative ease. Along the way we have learned things about her career as an artist and her short-lived marriage. It remains only to establish the details of her birth and our mission is complete. But it was on this last leg of the journey that some biographers went most astray, and not because they were invested in denial but precisely perhaps because they wanted so badly to find her. This chapter tells the story of how her birthday was discovered and a "real" name attached to the pseudonym of Gisèle d'Estoc. Only it turned out to be the wrong name at first.

In the 1960s a respected French critic, Armand Lanoux, announced in print that he had succeeded in identifying Gisèle d'Estoc as Marie Elise Courbe, born in Nancy in 1863.[1] This identification lasted well into the twentieth century (and in some places it is still how she is identified). Here the attentive reader of this book will notice that simple math throws up an obvious problem with this identification. Something is not right about the picture: we (you and I) now know that the person later known as Gisèle d'Estoc first exhibits at the Paris Salon in 1869. If a six-year-old (one born in 1863) were to achieve this distinction there surely would have been a mention of such genius somewhere in the history books. In retrospect, it seems obvious that these two dates—born 1863, exhibiting 1869—produce an impossible narrative, but Armand Lanoux and his cohort did not have all the information to hand. The details of Gisèle d'Estoc's artistic career, while known (or at least available in print) to the art world, were unknown to literary critic Lanoux, for example. Still, Lanoux could have seen some of the inconsistencies that were emerging, and sorting out why the problems were not immediately apparent raises questions about how assumptions one is not even aware of making can affect the way research is conducted.

Very little in the humanities comes from "new" knowledge, at least in the way that word is used in some of the sciences, where discovering things about the world (genes, antibiotics, new planets) is often the goal. Perhaps (re)discovering the true identity of Gisèle d'Estoc counts as new knowledge, but the interest of the fact is not so much the little nugget of knowledge as it is the journey to its discovery (the story of the story). Rather than producing a new object, the humanities often suggest new ways of looking at old things that have been known for a long time, but known imperfectly or known differently. New insight is based on challenging old assumptions, but one cannot challenge everything all at once (the Archimedean principle that to move the earth off course you must be standing on something other than the earth), so the trick is in knowing what to keep and what to change in the new paradigm.

What sometimes gets in the way of seeing things differently is the kind of automatic thinking that makes us stay in the same familiar ruts, the mental cruise control that is our "default" mode of being. Once paths of thought are established, it is sometimes difficult to change tracks, even to see that another way is possible. Automatic thinking is not a problem limited to biographical enterprises, however, nor even to the humanities, but rather is part of the human condition, rooted in the structures of thought in everyday life. It is a daily problem for everyone who drives or is driven, for example. In *Traffic: Why We Drive the Way We Do*, Tom Vanderbilt explains that most traffic accidents occur not in difficult driving conditions but in routine, easy ones. When conditions are difficult, we know to pay attention, but when things seem easy, we relax and rely on mental cruise control. The result is the diminished attention that leads to accidents. Vanderbilt explains that engineers sometimes respond by deliberately making roads more challenging than necessary in order to keep drivers more alert. Knowing the pitfalls in driving, engineers take them into consideration in their planning. There arc lessons here for the information highway as well. In the transmission of knowledge, we tend to assume that making things easy (for the reader, for the student) is a virtue, but there may be a price for staying on the narrative straight and narrow. When things are made easy for us, we sometimes forget to think precisely because we can.

One does not escape the problem of staying in ruts by flying rather than driving. Controlling air traffic is a complex task, and there are many more near misses than bear thinking about. Of course there are computer programs to help manage the business of keeping track of planes, but as Malcolm Gladwell has noted (in a review of *The Myth of the Paperless Office* by Abigail Sellen and Richard Harper), many flight controllers still prefer passing pieces of paper back and forth among themselves to keep track of the planes entering the airspace they are responsible for. "Air-traffic control depends on computers and radar. It also depends, heavily, on paper and ink," writes Gladwell (92). Gladwell is interested in the problem of why computer technology has not succeeded in replacing paper and in explaining the cognitive reasons why paper, while "messy," is sometimes better because it "enables a certain kind of thinking" (93). Thinking about anything even remotely complex is in itself a messy business, and imposing a structure prematurely can cause part of the necessary work of thinking to be lost, so automation is not always an improvement. A draft of a document written on a computer already has a beginning, a middle, and an end, for example, and does not lend itself to being reshuffled as easily as pieces of paper. The same text on sheets of paper can more easily be rearranged to produce a different pattern, to tell a different story, perhaps, or to allow a different perspective to emerge.

One cannot even escape the problem of automatic thinking by leaving the earth entirely. The automation (for example, by software or other protocols) that ought to make a job like flight control more manageable can become downright dangerous in more complex contexts. After the explosion of the NASA shuttle *Challenger* in 1986, there were many attempts to understand what went wrong. The problem was traced to a design flaw in some O-ring seals that had failed, but people struggled to understand why, given that NASA knew about this flaw, the launch proceeded anyway. Most accounts of the disaster made the decision makers look either stupid or callous because they overlooked what should have been obvious. But organizational sociologist Diane Vaughan offers a revisionist version of events in her book *The Challenger Launch Decision*. Her explanation emphasizes the way bad decisions come about incrementally in a culture in which anomalous information (in this case, reports that mechanical parts were not always operating as predicted) becomes normalized. In a culture of what Vaughan calls "the sociology of mistake" (xiv), there are no bad people, just flawed structures that arise from sheer banality, the banality of diffused responsibility and repetitions that allow theories to be taken for facts.

As the *Challenger* case illustrated, making the wrong guess about the danger signals can have catastrophic results, but many other attempts to assimilate and coordinate information can produce similar instances of anomaly about which a person (though it is seldom only one) must decide whether and how much attention to give them. Things are overlooked not because people are irresponsible or evil or lacking intelligence. Things are overlooked because if we paid attention to everything all the time, nothing would ever get done, and in deciding what not to pay attention to we sometimes get it wrong. In fact, we often get it wrong—it's just that most of the time the consequences are not as dramatic as an explosion that kills people.

Making mistakes is not unique to launching rockets. And Vaughan shows that it is not enough to follow established procedures in order to avoid making them. The "sociology of mistake" is not unique to NASA, by any means — rather, it is "relentlessly inevitable" wherever organization is involved (xv), and by organization I mean not only groups of people (even informal ones such as communities of scholars) but also the organization of thought. As we repeat certain tasks, so we tend to formalize the process. Initially, this tendency can have benefits (as described in Atul Gawande's work on the use of checklists in hospitals). For one thing, formalizing procedures can make it easier to teach someone else how to perform the same task; it facilitates the transmission of skills and knowledge. Formalization can also add a degree of safety by ensuring that certain steps are not accidentally forgotten, especially once the procedure becomes a frequently repeated routine. But checklists and safety protocols also bring their own problems. Recently, I thought I smelled a gas leak around the gas meter outside my house. I called the gas company. The representative took down the details of my report, then read me a list of safety precautions: switch off and do not use electrical appliances (everything? the refrigerator, too?); evacuate the premises (so as to be closer to the leak, which was *outside* the house?); do not operate motor vehicles (so evacuate the premises but *slowly*, on *foot*?); do not use the phone (we were talking on the phone when she told me this, with no apparent sense of irony).

The goal of the gas company in formulating these precautions was to be absolutely safe, and probably to avoid legal responsibility for an accident. My goal was to find a balance between safety and getting on with my life (I only *thought* I smelled a leak; who knew how long I would have to wait for the repair person to show up?). I could follow the instructions to the letter and turn off everything (even the refrigerator) and leave on foot until I was given the all clear (somehow, without using the phone), but this entailed serious disruption to my plans for that day.

The very comprehensiveness of the gas company's policies ("turn off *all* appliances") pretty much guaranteed that I would not follow all the instructions exactly. At the same time, the comprehensiveness itself was only an illusion. The instructions said nothing about smoking, for example. So, as I was evacuating the premises (on foot), my neighbor, who likes to smoke outdoors in his driveway, which happens to be near my gas meter, might have chosen that moment to take a break. Or, while I was avoiding using my motor vehicle, the city dump truck (it was trash day) might have chanced along at that moment and emitted a random spark (metal grinding on concrete) as it picked up my trash can next to my meter, blowing us all up (a fate I at least might have avoided if I had driven off at once in my car instead of having to move on foot).

Checklists can fail in two ways, then, by being both too complete and not complete enough. First, the more thorough they are, the less likely they are to be followed completely every time. Second, they attempt to anticipate all eventualities but they are inevitably incomplete (they cannot anticipate all possible factors, such as the smoking habits of my neighbor and the city's trash collection schedule). Thus, the problem with safety checks, as Vaughan testifies, is that we have a tendency to think that if we have performed all the safety checks on the list, the procedure is safe or foolproof.[2] In other words, it gives us a false sense of security. Nothing can go wrong because we did everything we were supposed to do.

Automatic thinking, then, is dangerous because it lulls us into a false belief of certainty. The "already known" is the basis for further knowledge and is not in need of constant reevaluation. If the solution to accidents "caused" by clear, straight roads is to create a bend in the road to make the driver sit up and pay attention, the challenge in intellectual endeavors is to keep creating unexpected bends on the old narrative paths in order to wake us up to seeing them in a new light. We think we know the story, but what happens when you retell it a different way: do you suddenly notice something that does not make sense, that no longer "adds up"? We must create (for ourselves as researchers) the circumstances in which we force ourselves to review—to look at once again and with our full attention—what it is we thought we already knew.

But how do you know when things don't add up, when a piece of the story is missing? It's not always obvious. Sometimes it's no more than a hunch. I went to a local bookstore in search of a book that had just been published about Virginia Woolf. Not sure where to start looking (would it be shelved with books by Woolf, under *W*, or under the author's name, for example?), I asked a clerk for help. He looked the book up on the store's computerized inventory and told me that they did not carry that book. I turned to leave the store, satisfied that he had answered my question. Purely as an afterthought, the clerk added that they didn't even have any books *by* Virginia Woolf. This last piece of (unsolicited) information brought me up short. That this particular store did not have this particular book *about* Virginia Woolf came as no great surprise to me. It was a book of general criticism, and not the sort of thing the average reader (the target customer of this kind of store) would be likely to buy, perhaps, so I found it quite credible that the store would not carry it. But that such a store would not even carry any books *by* Virginia Woolf I found quite *in*-credible. Something was wrong here. Somewhat sheepishly, I asked the clerk how he was spelling the author's name. "W-O-L-F," he replied. This, then, was the problem, one that had not occurred to me. The spelling corrected, the computerized inventory revealed that not only did the store carry books by Woolf, it had the very book I was looking for. Mission accomplished. And a lesson learned.

The lesson I learned was not the one about falling standards of education (young people today are so illiterate they can't even cry Woolf), nor the one about the limits of computers (garbage in, garbage out), but the one about how expectations (my own, in particular) shape results. I expected that the store might not carry the book I wanted, so I settled for the answer from a clerk (a third party) that it did not. It did not occur to me to think about the mental tasks involved in doing the clerk's job and where those might go wrong. I expected a negative answer, got one, and was ready to walk away thinking I knew something about the state of the universe in that particular store. What turned things around was a chance piece of information I didn't think to ask for. This additional fact changed the mental landscape and alerted me to the fact that there was a methodological problem. Once the search process changed, the facts changed.

This chapter tells the story of how the real identity of Gisèle d'Estoc was established, and it involves the same elements as the story of the big bad Woolf. Some people trusted the word of a third party when they should not have, and did not think to ask a question they should have thought of. In addition, when some things did not add up, they were reluctant to admit it and instead fell back on some expectations that, it turned out, would lull them into thinking they had an answer when they didn't.

In academic searches—in all searches, perhaps—it is important not only to know what you are looking for, but to anticipate what might prevent you from seeing it. Historian Anthony Grafton tells a revealing anecdote about electronic searches. It turns out that the character-recognition software used in digital library projects such as those of Google has a weakness: the search engine that enables a user to find a given word or words requires making a second copy of the digitized texts, and the software that makes the copy is less than a perfect reader. For example, it has a hard time distinguishing between the letters *u* and *n*, and so routinely mistakes one for the other in making copies. Grafton reports that if you enter the word *qualitas* into Google Book Search, you find about a couple of thousand references. But if you anticipate the mistake of the software and search for *qnalitas*, you will find another six hundred or so references that the first search failed to turn up (304). Ironically, Grafton notes, this is the same error (*n* for *u*) often made by medieval scribes who copied texts by hand. "Plus ça change," one might say, but the point is that knowing the weaknesses in how information is stored and accessed is important to the information you will find. "'Search is everything' has become a proverb," Grafton observes (295), and he is right, though of course we didn't need computers to discover this. Moreover, the perfect search must be, in some ways, imperfect. That is, to search thoroughly one must anticipate the mistakes that others might have made in the way information is stored. Finding the real

Gisèle d'Estoc illustrates this principle that search is everything and being able to tell when the search has gone off course is what separates successful searches from false positives (such as "Yes, you are right, we don't have this book"). Finding Gisèle d'Estoc shows that it is not enough to get the story right; you have to know enough to get it wrong, too.

The issue of d'Estoc's true identity was taken up and advanced by the Maupassant scholar Armand Lanoux, who presented the results of his research in his 1967 book *Maupassant le bel-ami*. By this time, Pierre Borel's assertions were still received with skepticism, but Lanoux noticed how much of Borel's version was turning out to have some truth to it. By 1967 it was generally accepted that Gisèle d'Estoc was a real person, for example, but ignorance of her true identity remained a major obstacle to full acceptance, and this was the scoop that Lanoux broke in this book, announcing that he had "found" Gisèle d'Estoc. His account of how he found her is an interesting one, and the fact that he describes his methodology—the "story of the story," if you like—enables readers today both to see why he came to the conclusions he did and also to see how he was misled and why he failed to notice.

At first Lanoux looked for traces of a Madame Desbarres, based on the name given in Ernest Raynaud's symbolist memoirs, which gave one of the first clues to d'Estoc's identity. There was also widespread acceptance of the claim that d'Estoc was from Nancy, which indicated where to begin looking for Madame Desbarres. But Lanoux ascertained that there were no births under the name Desbarres in Nancy for the years 1840–60, and the trail went cold. The break came when he was later contacted by the local departmental archivist, a Monsieur Delcamp, who obligingly thought to look beyond what was to be found in his own archive where the records of births, marriages, and deaths were kept. He thought to look at the holdings of the local library also.

Here Delcamp found a capital piece of the puzzle, as the last chapter recounted. He found a rare copy of a collection of short stories that d'Estoc published under the title *Noir sur blanc: Récits lorrains.*[3] It appeared under the pseudonym Gyz-El, but it was perhaps not hard for Delcamp to link this exotic-sounding Gyz-El to the homonymous Gisèle whose tracks he sought. Both on the index card and on the book itself (book number 3606), an anonymous but thoughtful librarian had penciled, "Mme Desbarres née Courbe." Lanoux recounts this discovery in a curiously impersonal way: "On peut donc consulter . . ." (393). Does this mean he confirmed Delcamp's report with his own eyes, or that he is taking it on faith (as I now do) that the card exists (or existed then)? The subject "on" leaves it vague, but I suspect (for reasons that will become clear below) that Lanoux himself never went back to Nancy to confirm the archivist's story.[4] Lanoux writes, "Je cherchai à Nancy" (I looked in Nancy) (393), but in fact the successful part of his search appears to have taken the form of a correspondence rather than a "site visit" (and one involving actual sight). Lanoux remains silent about who this Nancy librarian was, why he (or she?) wrote this gloss or when, how he knew, and whether he is any more trustworthy than the much-vilified Borel. But perhaps these details are immaterial. The point is that the librarian attaches a name to the pseudonym of Gyz-El/Gisèle, or rather two names, one of which (Desbarres) was already known but was not helpful, the other a vital missing clue, her birth name (Courbe), which provided something concrete that could be pursued. It is always easier to confirm or disprove a specific identification than it is to come up with a name ex nihilo, so this anonymous book defacer had in fact rendered a huge service to posterity.

Lanoux learned, then, that Gisèle d'Estoc, aka Madame Desbarres, was born a Courbe, and he was not slow to follow this chain of linked identities, but his mistake was not doing so in person. He once again relied on Monsieur Delcamp, the archivist, to conduct a search in the registry of births, marriages, and deaths.

The thing to know about looking for birth records in France is that, unlike in, say, England, they are not summarized in one central location (let alone available online), but remain in the departmental centers around the country. For genealogy, you have to go in person to a local archive. Here the original records are preserved, copied onto reels and reels of microfilm that the public may consult. The primary records of births, marriages, and deaths were originally recorded chronologically, as they happened. A local clerk would start writing down the prescribed details of births (or marriages or deaths) in the annual register, beginning on January 1 and continuing in the order in which events were reported for that year. If you already know the date of the occurrence, you can thus go directly to the primary record. In many cases, however, it is precisely the date you are seeking to ascertain, working with nothing more than a name. With nothing but this to go on, you would have to search through all the records for each year until you came to the name you were looking for, a potentially herculean task. So in order to facilitate later searches by name, the clerk would compile an alphabetical index at the end of each register at the end of the year. And every ten years, the raw data of this alphabetical listing was compiled by yet other clerks into a summary volume of all births (or marriages or deaths) in a given commune (the relevant French administrative unit), providing an index for a ten-year period in alphabetical (not chronological) order. As a result, researchers (whether scholars or family genealogists) can trace a given individual by working backward, consulting the alphabetical list in the summary volume, which will then direct them, both by date and number, to the exact place in the original records where the event is recorded with all its details. These ten-year summaries are a little quirky, however, in that they run from mid-decade to mid-decade, since they were begun when centralized government record keeping replaced church-based parish registers, a switch that did not wait for the beginning of a decade to happen. Thus, there are separate index volumes that run from 1823–32, 1833–42, 1843–52, 1853–62, 1863–72, and so on. So to find a birth record, you start with a name and a hypothesis about the decade in which the person was born and you go to that summary volume. In searching for the birth record of Madame Desbarres, née Courbe, Delcamp must have begun with the register for 1863–72, for he quickly turned up a likely prospect—the birth on August

9, 1863, of Marie Elise Courbe, the daughter of Alphonse Courbe, who was, as luck would have it, himself a sculptor.

Lanoux was not immediately convinced but thought that, on balance, "c'est probablement d'elle qu'il s'agit" (394). Everyone noticed the name problem, however. They had gone looking for a Marie Paule and had come up with a Marie Elise. Already in his initial report, Monsieur Delcamp flagged the issue but dismissed it as perhaps a choice on the part of the interested party: "Peut-être l'intéressée a-t-elle changé son nom de Marie-Elise en celui de Marie-Paule," he helpfully suggested (Lanoux 394). Lanoux was similarly willing to overlook what he described as the "léger flottement des prénoms" (the slight slippage in the first names). I must confess that this was one of the first gut feelings that made me uncomfortable about the identification of Gisèle d'Estoc as Marie Elise Courbe (there was also the problem of the dates, but we'll get to that). Even as recently as 2001, Gilles Picq, defending the identification and commenting on the change of given name, writes: "Mais, cela ne prouve rien! Nous sommes nombreux—encore—à avoir connu nos grands-mères—nées au siècle dernier—ayant adopté des prénoms autres que ceux choisis par leurs parents" (That doesn't prove anything! Many of us still remember our grandmothers—born in the last century [he means the nineteenth]—who adopted names other than the ones chosen by their parents) (*Laurent Tailhade* 264). It is one of the tritest and yet most profound observations of feminism that under patriarchy, women don't even get to have their own name. In a system in which girls typically receive their family name from their father, then change it to the name of their husband, women often end up virtually invisible to genealogy. Indeed, this is partly why d'Estoc was so difficult to trace in the first place: her married name was known, but it was only thanks to chance and a graphomaniac librarian that her birth name survived and could be reliably recovered. In such a system, the given name is often the only name women have "of their own." And of course many women do end up being known by a name other than the one given at birth, but there was something about the cavalier dismissal of the name Marie Paule that seemed to me too hasty. Marie Paule, Marie Elise, these critics seemed to shrug, what's the difference? The dropped "Marie" did not bother me: every other girl (and a good many boys) technically had the name "Marie" in Catholic France, and it was seldom retained in daily usage, but the difference between Paule and Elise was harder to overlook.

An even more compelling reason for rejecting this identification, however, is the problem of the dates. Once again, Lanoux was not blind to this issue, though ultimately it did not cause him to revise his ideas. Lanoux was fortunate enough to have known Borel in person and to have been able to question him about details of his claims. Alas, Borel died in 1964, before the publication of Lanoux's book and its new revelations, but Lanoux recalled some of Borel's statements and juxtaposed them with what he thought he had just discovered about Marie Elise Courbe. Borel claimed that d'Estoc had been painted in certain pictures, but one of the specifics he cited was *Bara* by Henner, from 1882. Lanoux recalls this detail with outrage (the capitals are his): "Alors, là, c'est IMPOSSIBLE, SI GISELE D'ESTOC EST BIEN NEE EN 1863. Le *Barra* [*sic*] du peintre Henner date de 1882. Elle aurait eu alors dix-neuf ans" (Here, this is impossible if Gisèle d'Estoc was indeed born in 1863. Henner's *Bara* [the proper spelling] dates from 1882. She would have been nineteen then). Lanoux, on the verge of finding Borel credible, cannot reconcile Borel's specifics with the birth date of 1863, and concludes not that the date of birth is wrong but instead that Borel "disait n'importe quoi!" (said any old thing) (396).

A date of birth in 1863 also throws into doubt another story retailed by Borel, this one concerning a friendship that caused a scandal in d'Estoc's hometown of Nancy. According to Borel, the adolescent Marie Paule had only one real friendship outside her family, and that was with another girl from Nancy whom he names as Marie Aimée. They had a number of things in common: both were aspiring artists and they shared an admiration for Joan of Arc (Nancy is in Lorraine, lest it be forgotten). Their "passionate friendship" caused gossip, and it was in order to put an end to the rumors that Marie

12. D'Estoc and her friend Marie Edmée Pau. (From Pierre Borel, *Maupassant et l'androgyne*)

Paule left Nancy and moved to Paris (*Maupassant et l'androgyne* 21–22). All of which would be so much talk were it not for the fact that Marie Aimée went on to write about Joan of Arc in works that, combined with the hints left by Borel, make it possible to trace her.[5]

Borel noted that "in reality" the friend's name was Marie Edmée X, that she was related to a war hero of World War I, that she left a painting of Joan of Arc at Domrémy, and that her diary had been recently published (see *Maupassant et l'androgyne* 21n1). Primed with this information, it is not hard for the researcher to trace Marie Edmée Pau, sister of the famous World War I general, and author—under the modest name simply of Marie Edmée—of *Histoire de notre petite soeur Jeanne d'Arc, dédiée aux enfants de la Lorraine* (1874) as well as of a diary (first published in the 1870s, after the Franco-Prussian War, but perhaps coming to Borel's attention only in a more recent edition republished in the run-up to World War II).[6]

The trouble is, this Marie Edmée Pau, born in Lyon in 1846 but reconnected to her maternal roots in Nancy after the death of her father in her childhood, died on March 7, 1871, when she was only twenty-four or twenty-five. Marie Elise Courbe would have been eight years old.

To compound this problem, Borel included a photograph of Marie Paule and Marie Edmée, in which both are of a similar (young adult) age and wear identical outfits in an almost symmetrically identical pose; Marie Paule is certainly more than eight years old (*Maupassant et l'androgyne*, facing 48). Granted, there are problems with the photograph: Marie Paule's right hand is draped on Marie Edmée's left shoulder, but her elbow seems impossibly rounded, as though the photograph had been somehow altered or doctored. Marie Edmée's right arm is around Marie Paule's waist, but her right hand, which we can just see on the left of the photo, appears unattached to any sleeve or wrist, giving it the appearance of some ectoplasmic manifestation. Of course much might be learned from examining the original of the photograph, but it is part of the "dossier d'Estoc" that, according to Borel, "disappeared" into a private collection in the United States around the middle of the twentieth century. There may be many questions about Borel's hazy recollection of exact dates, but the independent evidence (of publications, of photographs) makes it hard to accept both that Gisèle d'Estoc was a close friend and contemporary of Marie Edmée Pau and also that d'Estoc was born in 1863.[7] But this was the messy state of affairs after the publication of Lanoux's book and the paradigm that dominated the thinking about d'Estoc in the last third of the twentieth century.

A separate line of inquiry produced an important tangible piece of evidence at the close of the century. Nearly a hundred years after d'Estoc's death, her death certificate was finally (re)discovered, as we have seen earlier, by the critic Gilles Picq, an expert on d'Estoc's rival Laurent Tailhade. Picq took his cue from Pillard d'Arkaï's defense of d'Estoc in the Foyot bombing affair, but Pierre Cogny had been the first to draw attention to the document, which was also known to Lanoux.[8] In this broadsheet, "L'explosion du Restaurant Foyot: Justification de l'accusé," it was claimed that d'Estoc could not be involved because she lay mortally ill in bed at the time of the bombing. The broadsheet was dated "Nice, le 20/25 Avril 1894," so putting the fact of d'Estoc's terminal illness together with the provenance of the broadsheet suggested to Picq where and when to look, but Lanoux might have made the same inference if he had trusted the materials.

Picq announced his finding publicly on the occasion of the first Colloque des Invalides in 1997. (The conference proceedings were published the following year.) The topic of the symposium that year was "les à-côtés du siècle" (the "also-rans" of literature), initiating a series of colloquia that consistently privileged the arcane and marginal over the more typical "greats" emphasized by traditional (and institutionalized) academic inquiry.[9] Unlike the traditional academic conference of tightly scheduled twenty-minute presentations and hour-long plenaries, the Invalides colloquia were also known for their "alternative" conference ground rules that took seriously the etymology of the term *colloquium*: presentations were strictly limited to five minutes, followed by unlimited discussion time. It was in this context of specialists that Picq announced his finding and discussed its implications. Prior to this announcement, d'Estoc's death had been placed in 1906 (the BnF online catalog still gave this date as late as 2008). Picq reminded the audience of the debate accompanying the publication of the *Cahier d'amour* in 1939 and, just to complicate matters and stir debate once more, pointed out that since d'Estoc in fact died in 1894, she was dead before Harry Alis died in 1895, recalling that her confused claims about his death had been one of the stumbling blocks to acceptance of Borel's assertions in the first place.[10] Picq then reminded the audience of Lanoux's identification of d'Estoc as Marie Elise Courbe, born in 1863, before adding the details to be gleaned from the death certificate (signed by lover Pillard d'Arkaï, its guarantor of authenticity): Paule Courbe, widow of Parent Desbarres, born in Nancy, died in Nice on May 8, 1894, at the age of thirty-five. Picq notes that the given name problem remains (no mention of Elise on the official death certificate) but dismisses it summarily— "Ce qui ne veut rien dire car Gisèle put très certainement délaisser son prénom de baptême par choix esthétique" (It doesn't mean anything because Gisèle might have dropped the name she was christened with for aesthetic reasons) ("On destocke" 118). More troubling, however, is the fact that the death certificate would place her birth in 1859, rather than 1863 (1894 minus her stated age of thirty-five). He turns to the archives of Nancy for an explanation, finds that there is no birth record for a Paule Courbe between 1858 and 1860, and so formulates two hypotheses: either the recording clerk misheard the informants who came to register d'Estoc's death (they said she was thirty-one and the clerk heard—and wrote—thirty-five), or else d'Estoc had made herself out to be a little older than she really was to make the tall stories she told her lover Pillard d'Arkaï seem more chronologically plausible.

Either way, Picq did not challenge Lanoux's identification, since he had been unable to trace an earlier birth record in the 1858–69 range. The idea that Gisèle d'Estoc was Marie Elise stood, and was if anything even further confirmed. True, there was the name problem, and even worse, as Picq went on to acknowledge, the dating problem. The former was insignificant, he thought, but the latter was indeed troublesome because of the Marie Edmée Pau story, but in the remainder of his presentation on d'Estoc, he went on to elaborate a complicated explanation that would resolve the problem of chronology. It was not Marie Edmée Pau who was being referred to, since indeed she died in 1871 and d'Estoc would have been eight years old (if born in 1863); instead, it was another Pau, not the *sister* of the general but his *wife*, Marie Henriette (née de Guntz), born in 1859 (i.e., she was only about four years older than Marie Elise Courbe).

Picq's explanation succeeds in reconciling the apparently irreconcilable, but at what cost? The name problem (Marie Paule/Marie Elise) is dismissed; the "Pau" problem finds a solution, but one that creates its own set of confusions: Borel referred only to Marie Aimée/Edmée X, and she was only later identified as belonging to the Pau family; Picq privileges the family name Pau and connection to the military hero, but once again dismisses the fact that the given names do not match (this time Marie Aimée/Edmée has turned into Marie Henriette), not to mention the fact that the general's wife does not seem to have left any works about Joan of Arc, whereas this is an important point identifying Marie Aimée/Edmée.

The question is why any researcher would stop with the identification that d'Estoc is Marie Elise Courbe when there are still so many inconsistencies. Why is it preferable to believe that "Mme Pau" is Marie Henriette de Guntz, when Marie Edmée Pau seems a so much more obvious candidate? I believe the answer lies in the way the information in the Nancy archives is stored. As explained above, the birth records are usually accessed through the ten-year summaries, so someone looking for a Marie Paule Courbe might begin with the volume of births from 1863–72, as Lanoux's informant presumably did, and would find there the reference to Marie Elise Courbe. In looking for a reference to a birth in 1859, the date suggested by the death certificate, one would have to go back to a different summary volume of births, the one that runs 1853–62, as Picq presumably did when he checked for records on either side of 1859 (he was looking at the period 1858–60). There are no records of any Courbes—boys or girls—born in Nancy in this summary volume of the years 1853–62, so the trail would seem to go cold. What sort of perversity does it take to think of looking at yet another entirely separate volume, the summary of births 1843–52? Surely, if your starting point is 1863, it is already a stretch to be looking as early as 1853 (the beginning of the next-oldest volume). Lanoux's informant, Monsieur Delcamp, may well have thought to look in this volume for 1853–62 but, finding no references to Courbe, may have not looked any further because he had already heaved two large, dusty, leather-bound, handwritten volumes off the shelf and carried them to a table and leafed through until he found the Cs. What makes someone look or not look any further? Just how far back is it reasonable to go? I do not know the answer to those questions, but I do know that something made me look in the earlier volume, births 1843–52, even though it seemed so unlikely.

Well, not so unlikely, really, because I had already concluded that earlier was where we should be looking. To begin with there was the death certificate, putting her date of birth in 1859. But what if, instead of making herself out to be *older* than Pillard d'Arkaï, she did the thing more commonly ascribed to women and made herself out to be *younger*? She could well have been born before 1859. Then there were the dossiers I had found in the archives at the musée d'Orsay, suggesting that she had been exhibiting in Paris in the 1870s. Here I must acknowledge that I was acting on a tip from Gilles Picq himself who, following up on the rumor that d'Estoc had been an artist as well as a model, had found a reference to her in Bénézit's reference work *Dictionnaire des peintres, sculpteurs, dessinateurs et graveurs*. A trip to the archives of the musée d'Orsay confirmed that there were in fact three dossiers there that were worth noting (the two on the Courbe sisters and the one on Madame Desbarres).

The career of the artist Marie Paule Courbe can now be reconstructed in more detail (as chapter 5 has already showed). At the time, it was enough to confirm just the outline of her artistic career to convince me that the identification of Gisèle d'Estoc as Marie Elise Courbe could not be correct, no matter how one twisted the record.

Not only were the names Marie Paule Courbe and Paule Desbarres there on the dossiers, but the dates were prohibitive. If Courbe had indeed been born in 1863, then whatever her first name might be, she would had to have been a child prodigy to be exhibiting in the Salon in 1869. More likely, Marie Paule Courbe was at least a young woman, perhaps in her twenties, when she began to show her work, and that seemed to place her birth in the 1850s, with 1859 as the latest, rather than earliest, date to consider. Finally, there was the photograph of the young Gisèle d'Estoc with her friend Marie Edmée, who died in 1871. They appear similar in age; certainly Marie Edmée cannot be more than a few years older than her companion. If Marie Edmée was born in 1846, the woman known as d'Estoc could not have been born too many years later.

But still, was there any reason to look at the volume *preceding* the 1853–62 volume? It was a stretch. But then, why not? There were no Courbe births in that midcentury volume, and the alternatives were to accept the date of birth of 1863, which I found impossible to do, or simply to give up. So I looked at the volume of births for 1843–52. And there . . . well, I still nearly missed it. There are indeed some references to Courbes — Marguerite Paule Mathilde and Marie Isabelle Mathilde (on whom there was the empty dossier in the musée d'Orsay), not particularly promising — but the handwritten summary then moves from Courbe to Courcelles, and I was about to abandon the search when I noticed that human error had added yet another obstacle to the finding of Gisèle d'Estoc. The recording clerk who compiled the summary had forgotten one of the Courbes, and so he had inserted it later, out of its alphabetical sequence and after the Courcelles. There it was: Courbe, Marie Paule Alice, whose birth was registered on March 28, 1845. She was indeed quite a bit older than she had let on to Pillard d'Arkaï, but old enough to be the contemporary of Marie Edmée Pau born in 1846, old enough to be exhibiting in Paris in the 1870s. And she had not abandoned or changed her given name (at least not for official purposes; earlier chapters have shown how she reconstructed her public identity on several occasions).

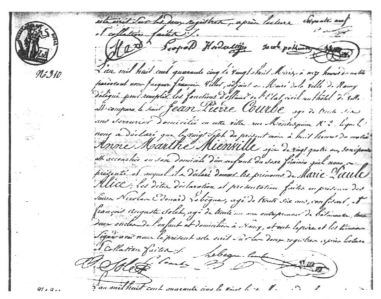

13. Birth certificate of Marie Paule Courbe from regional archive. (Archives départementales de Meurthe-et-Moselle, 5 Mi 394, R 148 N)

Based on this identification, I was able to search the archives and find out more about her family. Her father was not Alphonse Courbe the sculptor, promising as that had seemed given d'Estoc's sculpting career, but Jean Pierre Courbe, a locksmith, who was thirty-six years old at the time of her birth. Her mother was Anne Marthe Mienville, aged twenty-four, and they lived on the rue Montesquieu in Nancy. In *Maupassant et l'androgyne*, Borel had quoted an interview that d'Estoc gave to Pillard d'Arkaï in which she claimed to have been born "à l'ombre d'une vieille cathédrale, dans une maison d'ancien style où habitait, au rez-de-chaussée, un statuaire religieux" (in the shadow of an old cathedral, in an old-fashioned house with an artist who made religious statues living on the ground floor) (42). She went on to describe how the ringing of the cathedral bells would make the walls of the building vibrate and seemed to bring the religious statues to life, and d'Estoc could almost believe she was hearing voices like her idol Joan of Arc. The rue Montesquieu is about one block from Nancy's cathedral; once again, Borel proves to be an accurate guide.

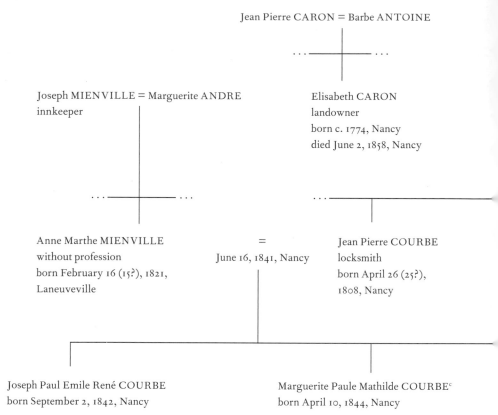

Jean Pierre CARON = Barbe ANTOINE

Joseph MIENVILLE = Marguerite ANDRE
innkeeper

Elisabeth CARON
landowner
born c. 1774, Nancy
died June 2, 1858, Nancy

Anne Marthe MIENVILLE
without profession
born February 16 (15?), 1821,
Laneuveville

=

June 16, 1841, Nancy

Jean Pierre COURBE
locksmith
born April 26 (25?),
1808, Nancy

Joseph Paul Emile René COURBE
born September 2, 1842, Nancy

Marguerite Paule Mathilde COURBE[c]
born April 10, 1844, Nancy

14. Courbe family tree, reconstructed based on archival research.
    a. Served as one of the witnesses at the marriage of his niece to Paul Parent
    Desbarres in Paris in 1875.
    b. There are no more births with the name "Courbe" in the ten-year summary
    for Nancy, 1843–52, and none listed in the summary volume for 1853–62.

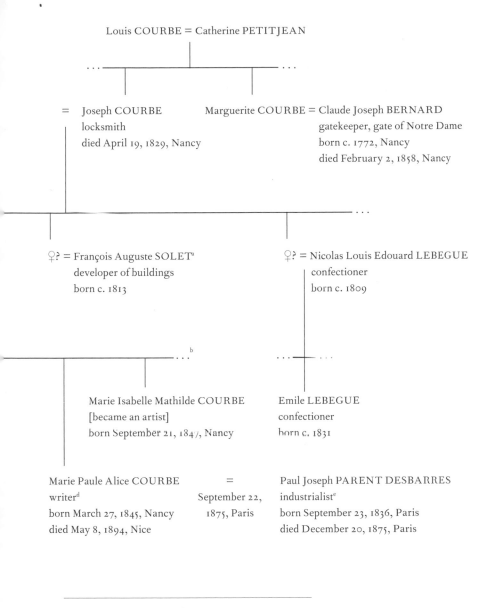

Louis COURBE = Catherine PETITJEAN

= Joseph COURBE
locksmith
died April 19, 1829, Nancy

Marguerite COURBE = Claude Joseph BERNARD
gatekeeper, gate of Notre Dame
born c. 1772, Nancy
died February 2, 1858, Nancy

♀? = François Auguste SOLET[a]
developer of buildings
born c. 1813

♀? = Nicolas Louis Edouard LEBEGUE
confectioner
born c. 1809

Marie Isabelle Mathilde COURBE
[became an artist]
born September 21, 1847, Nancy

Emile LEBEGUE
confectioner
born c. 1831

Marie Paule Alice COURBE
writer[d]
born March 27, 1845, Nancy
died May 8, 1894, Nice

=
September 22,
1875, Paris

Paul Joseph PARENT DESBARRES
industrialist[e]
born September 23, 1836, Paris
died December 20, 1875, Paris

c. Died young? The name "Paule" was given to the child born just a year later, and the name "Mathilde" to the child born in 1847.
d. Her death certificate lists her as a writer. Her marriage certificate lists her as "without profession."
e. According to the marriage certificate.

I cannot be sure that the following details about d'Estoc's family constitute an exhaustive account, but the records in Nancy permit at least a partial reconstitution of her family. Marie Paule Alice seems to have had an older brother, Joseph Paul Emile René, born on September 2, 1842, and a sister, Marguerite Paule Mathilde, born April 10, 1844. Perhaps this sister died young, however, because her second name, Paule, was given to the little girl born the following year who would grow up to become Gisèle d'Estoc, and Mathilde was the name given to Marie Isabelle Mathilde, born September 21, 1847, who would also grow up to become an artist.[11]

Paule/Gisèle's father Jean Pierre Courbe was born in April 1808 in Nancy (the birth was registered on the 26th), and his marriage certificate informs us that his father was Jacques Courbe, also a locksmith, who died in Nancy on April 19, 1829. Jacques's widow, Elisabeth Caron, was, however, still alive in 1841 to celebrate the marriage of her son Jean Pierre. Jean Pierre's bride, Anna Marthe Mienville, was also from Nancy, born on February 16, 1821, in the district of Laneuveville, and was thus, at age twenty, still a minor at the time of her marriage. Her parents were Joseph Mienville, an innkeeper, and Marguerite André, both of whom attended the wedding. Such were the modest antecedents of the future d'Estoc.

Death records reveal further details that extend our knowledge of this family. The death certificate of Paule/Gisèle's paternal grandmother, Elisabeth Caron, on June 2, 1858, states that her parents were Jean Pierre Caron and Barbe Antoine. One of the witnesses signing the declaration was Emile Lebegue, a grandson of the deceased, according to the document (and thus a cousin to our Gisèle). He was twenty-seven years old in 1858, which places his birth around 1831. A Lebegue also served as witness to the birth of Marie Paule Alice Courbe in 1845: Nicolas Edouard Lebegue, thirty-two, a confectioner, and probably the father of Emile. The other witness on the birth certificate was François Auguste Solet (twenty-eight, construction entrepreneur). Both witnesses were identified as brothers-in-law of Jean Pierre Courbe (and consequently uncles to Paule/Gisèle). Jean Pierre evidently had at least two sisters, then, since he acquired two brothers-in-law.

Beyond this point, it is possible only to speculate. To return to Marie Paule's paternal grandmother Elisabeth Caron who married Jacques Courbe, she was born around 1774 (as we may surmise from her having died in 1858 at the age of eighty-four), and probably her spouse was similar in age and thus born at around the same time. Perhaps the Marguerite Courbe, widow of Claude Bernard, whose death at the age of eighty-two is recorded on February 2, 1858, was sister to Jacques Courbe. Marguerite would have been born around 1776, thus she was about two years younger than Jacques's wife. Marguerite's parents (according to her death certificate) were Louis Courbe and Catherine Petitjean, so perhaps these were Jacques's parents, too.

A few more details about the family emerge from the marriage certificate of Marie Paule Alice Courbe with Paul Joseph Parent Desbarres in 1875 (in the Archives de Paris). This document seals the link between Mademoiselle Courbe and Madame Parent Desbarres that had so perplexed critics. As we saw earlier, Marie Paule Alice Courbe, daughter of Jean Pierre Courbe and Anne Marthe Mienville, married Paul Joseph Parent Desbarres, ten years her senior, on September 22, 1875, in the sixth arrondissement of Paris. Perhaps this Paul Joseph is the person d'Estoc wrote about in her letter to her friend Marie Edmée Pau that prompted the incredulous reply (quoted by Borel), "Vous avez, dites-vous, trouvé un homme digne de votre amour. Allons donc! Je n'en crois rien. Je ne vous vois pas en ménage[. . . .] Vous avez déjà beaucoup aimé et chaque fois vous avez cru que cet amour serait éternel" (You have, you say, found a man worthy of your love. Oh, come on! I don't believe a word. I can't see you settling down[. . . .] You have already loved many times and each time you thought that love would last forever) (*Maupassant et l'androgyne* 25).

Paul Joseph Parent Desbarres is described as an "industrialist" on the marriage certificate. It is a word that comes up in Borel's narrative when he describes d'Estoc's father. She is "fille d'un riche industriel" (*Maupassant et l'androgyne* 19). Was Borel confused? On Marie Paule Courbe's birth certificate, after all, her father was merely a locksmith. Although he might have been quite a wealthy one, it seems a stretch to describe this profession as that of an industrialist. On the other hand, the marriage certificate notes that at the time of her marriage, Marie Paule's parents were living with her at 99 rue de Rennes (also in the sixth arrondissement), and by this time her father's profession is given as "rentier," that is, his income derived from land. Perhaps the family had indeed come up in the world quite significantly in the intervening thirty years. Another hint comes from one of the witnesses to the marriage, François Auguste Solet, one of Marie Paule's uncles who, when he had signed her birth certificate, had been an "entrepreneur de bâtiments" (builder/developer) and was now (in 1875) identified as the mayor of St. Lager. Perhaps d'Estoc was not only marrying into a family of businessmen (her father-in-law was a publisher and bookseller), but also came from such a family and later represented her origins this way to others.

It is not impossible that Marie Paule Courbe's family was related to that of Marie Elise. It is especially tempting to imagine such a connection given that Alphonse Courbe was a sculptor and might have served as an informal teacher or patron to Marie Paule. But aside from the fact that Alphonse's family went by the name Courbe-Micholet, while Marie Paule's did not, there are other reasons to suspect that this connection, if it existed, was at best a very remote one. Alphonse Courbe was born in the Jura (in Lons-le-Saunier in 1832), whereas Jean Pierre Courbe was a native of Nancy, and while Jean Pierre's parents were named Joseph and Elisabeth Courbe, Alphonse's parents were Marie Joseph Cousin and Michel Courbe Micholet.

There is one more thing to note about Lanoux's identification of Gisèle d'Estoc as Marie Elise before consigning this false trail to the dustbin of history, and once again it has to do with how information is recorded. In this case, it is about the fact that births, marriages, and deaths are recorded separately—that is, in separate volumes on separate shelves (a compartmentalization not unique to France). Like Lanoux and his informant, I would not have thought to look at deaths as a way to learn more about births, but because I was looking into what else I could learn about Marie Paule Alice's family, I ended up looking at death records to find out some of the things recounted above, and there I came across a telling fact, one that was available to Lanoux and would have put an end to forty years of fruitless speculation if only anyone had thought to look for it. In the summary volume of deaths 1863–72, there is a reference to the death of Marie Elise Courbe. Her birth was registered on August 10, 1863, and that was the fact that the obliging Monsieur Delcamp took away from his research, but more interestingly her death was also recorded—though in a different volume that no one thought to look at—just a month later, on September 10, 1863. Marie Elise Courbe did not grow up to become Gisèle d'Estoc; in fact she did not grow up at all, for she died at just a month old. Ironically and sadly, Marie Elise Courbe has had a much longer life in literary history than she ever enjoyed in real life. It is hard to begrudge a child life, even if only a posthumous and fictitious one, but it is time, finally, to lay Marie Elise Courbe to rest once and for all.

Afterword

Final Lesson: There is no real beginning or end.

Once upon a time there was a woman who pretended to be Gisèle d'Estoc. For a while, some people doubted that this woman really existed, and then for a while after that, people thought that Gisèle d'Estoc was Marie Elise Courbe, born in 1863. But she wasn't, and now we know that, too. Gisèle d'Estoc was really Marie Paule Alice Courbe Parent Desbarres (1845–94), and now with this knowledge we can say that in a sense Marie Paule has finally become the woman she pretended to be all along; the connection between the two identities has been established. We have come full circle: there once was a woman who pretended to be someone else. The other identity took over, and people thought she no longer was who she was, but now we can see the connection again.

The Sanskrit scholar Wendy Doniger has written extensively about stories from around the world in which a woman pretends to be someone else and people fail to recognize her, even though her outward appearance has not changed significantly. It is such a common narrative pattern that the examples Doniger discusses range from ancient Sanskrit mythological texts to popular Hollywood films such as Alfred Hitchcock's *Vertigo* (1958). In this film, hero Scottie falls in love with Madeleine (supposedly an old friend's wife), who is really Judy acting the part of Madeleine. "Madeleine" dies (though not really) and when Scottie later meets Judy being herself, he does not recognize her, though she seems familiar (Freud would say "uncanny"). It takes a while for Scottie (James Stewart) to realize that Madeleine and Judy (both played by Kim Novak) are really the same person.

Doniger calls this pattern "the woman who pretends to be herself." The women she describes make little or no effort to disguise themselves, so although they seem to be impersonating someone else, they can hardly be said to be misrepresenting themselves. Indeed, as someone else, they are arguably even more really their true selves, Doniger suggests. The story of Gisèle d'Estoc is, I would contend, another variation on the same narrative: once upon a time, a woman pretended to be someone called Gisèle d'Estoc, and even though she never attempted to disguise herself in any other way, people found it hard, somehow, to see who she really was. The vast range of examples Doniger analyzes combine to suggest that we are strangely blind when we see the same person in a different context. What we see is largely a function of what we expect to see. But even stranger than this poor ability to recognize those we already know is what makes the scales of blindness eventually fall from our eyes. For what enables Jimmy Stewart to see that it was really Kim Novak all along is love. Or as Doniger puts it, "Love is what endures and survives when either consciousness or appearance is destroyed" (204). As a thousand clichéd films, sensational novels, and popular stories testify, we cling to the belief that true soul mates recognize one another even when their external appearance has changed—or seems to have changed, or even indeed *because* it has changed—because the bond between souls that are meant to be together is deeper than anything as superficial as their mere appearance. The paradox of masquerade, suggests Doniger, is that it really tells a deeper truth, but someone must love the person enough to notice that the traits they had overlooked as those of a stranger are in fact familiar.

For Doniger, this way of understanding identity as requiring the recognition of the other in order to truly be ourselves has an additional, postmodern, lesson. Rather than positing an inner core of self that puts on masks (different masks for different people at different times), a model of identity she ascribes to sociologist Erving

Goffmann, Doniger posits that there is only the surface.[1] There is no true inner self that can take off the mask: "We are never ourselves merely to ourselves but always in relation to others, even if only imagined others" (204). Being one's true self requires *putting on* the mask (pretending), not taking it off. This model of identity might be construed to mean that in order to discover Gisèle d'Estoc's true identity, it is not enough to look at (or for) her face, as this would only be a distraction (as indeed I tried to suggest in the interlude). It is only "in relation to others" that identity can be established.

The strange appearance of Gisèle d'Estoc can now be seen, on a closer look, to resolve itself into the features of Marie Paule Alice Courbe (just as, in retrospect, Madeleine can be seen to have been Judy all along), but can this recognition be said to be a transformation brought about by love? It's hard to think of "loving" Gisèle d'Estoc. She doesn't seem to have been a very lovable person, despite the fact that some people seem to have been in love with her, at least for a while (Marie Edmée Pau, M. Parent Desbarres, Rachilde, perhaps, Guy de Maupassant, Léo Pillard d'Arkaï . . .). I've lived with Gisèle d'Estoc for a long time and I have grown somewhat fond of her in that funny sort of way bred by familiarity, but to call it love? No, I don't think so (frankly, she seems too much like hard work).[2] So what accounts for the fact that I came to see that she was not the person she at first appeared to be? That the person other people thought they saw behind the mask of the pseudonym was not who I saw? If not love, then what? If love is a form of noticing in spite of the superficial distractions (if), then what makes it possible to see that Gisèle d'Estoc is not, and never was, Marie Elise? What made it possible to believe that the statement "There is a Gisèle d'Estoc, such that she is the author of a work called the *Cahier d'amour*" was not just an exercise in existential logic but had a referent in the real world? What makes these things possible is caring enough to notice. Not love, then, but caring (enough).

My caring started out as a niggle (not all caring is necessarily positive), the kind of niggle that pops up in your head during insomniac moments when you have nothing better to think about but the mind must perforce latch onto something. When I was working on a biography of Rachilde and came across the name of Gisèle d'Estoc, I tried to find out more about her. I read other works in which she was mentioned and combed through the footnotes, noticing that everyone was paraphrasing, choosing their words carefully so as to avoid literal plagiarism but basically repeating the same phrases that appeared to offer content but failed to provide enlightenment. It was clear that no one was quite sure who she was: the scholarly context of the footnote required an explanation of who d'Estoc was, but no one really had one. And that's how the niggle formed, like an irritating little grain of sand that keeps the oyster awake and makes it keep worrying the same spot. The footnotes bothered me; it was the beginning of caring, and caring meant a certain grumpiness with extant explanations that in turn required me to do something about them to relieve the irritation.

After digging around a little, after turning over many rocks to see what might be underneath, after sifting much evidence, I knew a little more. I came across the hypothesis that d'Estoc was Marie Elise Courbe. But anyone who took the trouble to notice this couldn't help also noticing that the pieces of the story did not hang together. It was like a jigsaw puzzle with pieces missing in which an impatient child has forced pieces that don't fit because they look like they *might* fit, that they *could* fit if you just thump them into place hard enough, and because it's just too tiresome to keep looking further (it's all just blue sky, after all . . .).[3] But the bad fit bothered me: how could someone born in 1863 be exhibiting in the Salons in the 1870s? If her name was Marie Elise, why did she change it to Marie Paule Alice? Yes, we all know women who change their names, but they don't simply forget their birth name, their official name, the one used on formal occasions when they have to state their identity for the record. It all made me stare very hard at the face of Gisèle d'Estoc and ask who really was behind the mask, and the more I invested in discovering the answer to that question, the more I cared and the more I noticed when things didn't fit.

Caring and noticing, these are the attributes of researchers. I might say, "Notice what you notice," but I have to admit that I am stealing this formulation from a friend (you know who you are) because others will surely notice the theft (you know who *you* are, too), as indeed they should. Caring and noticing are not confined to researchers in the humanities. Scientists have to care and notice as well: the bridge has to be built so as not to fall down, the medicine prescribed in the correct dosage, the cure for cancer to be found. But in the kind of stories that characterize the humanities, the emphasis in the narrative is more often on a nonapplied kind of caring, a caring for its own sake: one cares not because material things in the real world will be changed directly by that investment (bridges, sick patients), but because the idea itself is worth caring about. It matters to try to get it right, even if "it" is a story about someone who once existed in a galaxy long ago and far away (in France in the nineteenth century) whose life matters not a jot today.

But this is what stories have to offer the world. Stories may not save lives (at least, not in any direct causal sense—how they might prolong the desire to stay alive is another matter), but they teach us about noticing and caring, things that make life worth living. They teach us about loving the world because it's the only one we have and because the alternative is cold and dark.

Stories also teach us not to take things for granted, and the final lesson of biography is that despite the fact that specific stories always begin and end somewhere, in real life there are no such definitive markers. The story I have presented here about the life of Gisèle d'Estoc is certainly messy enough, but there is even more messiness to the narrative than I have let on. Let me tell you a story . . .

When I finally tracked down what I thought was the correct birth record for Marie Paule Courbe in the departmental archives in Nancy I was naturally quite excited and, yes, a little proud of myself. I had succeeded in finding new knowledge. I had actually gone to the archives and tracked down the materials even though I had had to come all the way from Texas to do it, whereas others who lived in Paris all their lives and for whom a trip to Nancy was a relatively easy excursion had not bothered. (It was only later that I began to understand how much easier it is to execute a long and complicated journey that requires planning than one you think you can do just about any day and therefore put off indefinitely because you can, like the family in Monica Ali's novel *Brick Lane* who, though living in London, have never seen the sights of London.) Well, pride goes before a fall, they say, so I should have seen it coming. I wrote up the results of my research and put together my findings about the family of origin of Marie Paule Courbe and published the article in French in *Histoires littéraires*, in a special issue on Maupassant. *Histoires littéraires* is the kind of journal that appeals to literary historians and private collectors (it consistently features previously unpublished work, like a more scholarly version of *Les oeuvres libres*), so it is the kind of venue that attracts a certain specialized (even nerdy) attention. In the following issue of the journal, there were two responses to my article, one of which I have already discussed (by Philippe Chauvelot, it featured two new photographs of d'Estoc, new at least to a contemporary audience, since one of the photos had been published in 1939 but not reproduced since). The other response was by Gilles Picq, the Tailhade specialist, who, among other things, pointed out (with some satisfaction, I rather think) that I was not the first one to find d'Estoc's birth certificate because "un mystérieux chercheur écossais nommé Mac Culloch" had left a handwritten copy of the certificate in a dossier at the museum of Toul in 1983 (251). (Toul, you will recall, is the town where some of d'Estoc's sculpture had survived for a while.) Further inquiry confirmed this fact.[4] A Mr. William McCulloch (or Mac Culloch) had written from the Hôtel La Cigogne to the museum's curator thanking him for his help and informing him that he had been able to establish the birth of Marie Paule (Alice) Courbe in Nancy on March 27, 1845. Who was McCulloch and what was his interest in d'Estoc? A clue was provided by the letter of introduction he had furnished when making contact with the curator, a letter that had been preserved in the files and came from Madame Dominique Hoyet, then director of the Institut français d'Ecosse, the French Institute in Edinburgh. As his name suggested, Mr. McCulloch had a Scottish connection. I tried writing to the French Institute, but it was unable to provide any leads, perhaps not surprisingly since twenty-five years had elapsed since the time in question. My correspondent could not locate any record of Mr. McCulloch, and Dominique Hoyet had since retired. So I still don't know who this pioneer of d'Estoc scholarship was, why he cared, or what else he might have discovered. As this biography has shown, all the pieces of the puzzle that made it possible to solve the riddle of d'Estoc's true identity were available to scholars well before 1983, so it was only a matter of time before someone put the pieces together; part of what I find surprising about the story is that it didn't happen sooner. But there it is: when I thought I was the first, I was still not the first. Perhaps McCulloch was not the first, either, but we don't know because a prior record of discovery has not yet surfaced.

And that is part of the story, too. Beginnings and endings do not have clear edges. For purposes of narration, one must choose a place to begin and a place to end, but these places are mere conventions, contingencies. There are no real beginnings, and no real endings, either, and so the story of Gisèle d'Estoc does not really end here. This book will end here, but that is not the same thing. Others will, I hope, continue the story and along the way it will acquire new twists in the plot; there may be additional chapters, unsuspected characters may emerge from the shadows, perhaps people will do surprising and creative things with tense. Other narratives can and will be written, but that is as it should be. This narrative ends with the story of two false starts, that of Mr. McCulloch, who started but didn't go anywhere (his story did not come back from the underworld), and my own, which was not the start I thought it was. And perhaps this is not the ending I think it is either. I rather hope not.

Chronology

1836 September 23. Birth of d'Estoc's future husband, Paul Joseph Parent Desbarres, in tenth arrondissement of Paris.

1841 June 16. Marriage of d'Estoc's parents, Jean Pierre Courbe, thirty-three, a locksmith of Nancy, and Anne Marthe Mienville, twenty, also of Nancy.

1845 March 27. Birth in Nancy of Marie Paule Alice Courbe.

1869 April 26. Birth in Nancy of Louis Joseph Pillard.

Marie Paule Courbe of 12 rue du Regard (sixth arrondissement of Paris) first exhibits in the Paris Salon. She exhibits again in 1870.

1871 Death of d'Estoc's friend Marie Edmée Pau, aged twenty-five. Marie Paule Courbe does not exhibit at the Salon this year.

1872 Marie Paule Courbe resumes exhibiting her work at the Salon, and continues to do so for the next few years, until 1878.

1875 September 22. D'Estoc (thirty) marries Paul Joseph Parent Desbarres (one day before his thirty-ninth birthday), industrialist, of 358 rue St. Honoré (first arrondissement). His parents live at 28 rue Cassette (sixth arrondissement). D'Estoc is living at 99 rue de Rennes (sixth arrondissement) with her parents, now "rentiers" (landowners).

December 20. Death of Paul Parent Desbarres, now of 66 rue de Rennes.

1880 After a two-year hiatus, Marie Paule Courbe begins exhibiting at the Salon again, but now under her married name (though a widow for five years).

December. Gisèle d'Estoc meets Guy de Maupassant? It is not certain if the meeting takes place in December of 1880 or January of 1881.

1881 Death of Marie Paule Courbe's in-laws, Louise Eulalie Caffieri (on May 7) and François Pierre Parent Desbarres (on September 8).

1882 Henner's painting Bara (for which d'Estoc reputedly served as model) is exhibited at the Salon.

1883 April 30. Death of painter Edouard Manet (if d'Estoc did any modeling for him, it would have to have been before this).

1883–84 Marie Paule Courbe does not exhibit at the Salon, but according to Borel she does exhibit at the "Blanc et noir" exhibition.

1884 Emile Bayard's painting *Une affaire d'honneur*, rumored to depict d'Estoc's duel with Emma Rouër, is shown at the Salon.

First attested use of the pseudonym Gisèle d'Estoc.

1885 Marie Paule Courbe exhibits at the Salon under her married name Desbarres. She now lives on the rue Caroline (in the artists' neighborhood of the Batignolles, in the seventeenth arrondissement), where she will spend her remaining years in Paris.

1886 Last known letter to d'Estoc from Guy de Maupassant.

1887 Publication in Nancy of *Noir sur blanc: Récits lorrains* under the pseudonym Gyz-El.

Publication in Paris of *La vierge-réclame*, her roman à clef about Rachilde.

First issue of the *Revue caudine* (in November?).

December. Second issue of the *Revue caudine* with contributions by "Gyz-El."

1888 Rachilde publishes *Madame Adonis*, her fictionalized portrait of d'Estoc.

A new work by G. d'Estoc, *La bande à Virgile*, is announced, but there's no sign that it was ever published.

September. Laurent Tailhade links the names of d'Estoc and Rachilde in print, leading to a lawsuit by d'Estoc.

1889 February 27. Tailhade and a colleague are acquitted, but d'Estoc later wins a fine on appeal.

Mid-May. Tailhade serves time in Sainte-Pélagie prison for not paying the fine.

D'Estoc's last-known exhibition at the Salon.

1890 Pillard living at 9 rue du Mont-Doré, "à cent pas" (a hundred paces) from d'Estoc (according to *Journal des interviews*).

1891 First (and only?) installment of *Psychologie de Jeanne d'Arc* published.

D'Estoc moves with Pillard d'Arkaï to Nice sometime in the early 1890s.

1892 Louis Pillard d'Arkaï publishes an interview with d'Estoc that leads to a lawsuit. D'Arkaï (now editor of the *Tribun du Midi*) and d'Estoc are sued for libel by Gustave Kahn and Léon Pilate (a poet from Nice), and both are fined 25 francs. (The exact grounds for the suit remain obscure; no copies of the original interview remain.) Pillard d'Arkaï publishes his version of the affair in the *Journal des Interviews* of August 4–10. Among other things, the article claims that d'Estoc's father is now dead, and that her "aged and infirm" mother is back in Nancy. It also announces new forthcoming work by "G.-J. d'Estoc," including "La Ville-femme (proses de Nice)," but there is no evidence that this work ever appeared.

1894 April 4. Bomb explosion at the Foyot restaurant; d'Estoc is suspected of having "planted" the bomb (literally, since it is hidden in a flowerpot).

April 20/25. Louis Pillard d'Arkaï publishes his broadside defending d'Estoc.

May 8. Death in Nice of "Paule Courbe, widow of Parent Desbarres" (i.e., d'Estoc).

1900 January 27. Pillard d'Arkaï marries Honorée Joséphine Carle in Vallauris.

1912–13 Publication of "Guy de Maupassant intime: Notes d'une amie" by "Mme X" in *La grande revue* in three installments (October 25, 1912; March 25, 1913; and April 10, 1913). This is later thought to be (1) a hoax; (2) the basis for the "cahier d'amour"; and (later still) (3) by someone else entirely.

1927   Pierre Borel publishes *Le destin tragique de Guy de Maupassant* in Paris.

1936   Ernest Raynaud publishes yet another volume of his memoirs of the fin de siècle, *En marge de la mêlée symboliste*.

1939   June. Borel publishes "Une adoratrice de Maupassant: Le cahier d'amour, confidences inédites" in *Les oeuvres libres*, which launches the d'Estoc controversy.

        July 15 and August 15. Auriant challenges Borel's claims in the *Mercure de France* and debate ensues.

1941   November. Borel publishes "Une amie inconnue de Guy de Maupassant" in *Le mois suisse*.

1944   Borel publishes *Maupassant et l'androgyne*, but war allegedly interferes with its distribution.

1950   August 1. Borel's 1941 article "Une amie inconnue de Guy de Maupassant," originally published in Switzerland in 1941, is republished in *La revue des deux mondes*.

1951   Borel publishes *Le vrai Maupassant* in Geneva.

1952   April. American critic Artine Artinian warns in "Maupassant and Gisèle d'Estoc" that the cahier is a hoax.

1958   Borel publishes "Une amoureuse inconnue de Maupassant" in *Les oeuvres libres*.

1962   Borel publishes "Guy de Maupassant et Gisèle d'Estoc" in *Les oeuvres libres*.

        Pierre Cogny summarizes the debate in his introduction to *Notre coeur* by Guy de Maupassant. As part of his research, Cogny unearths the broadside by Pillard d'Arkaï defending d'Estoc after the attentat Foyot. Lanoux will refer to it (and publish the Bn call number) in his 1967 book.

1963   September 21. Death of Pierre Borel (Frédéric Viborel) in Nice.

1966   Paul Ignotus summarizes the debate in his book *The Paradox of Maupassant* published in London.

1967 Armand Lanoux publishes *Maupassant le bel-ami*, in which he identifies d'Estoc as Marie Elise Courbe, born 1863.

May 24. Maupassant's letters to Gisèle d'Estoc are sold at public auction in Paris.

1973 Maupassant's letters to d'Estoc are published in his collected *Correspondance*.

1983 Death of Armand Lanoux.

March 30. William McCulloch writes from Edinburgh to the director of the musée de Toul (where one of d'Estoc's art works supposedly was) to say that he knows the true identity of Gisèle d'Estoc. The letter remains in the archive, and the information is not disseminated further.

1984 Alexandre Grenier publishes Maupassant's pornographic play *A la feuille de rose, maison turque*. In an appendix, he (re)publishes Maupassant's letters to d'Estoc, along with a commentary.

1986 Jacques-Louis Douchin publishes *La vie érotique de Maupassant*.

1987 Pictures of d'Estoc appear in the Pléiade's *Album Maupassant* (Réda).

1988 Joan Ungersma Halperin revives the debate around the Foyot attack in her book *Félix Fénéon: Aesthete and Anarchist in Fin-de-Siècle Paris*.

1993 Gisèle d'Estoc's *Cahier d'amour* is republished (by Arléa), edited by Jacques-Louis Douchin.

Philippe Oriol publishes *A propos de l'attentat Foyot* in a small print run by an independent press. Published for the first time are photos from the police archives that show, among other things, a reconstruction of the flowerpot bomb. Oriol also includes facsimiles of Pillard d'Arkaï's broadside and an account of the Kahn/Pilate affair.

1997 The diary of Louis-Pilate de Brinn'Gaubast is published. The preface and notes (by Jean-Jacques Lefrère and Philippe Oriol) shed further light on the grievances behind the Kahn/Pilate trial.

1998 Gilles Picq announces that d'Estoc's death certificate has been found.

2001 Gilles Picq's biography of Laurent Tailhade is published.

The photo of the flowerpot bomb appears on the cover of a special issue of *Yale French Studies*.

2003 The birth certificate of Marie Paule Alice Courbe, born 1845, is published in *Histoires littéraires* (Hawthorne, "De nouveau").

2006 Léo d'Arkaï, *Il***; suivi de "Pillard d'Arkaï, Bandit des terres" par Gilles Picq* published.

Notes

INTRODUCTION

1. Lear's poem is about the Akond of Swat, who I used to think was an entirely made-up character, someone who didn't really exist, like the dong with a luminous nose or the maritime owl and pussycat, so the parallel with opinion about Gisèle d'Estoc is not entirely gratuitous. In fact, an akond (or akhoond, to give it the contemporary spelling) is an Islamic community leader like a mullah (the one Lear wrote about died in 1877), and the region of Swat is real, too, and probably all too familiar to Lear's readers, who were steeped in the geography of the British Empire, though it was forgotten in my postcolonial, postpartition childhood, which saw only countries ("Pakistan," "India"). The war in Afghanistan and along the Pakistani borders has brought new attention to the Swat valley, a name one hears on the nightly news with some regularity. For the full text of Lear's poem, see, for example, http://www.nonsenselit.org/Lear/ll/akond.html (consulted on January 14, 2009).

2. For a brief overview, see, for example, Hamilton, *Biography*; and Lee.

3. Though the genre of "great lives" endures in recent works of biography such as Nigel Hamilton's *American Caesars*, which suggests by its very title a link between the ancient and the modern view of leadership.

4. See Claire Tomalin's review ("The Female Captive") of Colley's book.

5. All translations are my own.

6. Corbin describes the fine of 5.70 francs as "l'équivalent du produit d'une dizaine de journées de travail." Assuming a modern workweek of five days, this is the equivalent of two weeks' work. In the nineteenth century, of course, work was not quite so standardized.

Laborers may have worked six or even seven days a week—depending on the season, the availability, and their line of work—and been underemployed or out of work and without any income at other times. Thus, I acknowledge that I am simplifying the situation here in order to try to grasp what these fines represented.

7. A desire that gives its title to her metabiographical account of her search for the letters of Marcel Proust, *Other People's Letters*.

8. See Secrest, *Shoot the Widow*; and Curtiss.

9. See, for example, the biographies of Colette and Simone de Beauvoir by the team Claude Francis and Fernande Gontier. For an overview of some of the issues, see Wagner-Martin.

10. In resurrecting d'Estoc (as it were), I am mindful of some of the problems inherent in what Janet Beizer has called "salvation biography," that is, the attempt to overcompensate for the dearth of information about female role models and predecessors of the past by putting the words we want to hear but don't find into their reanimated mouths. Although some speculation and inference is inevitable, I am more interested for purposes of this project in the fact that records in fact speak their own words. While there may doubtless be interpretation involved in reading them, I am also interested in paying attention to those words themselves. For more on our (perhaps misplaced) desire to reanimate the dead, see also Heather Love, *Feeling Backward*.

11. See also her *Footsteps in Paris*.

12. To borrow from the title of Martha Vicinus's edited collection of essays about the stereotypes of the nineteenth-century woman.

1. TO HELL AND BACK

1. Atwood, *Negotiating with the Dead*. See especially chapter 6, "Descent" (153–80). For more stories of academic adventures in the archive, see Burton. In the words of one of the contributors to this volume, Craig Robertson, "Scholars who use archives need to critically analyze not only documents but also the institutions which house them" (77).

2. For more on the role of caves and other spaces that take the seeker away from light and life in order to bring about other states of consciousness associated with inspiration, see Ustinova.

3. The classic example of this genre in biography is Symons.

4. In the new dispensation of the Bibliothèque nationale de France, my

(admittedly limited) experience is that the concept of pollution has replaced theology. Instead of going to hell to read forbidden works, one goes to the "Salle T" (all the halls are lettered), but of course in French *Salle T* sounds exactly like *saletés*, filth.

5. The idea that "information wants to be free" is the contentious claim of Chris Anderson.

6. I am indebted to Ross Chambers for this insight.

7. See, among others, Douchin.

8. I am happy to be able to report that as of this writing, not only is the text available, it can even be downloaded digitally from the Bibliothèque nationale de France website. Change is often slow, sometimes surprisingly rapid, but always uneven.

9. Daeninckx compares it to a huge overturned table. The "book silos" look like "quatre pieds massifs et vitrés d'une gigantesque table renversée" (four massive, glassy legs of a giant upside-down table) (6). For Grafton, the building resembles "the set from some forgotten dystopian sci-fi film of the 1970s" (292).

10. Some interior designers (these would include my nephew, who is my source on this) maintain that good (efficient) design uses a simple binary code to signal nonverbally to the user whether to pull or push. The presence of a handle means "pull." If there is no handle, but rather a flat plate screwed to the door where you are meant to put your hand, it is a clue to "push." Thus, putting handles on a door that is meant to be pushed open just confuses the user by sending the wrong signal, and labeling the doors (push/pull) isn't necessary to begin with. The designers of the BnF do not subscribe to this way of thinking.

11. The library is very popular as a setting for fiction, of course (see Keen for some British examples), but fact is often stranger than fiction.

12. A second, later version on this theme may be viewed at the comic's website http://www.tmcm.com, but this second version is not as clever as the first, original panel, which dates from 1993.

13. If you are still not convinced that library research can constitute a hardship, see Steedman's description of the etiology of "Archive Fever" (17–19).

2. GISÈLE D'ESTOC AND WORLD WAR II

1. For an overview of trends in Maupassant's reputation, see Benhamou.

2. The Bibliothèque nationale de France rejects the suggestion that his real identity was Alexandre Hadjivassiliou but is otherwise unable to shed any light on his true identity.

3. Since Borel had done some advance publicity, as it were, for the "Love Diary" by publishing an article with an attention-grabbing headline in *Paris-soir* at the end of May in which he identified d'Estoc by name ("L'inconnue masquée qu'aima jusqu'au bord de la folie Guy de Maupassant est identifiée"), Auriant's claim to have learned the name only through Deffoux is a little odd. Assuming he was speaking in good faith, he must not have known about the *Paris-soir* article. Deffoux published a brief article (under the initials L. Dx) in *L'oeuvre* on July 23, 1939, under the heading "A propos de 'Gisèle d'Estoc,'" in which he informs readers of the "impudeur 'spectaculaire'" (the spectacular lack of shame) with which she tells the story of her alleged affair with Maupassant. While he goes on to cast doubt on Borel's story, Deffoux clearly uses d'Estoc's name, beginning with the headline itself (though always within a cordon sanitaire of quotation marks). It is not clear if it is Auriant or Deffoux who first labels the pseudonym as a "nom de guerre" (Deffoux does not use this term in his article but may have done so in a private conversation), but the choice of words is not without significance. On the one hand, of course, the warrior image is suggested by the pseudonym itself, since *estoc* is a word for sword (I shall have occasion to return to this image in the "Interlude"), and a *nom de plume*, or pseudonym, recalls a *nom de guerre*. But in everyday parlance, the *nom de guerre* was specifically the pseudonym used professionally by prostitutes (perhaps because of the perceived parallels between love and war, in which all is fair, for example). To the attuned reader, then, the reference to d'Estoc as this kind of warrior undermines her credibility by presenting her not simply as an admirer of Maupassant (a term Auriant puts in distancing quotation marks), but as a slut. I am grateful to Brigitte Mahuzier for drawing my attention to this usage of the term.

4. Frédéric-Louis Viborel was born at La Colle-sur-Loup (just outside Nice) on November 13, 1885, and died in Nice on September 21, 1963 (Picq, *Tailhade* 263n20).

5. Presumably Hélène Lecomte Du Nouy, née Oudinot (1855?–1915), she is thought to have written in collaboration with Maupassant (among others). The novel *Amitié amoureuse*, published under the pseudonym H.L.N., about the passionate but platonic friend-

ship between a man and woman who are married to other partners, may be read as a roman à clef (it is dedicated to Madame Laure de Maupassant) of this relationship.

6. Just to complicate matters, Auriant also refers to the "admiratrice" of Maupassant in his first intervention on the topic in the *Mercure* in July of 1939 (490).

7. Writing to the wife of a colleague, Madame Rachel Kahn, in 1894 about some insulting remarks d'Estoc had made in the press, Rachilde wrote: "Le meilleur système de châtiment à employer contre la d'Estoc c'est . . . *le silence!*" (The best way of punishing d'Estoc is . . . silence!) (see Shryock 148). For more on d'Estoc's attack on Kahn, see the discussion of the affair of the *Journal des interviews* below.

8. Not all copies were pulped, evidently. I was able to obtain the book through interlibrary loan, and later found my own copy to purchase through an online used book site.

3. A STORM IN A TEACUP

1. Along with the manuscript of the cahier, the "dossier en Amérique" contained the only known copy of d'Estoc's article on Michelangelo's androgyny, "Le secret de Michel-Ange." This article, from which Borel quotes, supposedly contained many proto-Freudian "pages brûlantes" about the genius of the artist and its relation to his sexuality (Borel, *Maupassant et l'androgyne* 39). Borel claims the article has been translated into many languages. I have not been able to trace the current whereabouts of this dossier, nor any trace of the article in other languages. In his book Lanoux affirmed that part of the dossier, at least, was in the collection of bibliophile Daniel Sickles (the collector, not the famous Civil War hero). Sickles has since died and his collection has been dispersed through sale, but I have not been able to trace these particular documents.

2. Tuchman states succinctly that "six heads of state were assassinated for [anarchism's] sake in the twenty years before 1914" (63).

3. Eisenzweig provides a useful summary of the main events of 1882–94 (23–25).

4. First noted by Jean Maitron, who is cited in Eisenzweig 26.

5. Even if they did not go back to the "raw material" of the press coverage of the day, books about anarchism began appearing almost immediately. While Jean Maitron's magisterial *Le mouvement anarchiste*

en France was not published until much later, those curious about this period of history in the 1930s might have consulted Joseph Garin's *L'anarchie et les anarchistes*, which appeared almost immediately, in 1885, or Félix Dubois's *Le péril anarchiste* of 1894, to mention but two examples of what was available.

6. The widening of the rue de Vaugirard led to its demolition in 1938 (Picq, *Tailhade* 122).

7. The quote is often invoked (see, for example, Weber 118), but often without the context, so that Tailhade seems hoist by his own petard. It was originally a quip at a dinner party but was picked up and quoted in the press the next day, so that what started as a casual table-talk witticism became something of an albatross around Tailhade's neck (see Tuchman 91; also Eisenzweig 127).

8. The case has been summarized recently by Lay. Those who favor Fénéon as the guilty party usually invoke Joan Halperin's 1988 biography of Fénéon, but her work has not gone undisputed. Philippe Oriol challenged her conclusions in his 1993 pamphlet *A propos de l'attentat Foyot*, but his work has not been widely disseminated and consequently many continue to blame Fénéon, even though Oriol's expert knowledge is more convincing. The impression often conveyed to the general public is that Fénéon's guilt can safely be assumed. Works of popular history such as David Sweetman's *Explosive Acts* (1999) slide from acknowledgment of doubt about the case to the tacit certainty that Fénéon must be guilty. For example, Sweetman goes from reporting what are merely rumors about Fénéon (13) to a fictionalized re-creation of the event in which Fénéon walks in the Luxembourg Gardens smoking a cigarette before planting the bomb and then taking a bus to Clichy (322–23) to deciding that Fénéon was "certainly guilty" (380). Sweetman concedes that Fénéon's guilt was never "irrefutably proven" (495), yet continues to refer to him as someone who combined anarchist theory with action. Fénéon's fictional work has recently become available in translation again, thanks to Luc Sante's translation of his *Novels in Three Lines*. Reviewing this work in the pages of the *London Review of Books*, Francophile British novelist Julian Barnes falls prey to the same logic of assuming Fénéon's guilt. Describing Fénéon's relationship to anarchism, Barnes states, "He supported the cause as journalist, editor and—almost certainly—bomb-planter" (9).

9. A photograph of a police re-creation of the bomb was recently fea-

tured on the cover of an issue of *Yale French Studies* devoted to "Fragments of Revolution" (Weber and Lay).

10. The title is sometimes mistakenly given as *Les gloires malsaines*, but the title page makes it clear that this is intended as the name of a series, even though this book is the only one, apparently, ever to have appeared in it.

11. All the illustrations suggest a similarly intimate knowledge of Rachilde's life and career. The first chapter, "Une gamine qui promet," depicts Rachilde showing a manuscript to a publisher or newspaper editor under the watchful eye of her mother. "L'homme-Vénus" illustrates the opening scene of *Monsieur Vénus*, and so on. The detailed knowledge displayed in both the content and illustrations of the book make the story of the clerk Le Hénaff, who supposedly drowned himself because of unrequited love for Rachilde, extremely suggestive to those interested in Rachilde.

12. D'Estoc may also have inspired the episode in Rachilde's novel *La marquise de Sade* (also of 1887) in which the heroine, Mary Barbe, brands with a hot iron a woman who makes sexual advances to her. Since the character of Mary Barbe is a thinly disguised self-portrait of Rachilde, this action may represent a fantasy of revenge. Since a *barbe* is a beard, it is easy to see the name as a form of masculinization, a pose Rachilde famously adopted, but this focus on gender may distract attention away from a related but different connotation of the name, the metal hook (or barb) on a weapon that makes it difficult to remove once it finds its target. Gisèle had her sword, or *estoc*, but Rachilde had her own barbs with which to counterattack. The character Madeleine in the novel *La Princesse des Ténèbres* (1896) also seems to draw on Rachilde's ambivalence about the relationship with d'Estoc. Madeleine reflects on a moment when she was tempted to choose to love herself, rather than a demonic man, but the love of self seems to hint at loving *someone like* herself, that is, another woman: "N'avait-elle point rêvé, jadis, d'aimer une seconde *elle-même* pour que leur passion, purement cérébrale, arrivée à son paroxysme, n'eût jamais le droit, ni le devoir, de descendre aux brutales prostitutions de la chair, lesquelles *déterminent* tout en leurrant les sens? Et si elle s'était dérobée à la dernière minute, c'est qu'elle avait eu d'insurmontables répulsions en présence du vice" (Had she not dreamed once, just for a second, of loving herself so that their purely cerebral passion, at its height, should never have the right nor the

need to lower itself to the brutal prostitutions of the flesh, which determine everything by deceiving the senses? And if she had begged off at the last minute, it was because she had felt insurmountable revulsion in the presence of vice) (142–43). I am grateful to Michael Finn for bringing this citation to my attention.

13. "Lettre grossière" are the words of Pierre Dufay, who edited and annotated Tailhade's *Lettres à sa mère, 1874–1891* in 1926 (see 178). This is another source of information about d'Estoc that the critics of the 1930s might have consulted, as she is clearly named (as Mme d'Estoc by Tailhade and as Mme G. d'Estoc in a note by Dufay).

14. Gilles Picq gives a summary of these events in his article "On destocke" and goes into more detail in his biography of Tailhade.

15. This was the affair of the *Journal des interviews*. This newspaper was an ephemeral publication in which d'Arkaï published an interview with d'Estoc that cast aspersions on the wife of Gustave Kahn, another literary figure associated primarily with symbolism (in April and August 1892). His wife, Elisabeth Dayre (she would later change her name to Rachel and convert to Judaism to make a statement during the Dreyfus affair), had a somewhat checkered past. In addition to collecting so many lovers from literary circles that she earned the nickname "the little anthology" ("la petite anthologie"), she was bisexual and reputed to have been d'Estoc's lover. Jehan Rictus (who would denounce d'Estoc in the Foyot affair) recorded in his diary, "De plus lesbienne elle couchait avec Jeanne d'Estoc (Mme Paul Parent Debarres [*sic*])" (qtd. in Lefrère 427). The exact nature of the dispute in this affair remains obscure—no surviving copies of the interview have been found—but the allegations were again discussed elsewhere in the press. One commentator, Aurélien Scholl, writing in August 1892, identified Pillard d'Arkaï as the editor of the *Tribun du Midi*, a newspaper based in Nice.

16. The *Tout Paris* had listed her as early as 1888 (under the name Mme Paule-P. Desbarres), noting that her reception day was Tuesday (the same day as Rachilde; one would have to choose sides if one wanted to belong to such a Salon!). She continued to be listed in 1889, 1890, 1891 (when the pseudonym d'Estoc was also included), and 1892.

17. I have been unable to confirm this claim since French death certificates do not record the cause of death.

18. According to an annotation on his birth certificate, Louis Pillard would later marry Honorée Joséphine Carle in Vallauris on January 17, 1900.

19. See the essay "Pillard d'Arkaï, bandit des terres" by Gilles Picq in d'Arkaï. Pillard d'Arkaï was not the only expatriate from Nancy who would gravitate to this corner of Paris. Maurice Barrès was living at 8 rue Caroline in 1895. Of course, by then d'Estoc was dead, but they had known many of the same people (such as the writer Gyp, about whom d'Estoc wrote a thinly disguised story in *Noir sur blanc*).

20. The title of the book was a coded reference to girls from Nancy (the "flowers") and a street with a bad reputation (the rue des Dominicains).

21. Borel adds in a footnote that the rue Caroline (in the seventeenth arrondissement) is now the rue Abel Truchet (*Maupassant et l'androgyne* 40), but it would appear he is confused: the *passage* Caroline has changed its name thus, but rue Caroline is still rue Caroline. D'Estoc lived at number 2 and had a studio at number 4 with a garden in between the two (see d'Arkaï's description). The building currently on this site (on the rue Caroline) appears to date from the twentieth century. (Number 2 on the former passage Caroline is now a hotel.) There is nothing visible from the street that would give us a sense of what it was like in d'Estoc's day, though in the Batignolles in general there are plenty of reminders of what the neighborhood must have been like when it was frequented by artists who maintained studios there.

22. The order of the letters given in Borel's *Maupassant et l'androgyne* is quite different from that given in the later edition edited by Jacques Suffel (Maupassant, *Correspondance*). Suffel acknowledges the problems in dating the letters, but seems to have had access to the originals that were sold at auction and therefore could take into consideration evidence such as postmarks on envelopes (in addition to internal evidence in the letters themselves, such as references to travel abroad). Borel presumably also had direct access to the letters when writing *Maupassant et l'androgyne*, but it is generally acknowledged that he is less accurate as a scholar. While I disagree with those who dismiss all his claims out of hand, as this book makes clear, it must be conceded that he is consistently unreliable when it comes to exact dates. For example, Borel brings François Tassart into the story at the beginning of his narrative, without taking into account the fact that Tassart could not have been privy to things that took place before he entered Maupassant's service in 1883. Borel's account of the d'Estoc-Maupassant relationship, "La solitude du faune," oc-

cupies an entire chapter of his book (60–153). Direct quotation of Maupassant's letters forms the basis of the narrative, complemented by what seem to be letters from d'Estoc. One in particular, addressed to "mon amant," is revealing of d'Estoc's investment in the relationship, suggesting that Maupassant is the only man capable of understanding her desire and ending with the rhetorical question "Ne sais-tu pas que je suis ta soeur en désirs 'interdits'?" (Don't you know that I am your [soul] sister when it comes to "forbidden" desires?) (124). To d'Estoc, Maupassant was a soul mate not so much as a lover but as a brother, someone who shared her tastes (for seducing women?). Borel also includes the texts of erotic poems that Maupassant included in his letters to d'Estoc, evidence that allows the supposition that these poems, at least, are also *about* d'Estoc. In between these documents, Borel fills in the background with scenes of what seem to be his own invention so that the narrative takes the form of a novelization that freely attributes thoughts and feelings to the participants.

23. Borel identifies the person in question as Catulle Mendès.

24. For an example of a critic who seems to take pleasure in pointing out d'Estoc's supposed youth, see Alexandre Grenier in *A la feuille de rose* 121.

25. D'Estoc would never run out of spite, or so it would seem. As late as 1892, in the *Pamphlet du jour* of September 28 (a broadside newspaper publication that appeared as a supplement to the *Journal des interviews* [about which more below]), d'Estoc attacked the feminist journalist Séverine. In a "private letter" to M. d'Arkaï published under the heading "Un fléau national" (A National Scourge), d'Estoc took her rival journalist to task for her writing skills: "Non-sens, faux-sens, contre-sens, solécismes et barbarismes, battologies et séverinades. Elle a usé de toutes les fautes connues . . . *et quibusdam aliis*." The article is signed with the byline G. J. d'Estoc and is followed by a list of examples of Séverine's bad prose (such as referring to someone as a "drinker of ambrosia," when everyone knows that ambrosia must be *eaten!*) under the heading "Touchée, Séverine!" which picks up on the general headline "Le duel de Mme Séverine avec M. Larousse."

26. There is a brief return to the *tu* form in a letter of 1884, but both the date and the exact identity of the addressee of the letter are uncertain (see *Correspondance* 2:164n1).

27. Maupassant's short story "La femme de Paul," about a young man who commits suicide because his girlfriend is a lesbian, dates from

1881 (it first appeared in the collection *La maison Tellier*). The story, about a man humiliated by the discovery of his female companion's preferences, displays a familiarity with lesbian subculture unusual for its time, and it is tempting to speculate—along with Louis Forestier, the editor of the Pléiade edition of Maupassant's stories—that d'Estoc may have served as an inspiration or informant for Maupassant in writing this story. See the note to this effect in *Contes et nouvelles* 1372–73.

28. Catulle Mendès (1841–1909), a poet and novelist associated primarily with the Parnassian movement and the fin de siècle, had his own complicated relationship to voyeurism and lesbianism. His first wife was Judith Gautier, daughter of the poet Théophile. They were married in 1866 but the marriage did not last, and Judith (who had her own career as a writer and orientalist) went on to spend her later life with another woman (Suzanne Meyer-Zundell) in a relationship that is often interpreted today to have involved more than mere companionship (see the biographies by Richardson and Knapp). Mendès went on to live with the composer Augusta Holmès (1847–1903), with whom he had five children. The couple split up in 1886, in other words not long after the kind of escapades described in this chapter. (Mendès would go on to marry Jeanne Nette [1867–1965], who published novels and poetry under the name Jane Catulle-Mendès.) Lesbianism was also a recurrent theme in Mendès's work. In addition to the short story "Lesbia" (in the collection of that name, 1887), Mendès published *Zo'har* in 1886 (discussed below in the "Interlude") and *Méphistophéla* in 1890 (the work for which he is often remembered today). In the preface to the 2005 edition of *Zo'har*, Michèle Friang sums up Mendès's reputation in the following terms: "Son oeuvre, pratiquement introuvable en dehors des bibliothèques spécialisées, est, de nos jours, presque inconnue, et aucune biographie conséquente ne lui a été consacrée" (His work, which is almost impossible to find except in specialized libraries, is almost unknown today, and no biography of any consequence has appeared of him) (7).

29. The theme recalls the role reversal explored in Rachilde's *Monsieur Vénus* of 1884, except that the narrator does not experience himself as feminized by the encounter.

30. D'Estoc's masculine appearance would seem to support Borel's claim that she served as the model for the famous painting of Bara (a boy hero of the recent Commune) by Jean-Jacques Henner that was ex-

hibited in 1882 (*Maupassant et l'androgyne* 37), in other words exactly around the time when d'Estoc's boyish physique would have been inspiring such gems of poetry in Maupassant. Of course there is some irony in the fact that Maupassant saw her figure as having nothing feminine about it, while Henner's painting was criticized when first it was shown for making the hero look too effeminate—the very thing that is sometimes mentioned to support the notion that d'Estoc was the model. She is thus both too masculine (to look like a woman to Maupassant) and yet too feminine (to be credible as a faithful representation of a boy in a painting) at the same time. Gilles Picq disputes Borel's claim based on a conversation with a curator of the Heller museum who maintained that two Italian boys were the model for the painting ("On destocke" 120).

31. It is true, however, that d'Estoc lived in close proximity to educational establishments on two occasions in the 1880s. In 1880 (possibly the year she met Maupassant), she gave her address as 6 rue Herran when she registered for the Salon. This very exclusive street (it is a private, gated road) in the sixteenth arrondissement (the only time d'Estoc ventured into such swanky surroundings) is next to the lycée Janson. A plaque set into the building at this address today shows that it was built in 1877; it was thus new when d'Estoc lived there just three years later. The following year, 1881, d'Estoc had apparently relocated to the Batignolles district, at 78 boulevard des Batignolles, once again near a school. (Again, the building bears the date of its construction, 1869.) Perhaps the proximity to colleges also explains how d'Estoc got her hands on her schoolboy outfits. Finally, we know that d'Estoc was living with her mother (and father) in the sixth arrondissement when she married in 1875, but there is no evidence to suggest that she continued living with them. Pillard d'Arkaï would later claim (in the affair of the *Journal des interviews* discussed below) that d'Estoc's mother had returned to Nancy.

32. Gilles Picq states only that it was "au début des années 1890" (*Tailhade* 260) and gives some details about Pillard d'Arkaï's journalism. The evidence suggests that d'Estoc was still living on rue Caroline when her work on Jeanne d'Arc began appearing, that is, in 1891, but the move to Nice may have occurred that same year or shortly thereafter. Her last exhibition at the Salon had been in 1889. If indeed she died after a prolonged illness (such as leprosy, as Borel claims), perhaps she had already begun to show serious symptoms,

which may account for the abandonment of her artistic career and the move to a healthier climate.

33. Curiously, when Pillard d'Arkaï later married, it was to a woman ten years his senior.

4. AN INTERLUDE

1. Such "petticoat duels" occurred at least as far back as the 1770s (Hopton 182). When Emile Zola wanted to show the extent to which Renée Saccard, the heroine of his incestuous novel *La Curée* (1872), was deranged, he had her want to fight a duel—and with pistols rather than swords—with the duchesse de Sternich because the latter spilled a glass of punch on her dress. See Zola 508.

2. A fencing club also plays a prominent role in Joséphin Péladan's novel *La gynandre* about the female equivalent of the androgyne. The main character, Tammuz, goes in search of the vice of lesbianism, but finds only female *gynandres*, parodies of virility.

3. If not, go to the musical's website http://www.lesmis.com, where it is part of the montage that greets you on the homepage (site consulted August 19, 2009).

4. Assuming that the rumor that the painting depicts d'Estoc is correct, the date of Bayard's work means that the duel took place before this date. The *Annuaire du duel* compiled by Ferréus in 1891 lists a duel between M. Destoc and M. de Bernis on November 16, 1883. The listing is based on an "écho de journal" and consisted of a "rencontre a l'épée [encounter with swords], à Montmorency." The listing is not conclusive, since the participants are listed as men ("Monsieur") and Destoc was a popular pseudonym, but it is suggestive. If indeed this was d'Estoc's duel, it is evidence of use of the pseudonym before 1884, which otherwise stands as the earliest attested use of the name by our subject.

5. It was not unusual for the popular press to depict such sensational events. An illustration of a duel between women that reputedly took place in Madrid also appeared in *Le petit parisien* in 1891 (see the back cover of Hopton).

6. Press reports of the painting were not limited to France. The Salon was also covered by the *New York Times*, where an article on May 18, 1884 ("New Pictures in Paris"), devoted an entire paragraph to Bayard's work. "Another original *succès*, which is sure under the guise of photographic reproduction to make the voyage around the

world, is the "affaire d'honneur" of Emile Bayard. It represents a duel between two women, nude to the waist. They are not ethereal types by any means; they rather incline to be vigorously developed specimens. The idea is a queer one, but it is full of interest, and a crowd around the painting testifies to its attraction for popular fancy. The witnesses are women, and they appear a trifle more scared than the combatants themselves" (4). The article's prediction that the painting would make the voyage around the world (in the manner of a Jules Verne hero so familiar to Bayard) would come true in the century to follow, as this chapter illustrates. Note that the article also manages to suggest something sexually deviant (without even mentioning the whip) by referring to the subject as a "queer" idea, though without naming anything as specific as Amazons.

7. Which is not to say that it was never fatal.

8. The fact that violets have become a marker of lesbian love makes Borel's re-creation a little suspect. In addition to their role in the poetry of lesbian icon Renée Vivien (where the flower derives its significance from the name of Vivien's closest friend, Violet Shillito), violets signify in a number of lesbian texts. See, for example, Edouard Bourdet's play *La prisonnière*.

9. For the morgue as popular spectacle and the way female corpses in particular were displayed for sexual titillation, see Zola's novel *Thérèse Raquin* and Vanessa Schwartz's *Spectacular Realities*.

10. See Lefrère and Goujon for some of the ways these circles overlapped. Rachilde's publisher Genonceaux was a bookseller who also retailed works by Catulle Mendès and Souillac. It is through court records that we know more about the real identity of Souillac. While managing to sound vaguely aristocratic and authentic (Souillac is indeed a real place), the name also seems to suggest the verb *souiller*, to soil, a tacit wink to readers that the novel knows it will appear "dirty." Behind the pseudonym was one Madame Lefèbvre. She was condemned to a month in prison and a fine of 100 francs when a second edition of *Zé'boïm* was published in 1889 with a racier cover that attracted the attention of the authorities (46).

11. Images available at http://www.nationalcigarmuseum.com (consulted on November 30, 2007).

12. The two films, American productions, were both titled *An Affair of Honor*. The 1897 adaptation by the American Mutoscope Company specifically referenced "the famous picture of this name" (with-

out mentioning Bayard) of a duel in which the women are "rivals in love" in its catalog description, while the 1901 version by the S. Lubin Company refers to the painting but construes the feud between the women as more specifically motivated by rivalry over a man. For more information, see http://www.imdb.com (site consulted July 13, 2011).

13. In this free adaptation the duel also resulted in death for one of the participants, another deviation from the version of the d'Estoc/ Rouër encounter, in which honor was satisfied without mortal threat.

14. The website gives further information. Babes with Blades (BWB) sponsors a play competition called "Joining Sword and Pen," which was "founded in 2005 to increase the number of quality scripts featuring fighting roles for women" (http://www.babeswithblades. org/wptest/?page_id=46). The website explains how "the inaugural theme was proposed by Fight Master David Woolley, inspired by the print of Emile Bayard's 'An Affair of Honor' that hung on his living room wall. Each entry to the contest was required to incorporate the moment depicted in the print: a duel between two women on a secluded country road. The competition netted the Babes over forty entries, from locales ranging from their native Chicago to South Africa and New Zealand" (http:///www.babeswithblades. org/?page_id=173). An excerpt from the resulting adaptation of Bayard's work can be seen on YouTube (http://www.youtube.com/ watch?v=jrE6nUYauBI). All sites consulted June 15, 2012.

15. See, for example, Alison Light, *Mrs Woolf and the Servants*, as well as Sarah Waters's fictional application of this theme, *Affinity*.

16. Art historian Mathilde Huet states that there is no mention of a painting titled *La réconciliation* in the Salon catalogs for the years 1884–87 (personal communication).

17. I am indebted to Mathilde Huet for reminding me about this double meaning of *balle*.

18. The volley (from *voler*, to fly) also characterizes both the exchange of gunfire, as in a duel, and the game of tennis. The volley shot in tennis exists as a verb from 1819 and as a noun from 1862. (I am grateful to Colleen McQuillen and Jennifer Forrest for both suggesting and helping to establish this connection.)

19. There would appear to be an etymological link between the French *estoc* and the English word *stock* (as in a "stockade," a fence made of sticks with sharp, pointy ends). An *estoc* can also refer to the trunk of a tree and, more figuratively, the genealogical "stock" from which

people descend, but dictionaries such as Littré and the *Trésor de la langue française* present this use of the word as a separate meaning. In colloquial French "frapper d'estoc et de taille" (to attack with both the sharp, business end of the sword and also to slash with the cutting edge) is to do something "de quelque manière que ce soit" (by all possible means) (as Littré puts it).

20. The *bulle* is an utterance, a communication: it can be the kind of bull that popes emit, a speech bubble in graphic fiction, or even, in a diminutive form, a bulletin.

21. The image is also reproduced, along with others, in the *Album Maupassant*, the definitive iconographic biography of the writer, but in a cropped version that shows d'Estoc only from the shoulders up (Réda 224). To see the details discussed here, it is necessary to consult Borel's book.

22. The jacket clearly fastens right over left, which would seem on the face of things to signal a feminine garment, but on the complication of such semiotics, see my discussion of this "code" in *Rachilde and French Women's Authorship* (145–47).

23. On the play of concealment and revelation that the veil made possible in late nineteenth-century Paris, see Kessler.

24. It is tempting to believe that this photograph is the one described in Catulle Mendès's novel *Zo'har* (of 1886). This novel forms a sort of parallel to Souillac's *Zé'boïm* in that both titles refer to accursed biblical cities destroyed along with Sodom and Gomorrah for their sins. The principal sin in *Zo'har* is that of incest between a half brother and sister. The mother of the sister, Stéphana (a minor character, she has died by the end of the first chapter), is the countess Giselle d'Erkelens, who among other things is "veuve morganatique" (morganatic widow) and travels widely "avec son amie, qui passait pour sa soeur" (with her [lady] friend, who was taken to be her sister) (24). She appears in photographs, including one in which she wears "presque pas de robe, le bras levé pour cacher le visage" (almost no dress, her arm raised to hide her face) (25).

25. This dynamic of nakedness combined with a hidden face makes it tempting to speculate that d'Estoc may have been the unidentified lunch companion who so impressed Henry James when he met Maupassant. Javier Marías writes: "[James's] enthusiasm for Maupassant knew no bounds, again thanks to a single visit: the French short-story writer had received him for lunch in the society

of a lady who was not only naked, but wearing a mask. This struck James as the height of refinement, especially when Maupassant informed him that she was no mere courtesan, prostitute, servant, or actress, but a *femme du monde*, which James was perfectly happy to believe" (39).

5. GISÈLE D'ESTOC WHEN SHE WAS REAL

1. The impressionists, for example, favored the café Guerbois near the place Clichy during the Second Empire, but at the beginning of the Third Republic switched to meeting at the Nouvelle Athènes on place Pigalle. Both of these would have been within walking distance for someone living in the Batignolles.

2. For a description of the role of the Salon in Paris life in the 1880s, see Davis, especially "Dancing on a Volcano" (155–76). Davis focuses on 1884, a year d'Estoc did *not* exhibit, but her descriptions capture the general atmosphere.

3. In 1886 Maupassant praised the "ravissants médallions" (ravishing medallions) in his review of the Salon that appeared in *XIXe siècle* (http://www.maupassant.free.fr/chroniq/salon.html [site consulted June 12, 2012]).

4. Her pseudonym shows a similar instability. Though she is most commonly referred to today as Gisèle d'Estoc, she was also the more oriental sounding Gyz-el when she was the author of *Noir sur blanc*, and she is variously referred to as Madame G. d'Estoc, and even G. Jeanne d'Estoc, assimilating the name of her countrywoman and apparent inspiration Jeanne d'Arc.

5. According to Marie-Jo Bonnet 34. Deschanel's article "Etudes sur l'antiquité, Sappho et les Lesbiennes" appeared in the *Revue des deux mondes* in 1847. In this overview, Deschanel argued that the island of Lesbos was famous for its courtesans and only courtesans were allowed to be educated in ancient Greek society, therefore an educated woman—one educated enough to write poetry (like Sappho)—was in all likelihood a courtesan. Not only that, she was likely to follow other practices of the island subculture, practices alluded to only indirectly as "preferring women." Deschanel takes an open-minded approach that favors accepting the truth over ideology, arguing that Sappho's poetry stands on its own merits, but his article also helped shift the cultural understanding of Sappho as an allusion to a woman writer (as the name had been for Madame de Staël at the begin-

ning of the nineteenth century, for example) to an allusion to sexual practices. Bonnet notes that the article appeared just three years before the poet Charles Baudelaire published his poem "Lesbos," one of the touchstones of lesbian representation in France in the nineteenth century. I am indebted to Mathilde Huet for bringing this reference to my attention. The contributions of Deschanel are also discussed by Joan DeJean in *Fictions of Sappho*, though her focus is on the way the figure of Sappho is represented rather than on the redefinition of what it means to be "lesbian."

6. A reproduction of the painting may be seen online at http://www. culture.gouv.fr/public/mistral/joconde_fr?ACTION=RETROU VER&FIELD_98=DENO&VALUE_98=Tableau&NUMBER=4 &GRP=366&REQ=((Tableau)%20%3ADENO%20)&USRNAM E=nobody&USRPWD=4%24%2534P&SPEC=1&SYN=1&IMLY =&MAX1=1&MAX2=1&MAX3=100&DOM=All (site consulted March 3, 2009). The reproduction is less than perfect, but sufficient to note that the anatomy of the naked body is presented very sketchily (a certain roundness is suggested, the hint perhaps of breasts, and a modest indeterminacy where the viewer would expect to find the penis of the boy hero Bara) and that the face is positioned away from the source of light so that it is somewhat obscured. If d'Estoc were indeed the model, it is interesting to note that once again her body is clearly offered for view while the features of her face are depicted only with the greatest reticence.

7. See http://www.artnet.com/artists/LotDetailPage.aspx?lot_ id=595B76E86A4A3CA (site consulted June 15, 2012).

8. The dictionary was published in several volumes from 1914 to 1921. The extract on Courbe specifies that it is from volume 1 of 1914. The annotation is dated September 1993.

9. There is, sure enough, a dossier on Mathilde Isabelle Courbe in the archives of the musée d'Orsay. It is entirely empty. Perhaps, like her sister, she might be traced through her married name. In 1881 Marie Isabelle Mathilde Courbe of 86 rue Laugier (seventeenth arrondissement) married Joseph Célestin Thévenin.

10. Courbe exhibited a portrait of A. Hiolle, also referred to as a "portrait de jeune fille," in 1872.

11. The information is corroborated by a search of the *livrets* for 1850–70 conducted by Laure de Margerie in 1979, which culled two references to works by Marie Paule Courbe in each of the years 1869 and 1870.

The results of the search are listed, along with information about who did it and when, in the dossier.

12. See Waquet. This work focuses on the branch of the family that stayed in provincial Clamecy, but the family tree clearly shows the place of Pierre François Desbarres, 1798–1881, though with no further detail about his line of descent. His parents were Etienne-Laurent, who went by the name Parent-Charley (1766–1808), and Hélène Faulquier (1767–1842). The family in general went by the name of Parent, but Waquet explains that they were so prolific "qu'ils ont dû souvent accoler le nom d'une propriété à leur patronyme, pour éviter les confusions" (they often had to add the name of their property to their patronymic in order to avoid confusion) (24). Thus there was a Parent de la Plante, a Parent des Vallées, a Parent de Chassy, and a Parent des Isles. This also explains the instability in the spelling of the name: it would have started out as Parent des Barres (as indeed it appears in certain records) before being assimilated into Parent Desbarres (or Parent-Desbarres).

13. The full title of his work is *Histoire complète de la Chine depuis son origine jusqu'à nos jours. Son étendue, sa chronologie, l'histoire de ses diverses dynasties et des empereurs qui ont régné sur ce vaste empire depuis sa fondation jusques et y compris le règne de l'empereur actuel Hien-Foung, aujourd'hui sur le trône, son gouvernement, son commerce, ses arts et métiers, etc., ses coutumes, sa langues, sa littérature, sa musique, etc., par mm. A.S. et D. et continuée jusqu'à nos jours par M. P. D.*

14. Archives de Paris, 5 Mi3/135.

15. For more on the family, see http://mapage.noos.fr/jcparent/n431. htm (site consulted July 6, 2011). Note, however, that this page does not list Paul Joseph among the children, so that the information is not complete and other siblings may have been overlooked, too.

16. Archives de Paris 5 Mi4/28.

17. Archives de Paris, 5 Mi3/226 (10e arrondissement décès 1872–1881).

18. Paul's older brother, Emile Antoine François Parent Des Barres, was still alive (presumably) in 1891, when his name appeared on a Parisian electoral roll that gave his address as 154 boulevard de Magenta (tenth arrondissement), but whether he maintained any contact with his widowed sister-in-law cannot be determined.

19. For more on Gyp and her origins in Nancy, see Silverman.

20. On the value of a donkey companion for a good story, see Holmes 16–17.

21. See the letter quoted in Borel, *Maupassant et l'androgyne* 50. The recipient is identified by Borel only as Louis C., who at the time was a medical student who would go on to become a well-known doctor. He also dabbled in art, and it was his work shown at the "Blanc et noir" exhibition that brought him to d'Estoc's attention. She wrote to express her admiration and subsequently led him on, accompanying him to brothels in her schoolboy outfit, but tired of him when he became too passionately attached to her. Mathilde Huet has suggested that this Louis C. might be the engineer and aeronaut Louis Capazza (1862–1928), who came to Paris in 1883. His work on hot-air balloons may have put him in touch with Maupassant, whose balloon was named *Le Horla*.

22. The names Marcel and Marcelle Désambres are not unlike Paul and Paule Desbarres (the different spellings of the first name both sound the same), but there is no suggestion that Rachilde intended to depict d'Estoc's husband (if she even knew him).

23. For example, "Marcel" Désambres hints at a mystery that Louise is unable to fathom. He suggests that if Louise knew the whole truth about him, she wouldn't be afraid and they would go to Paris together where he would give her "ce bonheur mystique que les hommes et ton époux lui-même ne sauraient t'offrir" (that mystical happiness that men and even your husband are unable to offer you) (58). When Louise still proves slow on the uptake, Désambres concludes that she is too innocent: "Il y a des péchés pour lesquels vous n'êtes pas mûre encore, mon joli fruit défendu" (There are sins for which you are not yet ready [ripe], my pretty forbidden fruit) (58).

24. Of course, in a patronymic naming system, "Carini" is Marcelle's father's name, and so could be considered a "man's name," but then one would have to say the same of "Désambres," which was her husband's name. It, too, is "un nom d'homme," not "un nom de dame."

25. There are other signs that *Madame Adonis* was hastily written. The age of Madame Bartau, Louis's mother, is given as forty-four on page 61, but a few months later she declares that she is fifty (143).

26. See, for example, the recent retelling of d'Estoc's story in *Maupassant et le joli collégien* with text by François David and illustrations by Charlotte Mollet, in which d'Estoc is a "toute jeune fille" (n.p.).

6. GISÈLE D'ESTOC AND WHO SHE WASN'T

1. Lanoux refers to Marie Elise, although the archives also give the

spelling Marie Elisa. There were often multiple spellings of names (we have seen the example of des Barres/Des Barres/Desbarres), so I have adopted Lanoux's spelling for convenience.

2. Vaughan discussed this phenomenon in connection with the *Columbia* shuttle accident on National Public Radio's news show *All Things Considered* on May 5, 2003. See http://www.npr.org/templates/story/story.php?storyId=1252749 (site consulted on March 11, 2009).

3. Although it was published in the same year as her scathing attack on Rachilde, *La vierge-réclame*, and the first issue of her journal *La revue caudine*, Borel claimed that she told him it was her first work (*Maupassant et l'androgyne* 44). Of course she could have meant it was the first work she wrote, even if it was only published later.

4. I am reminded of the importance in biography of what Antonia Fraser calls "optical research," or, in less grand-sounding terms, "going to places and looking at them" (113). Sometimes it is the only way to know, as when Richard Holmes doubted whether Mary Wollstonecraft could be trusted when she said that she had seen Louis XVI being taken from the Temple prison to his trial at the Convention. She claimed to have seen the cortège from her window on the rue Meslay, but Holmes could not see how that was possible, given that the route would have taken a parallel street, the boulevard Saint-Martin. But he confesses, "The solution became clear the moment I walked over the same ground": Wollstonecraft's digs at number 22 stood on an elevated part of the street (99).

5. For more on the role of Joan of Arc in fin-de-siècle France, see "On the Boulevards: Representations of Joan of Arc in the Popular Theater" in Datta 142–78.

6. Gilles Picq has since reported that the original manuscript of Marie Edmée Pau's diary contains references to Gisèle d'Estoc that were edited out of the published version, confirming the connection ("Et encore du nouveau").

7. Note that Picq attempted such a reconciliation in "On destocke."

8. Lanoux even provides its call number — B.N. Fol L b 11 358 — in *Maupassant le bel-ami* (379). A facsimile version of the article subsequently appeared in the pamphlet *A propos de l'attentat Foyot* published by a small, independent press in Paris in 1993 (Oriol).

9. Subsequent topics (all with a literary focus) have included failures (1998), romans à clef (1999), hoaxes (2000), "what I don't know"

(2001), madmen (2002), punching bags ("têtes de turc," 2003), Paris, its life, and work (2004), censorship (2005), curiosities (2006), prizes (2007), and publicity (2008).

10. Just to review that argument, in the "Love Diary," the author (Borel was claiming this was d'Estoc) claimed that Maupassant's friend died on one date when history shows he died on another. Auriant had maintained that this mistake proved that the memoir was a fake. Borel countered that it was the sort of mistake a fraud would have been careful not to make, showing that the memoir was genuine.

11. The brother, too, may have died young. Pillard d'Arkaï would later claim that "elle n'a pas eu de frère" (she never had a brother). See the *Journal des Interviews* of August 4–10, 1892, p. 2, column 3, reproduced in facsimile at the end of Oriol.

AFTERWORD

1. On the superficial and lack of depth as characteristics of the postmodern, see Jameson.

2. This despite the fact that biographer Richard Holmes believes that love is one of the two essential elements of biography. He describes the relationship between biographer and subject as "a type of hero- or heroine-worship, which easily develops into a kind of love affair" (66). This stage in which the biographer identifies with the subject may be both "pre-biographic" and "in a sense pre-literate," but it is nevertheless essential, he claims. "If you are not in love with them you will not follow them—not very far, anyway. But the true biographic process begins precisely at the moment, at the places, where this naïve form of love and identification breaks down" (67).

3. For more on the metaphor of the jigsaw puzzle as the organizing principle of (auto)biography, see Drabble.

4. I am grateful to Mathilde Huet for communicating a copy of the letter.

Works Cited

Ali, Monica. *Brick Lane*. New York: Scribner, 2003.

Anderson, Chris. *Free: The Future of a Radical Price*. New York: Hyperion, 2009.

André-Maurois, Simone. "Histoire d'une correspondance." In George Sand–Marie Dorval, *Correspondance inédite*. Paris: Gallimard, 1953. 13–202.

d'Arkaï, Léo. *Il***; suivi de "Pillard d'Arkaï, Bandit des terres" par Gilles Picq*. Châlons-en-Champagne: Cynthia 3000, 2006.

Artinian, Artine. "Maupassant and Gisèle d'Estoc: A Warning." *Modern Language Notes* (April 1952): 251–53.

Atwood, Margaret. *Negotiating with the Dead: A Writer on Writing*. Cambridge: Cambridge University Press, 2002.

Auriant. Letter in "Petite histoire littéraire et anecdotes." *Mercure de France*, August 15, 1939, 240–47.

———. "Petite histoire littéraire et anecdotes." *Mercure de France*, July 15, 1939, 487–500.

Bair, Deirdre. *Simone de Beauvoir: A Biography*. New York: Summit, 1990.

Barnes, Julian. "Behind the Gas Lamp." *London Review of Books*, October 4, 2007, 9–11.

Beizer, Janet. *Thinking through the Mothers: Reimagining Women's Biographies*. Ithaca: Cornell University Press, 2009.

Bénézit, Emmanuel. *Dictionnaire des peintres, sculpteurs, dessinateurs et graveurs*. Rev. ed. Vol. 3, *Da-Forain*. Paris: Gründ, 1950.

Benhamou, Noëlle. "Redécouvrir Maupassant." *Histoires littéraires* 32 (2007): 73–113.

Bibliothèque nationale. *Catalogue générale des livres imprimés de la bibliothèque nationale*. Vol. 48. Paris: Imprimerie nationale, 1912.

Bonnet, Marie-Jo. *Un choix sans équivoque: Recherches historiques sur les relations amoureuses entre les femmes, XVIe–XXe siècle.* Paris: Denoël, 1981.

Borel, Pierre. "Une adoratrice de Maupassant: Le cahier d'amour, confidences inédites." *Les oeuvres libres* 216 (June 1939): 71–100.

———. "Une amie inconnue de Guy de Maupassant." *Le mois suisse* 32 (November 1941): 142–68. Rpt. in *La revue des deux mondes*, August 1, 1950, 481–97.

———. "Une amoureuse inconnue de Maupassant." *Les oeuvres libres* 151 (1958): 121–44.

———. *Le destin tragique de Guy de Maupassant.* Paris: Editions de France, 1927.

———. "Guy de Maupassant et Gisèle d'Estoc." *Les oeuvres libres* 195 (1962): 137–80.

———. Letter in "Petite histoire littéraire et anecdotes." *Mercure de France*, August 15, 1939, 240–42.

———. "L'inconnue masquée qu'aima jusqu'au bord de la folie Guy de Maupassant est identifiée." *Paris-soir*, May 28, 1939, 2.

———. *Maupassant et l'androgyne.* Paris: Editions du livre moderne, 1944.

———. *Le vrai Maupassant.* Geneva: Cailler, 1951.

Burton, Antoinette, ed. *Archive Stories: Facts, Fictions, and the Writing of History.* Durham: Duke University Press, 2005.

Chauvelot, Philippe. "Et encore du nouveau sur Gisèle d'Estoc." *Histoires littéraires* 17 (2004): 251–52.

Cogny, Pierre. Introduction. *Notre coeur* by Guy de Maupassant. Paris: Librairie Marcel Didier, 1962. vii–xlvii.

Colley, Linda. *The Ordeal of Elizabeth Marsh: A Woman in World History.* London: Harper, 2007.

Cook, Blanche Wiesen. *Eleanor Roosevelt.* 2 vols. New York: Viking, 1992–93.

Corbin, Alain. *Le monde retrouvé de Louis-François Pinagot: Sur les traces d'un inconnu, 1798–1876.* Paris: Flammarion, 1998.

Curtiss, Mina Kirstein. *Other People's Letters: In Search of Proust.* Boston: Houghton Mifflin, 1978.

Daeninckx, Didier. *Nazis dans le métro.* Paris: Librio, 1998.

Datta, Venita. *Heroes and Legends of Fin-de-Siècle France: Gender, Politics, and National Identity.* New York: Cambridge University Press, 2011.

David, François. *Maupassant et le joli collégien*. [N.p.]: Esperluète, [2009].

Davis, Deborah. *Strapless: John Singer Sargent and the Fall of Madame X*. New York: Jeremy P. Tarcher/Penguin, 2003.

Deffoux, Léon. "A propos de 'Gisèle d'Estoc.'" *L'oeuvre*, July 23, 1939, 7.

DeJean, Joan. *Fictions of Sappho, 1546–1937*. Chicago: University of Chicago Press, 1989.

Deschanel, Emile. "Etudes sur l'antiquité, Sappho et les Lesbiennes." *Revue des deux mondes*, June 15, 1847, 330–55.

DiBattista, Maria. *Imagining Virginia Woolf: An Experiment in Critical Biography*. Princeton: Princeton University Press, 2009.

Doniger, Wendy. *The Woman Who Pretended to Be Who She Was: Myths of Self-Impersonation*. New York: Oxford University Press, 2005.

Douchin, Jacques-Louis. *La vie érotique de Maupassant*. Paris: Suger, 1986.

Drabble, Margaret. *The Pattern in the Carpet: A Personal History with Jigsaws*. New York: Houghton Mifflin, 2009.

Dubois, Felix. *Le périle anarchiste: L'organisation secrète du parti anarchiste, origines et historique, la propagande anarchiste sous toutes ses formes, la doctrine et ses précurseurs, etc., psychologie de l'anarchiste, les résultats*. Paris: Flammarion, 1894.

Eisenzweig, Uri. *Fictions de l'anarchisme*. Paris: Christian Bourgois, 2001.

d'Estoc, Gisèle. *Cahier d'amour, suivi de Guy de Maupassant, Poèmes érotiques*. Ed. Jacques-Louis Douchin. Paris: Arléa, 1993. Rpt. 1997.

———. "Un fléau national." *Pamphlet du jour*, September 28, 1892.

———. *Psychologie de Jeanne d'Arc*. Paris: J. Strauss, 1891. Trans. Melanie Hawthorne. "The Psychology of Joan of Arc." *Nineteenth-Century Women Seeking Expression: Translations from the French*. Ed. Rosemary Lloyd. Liverpool: University of Liverpool, 2000. 124–39.

———. *La revue caudine*. Paris: 1887–88.

———. *La vierge-réclame*. Paris: Librairie Richelieu, 1887.

Farge, Arlette. *Le goût de l'archive*. Paris: Seuil, 1997.

Fénéon, Félix. *Novels in Three Lines*. Trans. Luc Sante. New York: NYRB, 2007.

Ferréus. *Annuaire du duel, 1880–1889*. Paris: Perrin et Cie, 1891.

Francis, Claude, and Fernande Gontier. *Colette*. [Paris]: Perrin, 1997. Trans. *Creating Colette*. 2 vols. South Royalton VT: Steerforth, 1998–.

———. *Simone de Beauvoir*. Paris: Perrin, 1985. Trans. Lisa Nesselson. *Simone de Beauvoir: A Life, a Love Story*. New York: St. Martin's, 1987.

Fraser, Antonia. "Optical Research." *Lives for Sale: Biographers' Tales.* Ed. Mark Bostridge. London: Continuum, 2004. 113–17.

Friang, Michèle. Preface. *Zo'har* by Catulle Mendès. Lyon: Editions Palimpseste, 2005. [5–16.]

Garin, Joseph. *L'anarchie et les anarchistes.* Paris: Guillaumin, 1885.

Gawande, Atul. "The Checklist." *New Yorker*, December 10, 2007, 86–95.

———. *The Checklist Manifesto: How to Get Things Right.* New York: Metropolitan Books, 2009.

Gladwell, Malcolm. "The Social Life of Paper: Looking for Method in the Mess." *New Yorker*, March 25, 2002, 92–96.

Glendinning, Victoria. *Vita: The Life of V. Sackville-West.* New York: Quill, 1983.

Gordon, Lyndall. *Charlotte Brontë: A Passionate Life.* New York: Norton, 1995.

———. *Lives Like Loaded Guns: Emily Dickinson and Her Family's Feuds.* New York: Viking, 2010.

———. *Vindication: A Life of Mary Wollstonecraft.* New York: HarperCollins, 2005.

———. *Virginia Woolf: A Writer's Life.* New York: Norton, 1984.

Grafton, Anthony. *Worlds Made by Words: Scholarship and Community in the Modern West.* Cambridge MA: Harvard University Press, 2009.

Gyz-El. *Noir sur blanc: Récits lorrains.* Nancy: Imprimerie A. Voirin, 1887. Includes "Un mariage manqué." Trans. Melanie Hawthorne. "A Missed Marriage." *Nineteenth-Century Women Seeking Expression: Translations from the French.* Ed. Rosemary Lloyd. Liverpool: University of Liverpool, 2000. 124–39.

Halperin, Joan Ungersma. *Félix Fénéon: Aesthete and Anarchist in Fin-de-Siècle Paris.* New Haven: Yale University Press, 1988.

Hamilton, Nigel. *American Caesars: Lives of the Presidents from Franklin D. Roosevelt to George W. Bush.* New Haven: Yale University Press, 2010.

———. *Biography: A Brief History.* Cambridge MA: Harvard University Press, 2007.

Hawthorne, Melanie. "De nouveau du nouveau sur Gisèle d'Estoc, amante de Maupassant." *Histoires littéraires* 16 (2003): 77–84.

———. *Rachilde and French Women's Authorship: From Decadence to Modernism.* Lincoln: University of Nebraska Press, 2001.

Heilbrun, Carolyn. *Writing a Woman's Life.* New York: Norton, 1988.

Holmes, Richard. *Footsteps: Adventures of a Romantic Biographer.* New York: Viking, 1985.

Holroyd, Michael. *Basil Street Blues: A Memoir.* New York: Norton, 2000.

Hopton, Richard. *Pistols at Dawn: A History of Dueling.* London: Portrait, 2007.

Hughes, Kathryn. *George Eliot: The Last Victorian.* New York: Cooper Square, 2001.

―――. *The Short Life and Long Times of Mrs. Beeton.* London: Fourth Estate, 2005.

Ignotus, Paul. *The Paradox of Maupassant.* London: University of London Press, 1966.

Jameson, Fredric. *Postmodernism; or, The Cultural Logic of Late Capitalism.* Durham: Duke University Press, 1990.

Kakutani, Michiko. "A. S. Byatt's Bumbling Literary Sleuth Ends Up Clueless." Rev. of *The Biographer's Tale* by A. S. Byatt. *New York Times,* January 23, 2001, http://www.nytimes.com/2001/01/23/arts/23KAKU.html.

Keen, Suzanne. *Romances of the Archive in Contemporary British Fiction.* Toronto: Toronto University Press, 2004.

Kessler, Marni Revi. *Sheer Presence: The Veil in Manet's Paris.* Minneapolis: University of Minnesota Press, 2006.

Knapp, Bettina L. *Judith Gautier, Writer, Orientalist, Musicologist, Feminist: A Literary Biography.* Dallas: Hamilton Books, 2004.

Lami, Stanislas. *Dictionnaire des sculpteurs de l'école française au dix-neuvième siècle.* Paris: E. Champion, 1914.

Lanoux, Armand. *Maupassant le bel-ami.* Paris: Arthème Fayard, 1967.

Lay, Howard G. "*Beau geste!* On the Readability of Terrorism." *Fragments of Revolution.* Ed. Caroline Weber and Howard G. Lay. Spec. issue of *Yale French Studies* 101 (2001): 79–100.

Lecomte du Nouy, Hélène. *L'amitié amoureuse.* Paris: Calmann-Lévy, 1897.

Lee, Hermione. *Biography: A Very Short Introduction.* New York: Oxford University Press, 2009.

―――. *Edith Wharton.* London: Chatto & Windus, 2007.

―――. *Virginia Woolf.* New York: Knopf, 1997.

―――. *Willa Cather: Double Lives.* New York: Pantheon, 1989.

Lefrère, Jean-Jacques. *Les saisons littéraires de Rodolphe Darzens.* Paris: Fayard, 1998.

Lefrère, Jean-Jacques, and Jean-Paul Goujon. *Deux malchanceux de la littérature fin de siècle: Jean Larocque et Léon Genonceaux*. Tusson (Charente): Du Lérot, 1994.

Lefrère, Jean-Jacques, and Philippe Oriol. Preface. *Le journal inédit de Louis-Pilate de Brinn'Gaubast*. Paris: Pierre Horay, 1997.

Light, Alison. *Mrs Woolf and the Servants: The Hidden Heart of Domestic Service*. London: Fig Tree, 2007.

Lipton, Eunice. *Alias Olympia: A Woman's Search for Manet's Notorious Model and Her Own Desire*. New York: Scribner's, 1992.

Love, Heather. *Feeling Backward: Loss and the Politics of Queer History*. Cambridge MA: Harvard University Press, 2007.

MacFarquhar, Larissa. "The Deflationist: How Paul Krugman Found Politics." *New Yorker*, March 1, 2010, 38–49.

Maddox, Brenda. *George Eliot in Love*. New York: Palgrave Macmillan, 2010.

———. *Nora: The Real Life of Molly Bloom*. Boston: Houghton Mifflin, 1988.

———. *Rosalind Franklin: The Dark Lady of DNA*. New York: HarperCollins, 2002.

Maitron, Jean. *Le mouvement anarchiste en France*. 2 vols. Paris: François Maspéro, 1975.

Malcolm, Janet. *Iphigenia in Forest Hills: Anatomy of a Murder Trial*. New Haven: Yale University Press, 2011.

———. *The Journalist and the Murderer*. New York: Knopf, 1990.

———. *The Silent Woman: Sylvia Plath and Ted Hughes*. New York: Knopf, 1994.

———. *Two Lives: Gertrude and Alice*. New Haven: Yale University Press, 2007.

Marías, Javier. *Written Lives*. New York: New Directions, 2006.

Masters, Alexander. *Stuart: A Life Backwards*. London: Fourth Estate, 2005.

Maupassant, Guy de. *A la feuille de rose, maison turque, suivi de la correspondance de l'auteur avec Gisèle d'Estoc et Marie Bashkirtseff et de quelques poèmes libres*. Ed. Alexandre Grenier. Paris: Encre, 1984.

———. "Au Salon." http://www.maupassant.free.fr/chroniq/salon. html (site consulted June 12, 2012).

———. *Contes et nouvelles*. Vol. 1. Ed. Louis Forestier. Paris: Gallimard-Pléiade, 1974.

———. *Correspondance*. 3 vols. Ed. Jacques Suffel. Geneva: Edito-Service, 1973.

Mendès, Catulle. *Zo'har*. Lyon: Editions Palimpseste, 2005.

Middlebrook, Diane Wood. *Anne Sexton: A Biography*. Boston: Houghton Mifflin, 1991.

———. *Suits Me: The Double Life of Billy Tipton*. Boston: Houghton Mifflin, 1998.

Mme X. "Guy de Maupassant intime: Notes d'une amie." *La grande revue*, October 25, 1912, 673–709; March 25, 1913, 217–33; and April 10, 1913, 519–33.

"A New Music Hall Sketch." *New York Times*, December 27, 1898, 7.

"New Pictures in Paris." *New York Times*, May 18, 1884, 4.

Oriol, Philippe. *A propos de l'attentat Foyot: Quelques questions et quelques tentatives de réponses, ainsi que quelques documents reproduits dont le journal des interviews*. Paris: Au fourneau, 1993.

Péladan, Joséphin. *La gynandre*. Paris: Dentu, 1891.

Picq, Gilles. "Et encore du nouveau sur Gisèle d'Estoc." *Histoires littéraires* 17 (2004): 251.

———. *Laurent Tailhade; ou, De la provocation considéréee comme un art de vivre*. Paris: Maisonneuve et Larose, 2001.

———. "On destocke Gisèle; ou, Comment donner de la chair à un ectoplasme." *Les à-côtés du siècle*. Ed. Jean-Jacques Lefrère and Michel Pierssens. Tusson: Du Lérot, 1998. 117–25.

Rachilde. *Madame Adonis*. Paris: Monnier, 1888.

———. *La marquise de Sade*. Paris: Monnier, 1887.

———. *Monsieur Vénus*. Brussels: Brancart, 1884.

———. *La Princesse des Ténèbres*. Paris: Calmann Lévy, 1896.

Raynaud, Ernest. *En marge de la mêlée symboliste*. Paris: Mercure de France, 1936.

———. *La mêlée symboliste: Portraits et souvenirs*. 3 vols. Paris: La renaissance du livre, 1918–22.

Réda, Jacques, ed. *Album Maupassant*. Paris: Gallimard-Pléiade, 1987.

Richardson, Joanna. *Judith Gautier: A Biography*. New York: Franklin Watts, 1987.

Saint-Albin, Albert de. *A travers les salles d'armes*. Paris: Librairie illustrée, [n.d.].

Scholl, Aurélien. "Retour à Paris." *L'echo de Paris*, August 26, 1892, 1.

Schwartz, Vanessa R. *Spectacular Realities: Early Mass Culture in Fin-de-Siècle Paris*. Berkeley and Los Angeles: University of California Press, 1998.

Secrest, Meryle. *Shoot the Widow: Adventures of a Biographer in Search of Her Subject*. New York: Knopf, 2007.

Shryock, Richard, ed. *Lettres à Gustave et Rachel Kahn (1886–1934)*. Sainte-Genouph: Nizet, 1996.

Silverman, Willa. *The Notorious Life of Gyp: Right-wing Anarchist in Fin-de-Siècle France*. New York: Oxford University Press, 1995.

Souhami, Diana. *Gertrude and Alice*. London: Pandora, 1991.

————. *Gluck, 1895–1978: Her Biography*. London: Pandora, 1989.

————. *Mrs. Keppel and Her Daughter*. New York: St. Martin's, 1997.

————. *The Trials of Radclyffe Hall*. London: Trafalgar Square, 1998.

————. *Wild Girls: Paris, Sappho, and Art; The Lives and Loves of Natalie Barney and Romaine Brooks*. New York: St. Martin's, 2005.

Souillac, Maurice de. *Zé'boïm*. Paris: Alphonse Piaget, 1897.

Spurling, Hilary. *Ivy: The Life of I. Compton-Burnett*. New York: Knopf, 1984.

————. *Pearl Buck in China: Journey to the Good Earth*. New York: Simon & Schuster, 2010.

Steedman, Carolyn. *Dust: The Archive and Cultural History*. New Brunswick: Rutgers University Press, 2001.

Sweetman, David. *Explosive Acts: Toulouse-Lautrec, Oscar Wilde, Félix Fénéon and the Art and Anarchy of the Fin de Siècle*. New York: Simon & Schuster, 1999.

Symons, A. J. A. *The Quest for Corvo: An Experiment in Biography*. 1934. Baltimore: Penguin, 1966.

Tabarant, Adolphe. *Manet et ses oeuvres*. Paris: Gallimard, 1947.

Tailhade, Laurent. Letter in *Le décadent*, September 15–30, 1888, 14–16.

————. *Lettres à sa mère, 1874–1891*. Ed. Pierre Dufay. Paris: R. Van den Berg et L. Enlart, 1926.

————. "Notes sur Charles Cros." *Le décadent*, September 1–15, 1888, 1–5.

Tindall, Gillian. *Footsteps in Paris: A Few Streets, a Few Lives*. London: Chatto & Windus, 2009.

————. *The Journey of Martin Nadaud: A Life and Turbulent Times*. New York: St. Martin's, 2000.

Tomalin, Claire. "The Female Captive." *Guardian Review*, May 26, 2007, 7.

————. *Katherine Mansfield: A Secret Life*. London: Viking, 1987.

————. *The Life and Death of Mary Wollstonecraft*. New York: Harcourt Brace Jovanovich, 1974.

Toth, Emily. *Inside Peyton Place: The Life of Grace Metalious*. New York: Doubleday, 1981.

————. *Kate Chopin*. New York: Morrow, 1990.

Tuchman, Barbara W. *The Proud Tower: A Portrait of the World Before the War, 1890–1914*. New York: Macmillan, 1966.

Tunzelmann, Alex von. *Indian Summer: The Secret History of the End of an Empire*. New York: Henry Holt, 2007.

Ustinova, Yulia. *Caves and the Ancient Greek Mind: Descending Underground in the Search for Ultimate Truth*. New York: Oxford University Press, 2009.

Vanderbilt, Tom. *Traffic: Why We Drive the Way We Do (and What It Says about Us)*. New York: Knopf, 2008. .

Vaughan, Diane. *The Challenger Launch Decision: Risky Technology, Culture, and Deviance at NASA*. Chicago: University of Chicago Press, 1996.

Vicinus, Martha, ed. *Suffer and Be Still: Women in the Victorian Age*. Bloomington: Indiana University Press, 1973.

Wagner-Martin, Linda. *Telling Women's Lives: The New Biography*. New Brunswick: Rutgers University Press, 1994.

Waquet, Simone. *Une dynastie républicaine dans la Nièvre: Les Parent (Clamecy, 1796–1885)*. Gueugnon, Saône-et-Loire: Imprimerie gueugnonnaise, 1987.

Waters, Sarah. *Affinity*. New York: Riverhead, 2000.

Weber, Caroline, and Howard G. Lay, eds. *Fragments of Revolution*. Spec. issue of *Yale French Studies* 101 (2001).

Weber, Eugen. *France: Fin de Siècle*. Cambridge MA: Harvard University Press, 1986.

Wroe, Ann. *Being Shelley*. London: Jonathan Cape, 2007.

Zackheim, Michele. *Violette's Embrace*. New York: Riverhead, 1996.

Zola, Emile. *Les Rougon-Macquart*. Vol. 1. Ed. Henri Mitterand. Paris: Gallimard-Pléiade, 1960.